Y0-BQN-825

Library Acquisitions

LIBRARY SCIENCE TEXT SERIES

Library Acquisitions

A Classified Bibliographic Guide to the Literature and Reference Tools

BOHDAN S. WYNAR

1968

LIBRARIES UNLIMITED, INC. ROCHESTER, N. Y.

LIBRARY SCIENCE TEXTS SERIES

Science and Engineering Reference Sources
A Guide to Library of Congress Classification
Introduction to Cataloging and Classification, 3d ed.
Introduction to Bibliography and Reference Work, 4th ed.
Guide to Reference Materials in Political Science, 2 vols.

Library of Congress Card No. 68-26144

Libraries Unlimited, Inc.
P. O. Box 9842
Rochester, New York 14623

Printed in the United States of America

INTRODUCTION

The purpose of this work is to provide order librarians, and those responsible for the organization and administration of acquisition departments, with a comprehensive bibliographic guide to standard practices as expressed in the literature, and to list selected reference tools for various aspects of order work and book selection. The articles and books listed cover problems of acquisition work in all types of libraries university, college, school, public, and special.

The selection of material in this guide is intended to provide comprehensive coverage of topics over the broad spectrum of acquisition work, thus providing direct assistance to order librarians who wish to examine current and useful articles and books on specific routines or problems in order work. The criteria applied in the selection varied with the topic surveyed taking into consideration the obvious fact that some topics are heavily represented in the literature, while others receive minor attention, or are rarely discussed. The relative importance of the topic in the general framework of acquisition activities was also considered and frequently necessitated inclusion of items of rather poor quality but which do provide some practical information, experience or guidance on an important problem. Items of repetitious nature and ones which contributed little in the way of new approaches are omitted. The recency of information and the possibility of applying the methods to other libraries of similar type were used as other major selection criterion. This guide is limited primarily to American materials, nevertheless many other English language monographic and serial items are included. Most non-descriptive entries are annotated.

The material in this guide is arranged in five chapters and subdivided by topic: Chapter I, The Role of Technical Services in the Library; Chapter II, Organization and Administration of Acquisitions; Chapter III, Publishing; Chapter IV, Purchases; and Chapter V, Cooperative Acquisitions, Gifts and Exchanges. The structure of each chapter is determined by the problems peculiar to that aspect of acquisitions, e.g. Chapter IV is subdivided into three sections:

Order Routines, The Use of Mechanized Equipment, and Special Problems in Acquisitions. Numerous subheadings are used for specific types of materials, such as: Foreign Materials, Microforms, Maps, Audio-Visual Materials, etc.

The first two chapters are devoted primarily to management problems: Chapter I surveys technical services in its relationship to library operations in general. One of the problem areas in administration of acquisitions is the lack of sufficient application of more sophisticated managerial and administrative skills to routine library operations. Consequently, special provision is made to include some essential professional material in such areas as operational research, personnel management, budgeting and cost accounting, statistical evaluations, work measurements, and other aspects of managerial science and research that can and must be utilized by efficient library management. Chapter II continues this approach within the framework of the acquisitions department but stresses the library literature.

Chapter III, Publishing, is limited to materials that provide the order librarian with a minimum background in the historical aspects of publishing, the book trade, statistics of the book industry, and copyright. The main body of material, including lists of reference tools, is in Chapter IV, Purchases. Chapter V, Cooperative Acquisitions, Gifts and Exchanges completes the work.

In using this guide it is hoped that the reader will find the detailed Table of Contents and "see also" references in the bibliography useful in providing subject access to the material. Some duplication of entries was deemed necessary, in certain cases, to avoid excessive cross-references to different parts of the guide. It should be observed that material arranged in any one section may have several other possible uses, and the order librarian should become familiar with the scope and content of each section. The school librarian, for example, will find specific sections in Chapter I, "Organization of Technical Services-School Libraries" p. 56, Chapter II, "Developing Acquisition Programs (selection) School Libraries" p. 94, and Chapter IV, "Ordering for School Libraries" p. 244. Equally important material is found in other sections, not specified or limited to school libraries, e.g. Chapter IV, "Order Routines" p. 131, "Out-of-Print Materials" p. 163, "Government Publications" p. 195, "Paperbound Books" p. 221, and "Audio-Visual Materials" p. 224.

In addition to descriptive material represented in monographic writings, proceedings of conferences, and periodical articles, the reader will find--in the second part of many sections--a selective annotated list of directories, verification aids, bibliographic tools, and other essential reference works useful in placing orders for a given category of materials. So, for example, such lists of reference tools are provided for in-print domestic and foreign materials, out-of-print materials, reprints, microforms and xerographic prints, government publications, manuscripts, technical reports, ephemera, etc. In several sections, e.g. out-of-print books, or rare books and manuscripts, annotated lists of pertinent serials and periodicals are also included.

While surveying and evaluating the literature on a given subject in acquisition work, it became apparent to the author that this guide may serve as some measure for the quantitative as well as qualitative analysis of existing literature, indicating those areas receiving attention--perhaps excessive attention--and those being neglected.

The analysis of the literature will also show that material on such traditional aspects of acquisition work, as for example, gifts and exchanges, is quite uneven in quality ranging from a few good descriptive studies to a number of largely repetitious reports of "how we do it in our library" type. Such problems as proper channelling of gift solicitations, or cost analysis of domestic and foreign exchanges are for all practical purposes not represented.

In conclusion it should be noted that one of the most important problems in acquisition work that hardly can be categorized as that of acquisition technique, is the problem of the relationship between the order librarian or library administrator, and the book producer and the book market. One has to take for granted that an acquisition librarian needs not only technical skills in order to establish a business-like relationship with the book market, but at the same time, he must possess certain intellectual capacities. To develop a collection for a specific educational purpose, the librarian needs a broad background in historical and current literature that goes far beyond bibliographic knowledge of certain titles or recommended "buying lists." It is also quite obvious that such knowledge can be absorbed only by years of practical experience and study, and in this respect little can be gained from reading two or three articles on the subject, or glancing through some bibliographic guides. We hope that this book, as the first attempt of a more comprehensive bibliographic coverage of this important area of library activity, will indirectly reveal to a careful reader some of the idiosyncrasies of this learning process--sometimes so well-hidden in the voluminous literature pertaining to building up library resources as a cumulative storehouse of human knowledge.

March 14, 1968.

B. S. W.

TABLE OF CONTENTS

CHAPTER V

COOPERATIVE ACQUISITIONS, GIFTS AND EXCHANGES

CHAPTER I

THE ROLE OF TECHNICAL SERVICES IN THE LIBRARY

---

1. HISTORICAL BACKGROUND

a. Bibliographies

"The Literature of Library Technical Services," In: Illinois, University. Library School. Urbana, 1963. 46 p. (Occasional Papers, No. 58).

> Originally published in 1960, this bibliographic essay has been updated and revised.

Schultze, G. Documentation Source Book. New York, Scarecrow Press, 1965. 554 p.

> A selective bibliography emphasizing the practical aspects and the state of the art of librarianship and documentation.

Wynar, B. Syllabus for Technical Processes in Libraries. Denver, University of Denver Graduate School of Librarianship, 1962. 115 p.

> Contains a selective annotated bibliography preceded by topical outlines covering major areas of technical processes.

b. Review Articles

Tauber, M. F. "Technical Services in 1960," Library Resources and Technical Services, 5:100-104, Spring, 1961.

__________. "Technical Services in 1961," Library Resources and Technical Services, 6:101-109, Spring, 1962.

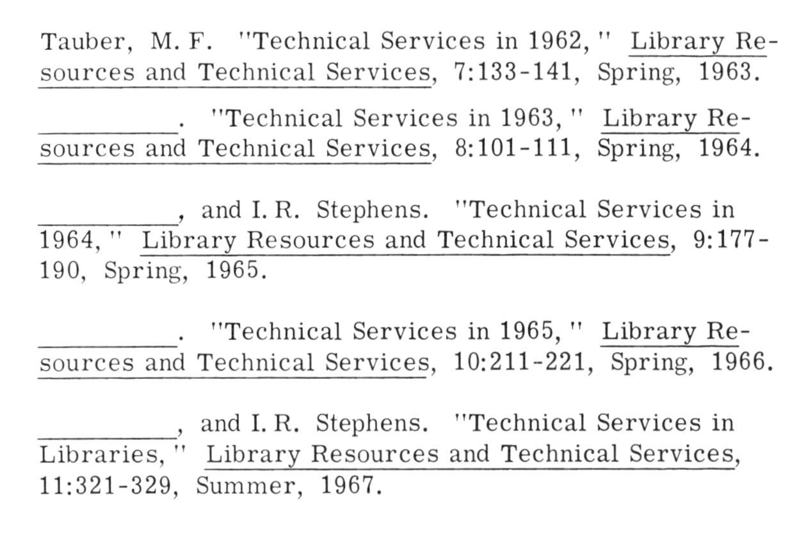

Tauber, M. F. "Technical Services in 1962," *Library Resources and Technical Services*, 7:133-141, Spring, 1963.

__________. "Technical Services in 1963," *Library Resources and Technical Services*, 8:101-111, Spring, 1964.

__________, and I. R. Stephens. "Technical Services in 1964," *Library Resources and Technical Services*, 9:177-190, Spring, 1965.

__________. "Technical Services in 1965," *Library Resources and Technical Services*, 10:211-221, Spring, 1966.

__________, and I. R. Stephens. "Technical Services in Libraries," *Library Resources and Technical Services*, 11:321-329, Summer, 1967.

c. Textbooks and Manuals

See also pp. 81-82.

Corbin, J. B. *A Technical Services Manual for Small Libraries*. Austin, Texas, Library and Historical Commission, 1965. (Monograph No. 3, Texas State Library).

Randall, W. M. ed. *The Acquisition and Cataloging of Books*. Chicago, University of Chicago Press, 1940. 408 p.

> Papers presented before the 1940 Library Institute at University of Chicago emphasizing recent problems and trends.

Tauber, Maurice Falcolm. *Technical Services in Libraries: Acquisitions, Cataloging, Classification, Binding, Photographic Reproduction and Circulation Operations*. New York, Columbia University Press, 1954. 487 p. (Columbia University Studies in Library Service, No. 7).

> A survey of library technical services associated with procurement, recording, preservation, and handling of library materials.

2. ADMINISTRATIVE ORGANIZATION

a. Principles of Management and Operational Research

Abbott, F., and L. A. Thompson. The Executive Function and Its Compensation. Charlottesville, Graduate School of Business Administration, The University of Virginia, 1957.

Alberts, Henry H. Principles of Organization and Management. 2d ed. New York, Wiley, 1965. 676 p.

Includes an interpretation from such fields as economics, operations research, information theory, semantics, psychology, and electronic data processing.

American Management Association. Finance Division. Operations Research Applied, New Uses and Extensions. New York, 1957.

Argyris, C. Integrating the Individual and the Organization. New York, Wiley, 1964.

Baker, B. N., and R. L. Eris. An Introduction to PERT-CPM. Homewood, Ill., Irwin, 1964.

Barnard, C. I. Organization and Management. Cambridge, Harvard University Press, 1948. 244 p.

Barnes, R. M. Motion and Time Study. 4th ed. New York, Wiley, 1958.

Beach, D. C. Personnel: The Management of People at Work. New York, Macmillan, 1965.

Birn, Serge A. Measurement and Control of Office Costs; Master Clerical Data. New York, McGraw-Hill, 1961. 318 p.

The MTM-based standards of clerical activities developed by the Birn Company.

Brown, Ray E. Judgement in Administration. New York, McGraw-Hill, 1966. 225 p.

The major emphasis is on causes of failure in administration.

Calhoon, R. P. Managing Personnel. New York, Harper and Row, 1963.

Cantor, N. The Learning Process for Managers. New York, Harper, 1958. 154 p.

Chapanis, A. Research Techniques in Human Engineering. Baltimore, Md., John Hopkins Press, 1959. 316 p.

Human engineering is the name applied to that brand of modern technology which deals with ways of designing machines, operations, and work environments so that they match human capacities and limitations. The purpose of this work is to describe some of the methods available to the human engineer in operational research.

Churchman, Charles West, et al. Introduction to Operations Research. New York, Wiley, 1957.

Clover, Vernon T. Business Research: Basic Principles and Techniques. Lubbock, Tex., Rodgers Litho, 1958. 394 p.

Presents basic procedures for conducting scientific managerial research.

Cochran, W. G., and G. M. Cox. Experimental Designs. 2d ed. New York, Wiley, 1957. 611 p.

An advanced textbook describing the principles of analysis of variance and computational methods.

Chorafas, Dimitris N. Operations Research for Industrial Management. New York, Reinhold, 1958.

Churchman, C. West. *Introduction to Operations Research* New York, Wiley, 1957. 645p.

An advanced text on the application of scientific method to operations research, with the emphasis on industrial problems.

Cooper, A. M. *How to Supervise People.* 4th ed. New York, McGraw-Hill, 1958. 250p.

Dahl, Robert Alan. *Social Science Research on Business: Product and Potential.* New York, Columbia University Press, 1959.

Dale, Ernest. *Management: Theory and Practice.* New York, McGraw-Hill, 1965. 743p.

A basic text in the field of management providing an analysis of managerial responsibilities and operations.

Dalton, M. *Men Who Manage.* New York, Wiley, 1959. 318p.

Sociological aspects of individuals in management situations.

Davies, K. *Human Relations in Business.* New York, McGraw-Hill, 1957.

Dean, Burton V. *Operations Research in Research and Development.* New York, Wiley, 1963. 289p.

Edited proceedings of a conference at Case Institute of Technology. Twelve chapters cover the development of scientific methods for use in research and development management.

Dimock, Marshall Edward, and Gladys Ogden Dimock. *Public Administration.* 3d ed. New York, Holt, Rinehart and Winston, 1964. 410p.

A non-technical textbook on the subject.

Drucker, P. F. The Practice of Management. New York, Harper, 1954. 404p.

Eddison, R. T., et. al. Operational Research in Management. New York, Wiley, 1962. 330p.

Of special interest is the chapter on the relation between operational research and other management techniques.

Ewing, D. H., and D. Fenn. Incentives for Executives. New York, McGraw-Hill, 1962.

Ferber, Robert. Research Methods in Economics and Business. New York, Macmillan, 1962.

Flippo, Edwin B. Principles of Personnel Management. 2d ed. New York, McGraw-Hill, 1966. 562p.

A basic textbook for use in college courses in personnel management.

Ford, G. B. Building a Winning Employee Team. New York, American Management Association, 1964.

Fox, William M. The Management Process: An Integrated Functional Approach. Homewood, Ill., Irwin, 1963. 460p.

Covers the role of probability in decision making, the formulating of organic sub-functions of planning, organizing and controlling, and the new planning and control system known as PERT.

Fuhre, W. J. Work Measurement and Production Control with the FAST System. Englewood Cliffs, N. J., Prentice-Hall, 1963. 211p.

Hansen, B. L. Quality Control: Theory and Applications. Englewood Cliffs, N. J., Prentice-Hall, 1963.

Harc, Van Court. System Analysis: A Diagnostic Approach. New York, Harcourt, Brace and World, 1967. 544 p.

A survey of systems analysis that emphasizes pattern formulation and diagnosis in a wide range of fields.

Hertz, D. B. The Theory and Practice of Industrial Research. New York, McGraw-Hill, 1950. 385 p.

The first four chapters present theoretical, background, and analytical materials on creative mentalities, problem solving, and scientific method. The remainder of the book attempts to apply these concepts to industrial research.

Hutchinson, John G. Organizations: Theory and Classical Concepts. New York, Holt, Rinehart, and Winston, 1967. 150 p.

Basic functions underlying the various theories of management.

Johnson, J. Statistical Cost Analysis. New York, McGraw-Hill, 1960. 197 p.

The purpose of this book is to provide an up-to-date and comprehensive survey in the field of statistical cost functions.

Kleinmutz, Benjamin, ed. Problem Solving: Research, Method, and Theory. New York, Wiley, 1966. 406 p.

A symposium of major viewpoints on problem solving.

Koontz, Harold D., and Cyril J. O'Donnel. Principles of Management. 3d ed. New York, McGraw-Hill, 1964. 608 p.

A standard text on the theory of managing process, viewed operationally. Contents: The basis of management. Planning. Organization. Staffing. Direction. Control.

Lepawsky, A. Administration. New York, Knopf, 1949.

Lehrer, Robert N. *Work Simplification*. Creative Thinking about Work Problems. Englewood Cliffs, N.J., Prentice-Hall, 1957. 394 p.

An elementary textbook on the procedures designed to make human work more effective. Of special interest are chapters on principles of effective work, work simplification programs in business and technology, and work organization.

Lewin, Richard I., and C.A. Kirkpatrick. *Quantitative Approaches to Management*. New York, McGraw-Hill, 1965, 365 p.

An introduction to some of the quantitative techniques which demands only a modest background in mathematics.

Likert, Rensis. *New Patterns of Management*. New York, McGraw-Hill, 1961.

Primarily concerned with the problems of organizing human resources and activity and is written especially for those actively engaged in management and supervision. Of special interest is the chapter on some emphirical tests of the newer theory.

Line-Staff Relationships in Production. New York, American Management Association, 1956. 135 p. (Special Report, No. 18).

Lowry, S.M., et. al. *Time and Motion Study*. 3d ed. New York, McGraw-Hill, 1940.

Likert, R. *New Patterns of Management*. New York, McGraw-Hill, 1961. 279 p.

McCloskey, Joseph F., and Florence N. Trefethen, eds. *Operations Research for Management*. Baltimore, Md., John Hopkins University Press, 1954.

Malcolm, G.D. *Management Control Systems*. New York, Wiley, 1960. 375 p.

Maynard, H. B., ed. Handbook of Business Administration. New York, McGraw-Hill, 1967. 1 v. (various paging).

Of special interest are chapters on research and development, financial management, management of human resources and office management. Includes bibliographies.

Maynard, H. B. Practical Control of Office Costs. Greenwich, Conn., Management Pub. Corp., 1960. 160 p.

Mesarovie, M. D. Views on General Systems Theory. New York, Wiley, 1964. 178 p.

The proceeding of the second systems symposium held at Case Institute in 1963.

Miller, R. W. Schedule, Cost, and Profit Control with PERT. New York, McGraw-Hill, 1963.

Nadler, Gerard. Motion and Time Study. New York, McGraw-Hill, 1955. 612 p.

Of special interest is the chapter on philosophy of motion and time study and analysis of work with good examples of product process chart, form process chart, man process chart, operation chart, multi-activity chart, and other analysis techniques.

Niebel, B. W. Motion and Time Study. 4th ed. Homewood, Ill., Irwin, 1967. 628 p.

A standard text on the subject with chapters on the operation and flow process charts, operation analysis, work sampling performance rating and other pertinent topics.

Neuschel, Richard F. Management by System. 2d ed. New York, McGraw-Hill, 1960. 359 p.

Of special interest are chapters on the ingredients of a successful procedures improving program and procedures analysis.

Niles, H., et. al. *The Office Supervisor: His Relations to Persons and to Work.* 3d ed., New York, Wiley, 1959. 307 p.

Paterson, Elmore, E. Grosvenor Plowman, and Joseph M. Trickett, *Business Organization and Management.* Homewood, Ill., Irwin, 1962. 354 p.

The principal subjects covered are the organizational hierarchy, departmentation, line and staff, picturing organizational relationships, and inter- and intra-functional organization.

Prince, Thomas R. *Information Systems for Management Planning and Control.* Homewood, Ill., Irwin, 1966. 600 p.

The case studies included in this volume do not require the reader to have a familiarization with any given computer program; however, it is desirable for the reader to complete instruction in some computor planning language.

Redfield, C. E. *Communication in Management.* Chicago, The University of Chicago Press, 1953. 314 p.

Richards, Max D., and Paul S. Green-Law. *Management Decision Making.* Homewood, Ill., Irwin, 1966. 578 p.

Employs mathematical and model building concepts.

Rourke, Francis E., and Glenn E. Brooks. *The Managerial Revolution in Higher Education.* Baltimore, Md., John Hopkins Press, 1966. 184 p.

A description of recent changes in the management of colleges and universities.

Rowlend, V. K. *Management Performance Standards.* New York, American Management Association, 1960.

Sasieni, Maurice, et. al. *Operation Research - Methods and Problems.* New York, Wiley, 1959.

Schell, E. H. *Technique of Executive Control.* 8th ed. New York, McGraw-Hill, 1957. 357 p.

Scott, William G. Human Relations in Management: A Behavioral Science Approach. Homewood, Ill., Irwin, 1962. 456 p.

An introductory text on the subject providing an analytical treatment of individual, small group, and organizational behavioral.

Scott, W. G., et. al. Personnel Management: Principles, Practices and Points of View. New York, McGraw-Hill, 1954.

Shuchman, Abe, ed. Scientific Decision Making. New York, Holt, Rinehart, and Winston, 1963. 576 p.

Fifty articles on the nature, methods, and applications of operations research.

Stahl, O. G., ed. Public Personnel Administration. New York, Harper, 1962. 304 p.

Stone, C. H., and W. E. Kendall. Effective Personnel Selection Procedures. Englewood Cliffs, N. J., Prentice-Hall, 1956.

Strauss, G. Personnel: The Human Problems of Management. New York, Prentice-Hall, 1960.

Systems and Procedures Association. A Guide to Office Clerical Time Standards. Detroit, 1960. 169 p.

Tead, O. The Art of Administration. New York, McGraw-Hill, 1951. 223 p.

Terry, George R. Principles of Management. 4th ed. Homewood, Ill., Irwin, 1964. 837 p.

Included are recent managerial developments and techniques such as PERT, Rhochrematics, RAMP, Causative Thinking, Project Organization, Quantitative Measurements, Modern Organizational Concepts, and recent developments in motivation.

Urwick, L. F. Some Notes on the Theory of Organization. New York, American Management Association, 1952.

Weimer, Arthur M. Business Administration: An Introductory Management Approach. 3d ed. Homewood, Ill., Irwin, 1966. 700 p.

A classic text on the subject.

Young, Stanley, and Charles E. Summer. Management: A System Analysis. Glenview, Ill., Scott Foresman, 1966. 436 p.

A standard textbook on the subject.

b. Principles of Statistical Analysis

Adler, Irving. Probability and Statistics for Every Man. New York, Day, 1963. 256 p.

Alder, Henry L. and Edward B. Roessler. Introduction to Probability and Statistics. 2d ed. San Francisco, W. H. Freeman, 1962. 289 p.

A non-mathematical introduction.

Arkin, Herbert. Statistical Methods. 4th ed. rev. New York, Barnes & Noble, 1956. 226 p.

A standard manual, giving a condensed and succinct treatment of the subject.

Bryant, Edward C. Statistical Analysis. 2d ed. New York, McGraw-Hill, 1966. 325 p.

A basic text in inferential statistics. Includes a simplified treatment of sampling.

Cochran, William G. Sampling Technique. 2d ed. New York, Wiley, 1963. 413 p.

This is a textbook on elementary level including basic principles of random and stratified sampling.

Croxton, Frederick E. Applied General Statistics. 3d ed. New York, Prentice-Hall, 1967. 754 p.

Of special interest are chapters on graphic presentation.

Dening, William E. Some Theory of Sampling. New York, Wiley, 1950. 602 p.

Dixon, W. J., and F. J. Massey. Introduction to Statistical Analysis. New York, McGraw-Hill, 1957. 488 p.

A basic text in statistics, requiring no mathematical background beyond algebra.

Dornbusch, S. M., and C. F. Schmid. A Primer of Social Statistics. New York, McGraw-Hill, 1955. 251 p.

Written to give the student an appreciation of statistics as a universal way of thinking, to make him aware of the strengths and weaknesses of the systems, besides developing the basic skills. Various methods of presenting statistical information, plus methods of computation are given.

Fisher, Ronald H. Statistical Methods for Research Workers. 13th ed. New York, Hafner, 1958. 356 p.

An introductory text to inferential statistics.

Fisher, Ronald H. Statistical Methods and Scientific Inference. 2d ed. New York, Hafner, 1959. 178 p.

Franzblau, Abraham N. A Primer of Statistics for Non-Statisticians. New York, Harcourt, Brace, 1958. 150 p.

Designed for the consumer of statistics, this book provides only the essentials of the subject.

Grant, Eugene L. Statistical Quality Control. 3d ed. New York, McGraw-Hill, 1964. 630 p.

Introduction to statistical techniques that can be used to reduce costs, improve quality of products, etc.

Guenter, William C. *Concepts of Statistical Inference.* New York, McGraw-Hill, 1965. 353 p.

A basic text at the pre-calculus level.

Guest, Lester. *Beginning Statistics.* New York, Thomas Y. Crowell, 1957. 255 p.

The book covers the basic concepts necessary for students in the field of social sciences: frequency distributions, indices of central tendency and variability, the normal curve, Pearson correlation, regression and prediction, and simple sampling statistics.

Hauser, P. M., and W. R. Leonard. *Government Statistics for Business Use.* New York, Wiley, 1956. 440 p.

Hoel, P. G. *Elementary Statistics.* New York, Wiley, 1966. 351 p.

This book is designed for a one-semester course for students whose background in mathematics is limited to high school algebra.

McCarthy, Philip J. *Introduction to Statistical Reasoning.* New York, McGraw-Hill, 1957. 292 p.

An introductory text for those with a non-mathematical background.

Moroney, M. J. *Facts from Figures.* Baltimore, Md., Penguin Books, 1956. 472 p.

Munroe, M. E. *The Theory of Probability.* New York, McGraw-Hill, 1951. 210 p.

Presents in terms of integrals studied in first-year calculus on outline of the mathematical framework and a number of the more important results of modern investigations in probability theory.

Rickmers, Albert D., and Hollis N. Todd. *Statistics: An Introduction.* New York, McGraw-Hill, 1967. 585 p.

A basic text for undergraduate students.

Senders, Virginia L. Measurement and Statistics. New York, Oxford University Press, 1958. 594 p.

Slonim, Morris James. Sampling in a Nutshell. New York, Simon and Schuster, 1960. 145 p.

A very simplified treatment of sampling which is particularly of interest to the layman.

Sprowls, R. Asy. Elementary Statistics. New York, McGraw-Hill, 1955. 392 p.

Wadsworth, George A., and Joseph L. Bryan. Introduction to Probability and Random Variables. New York, McGraw-Hill, 1960. 292 p.

An introduction to mathematical theory and practical applications of probability.

Wallis, Wilson A., and Harry V. Roberts. Statistics: A New Approach. Glencoe, Ill., Free Press, 1956. 646 p.

An introductory text for the non-mathematician.

Weiss, Lionel. Statistical Decision Theory. New York, McGraw-Hill, 1961. 208 p.

Covers the subject at an intermediate mathematical level.

Wolf, Frank L. Elements of Probability and Statistics. New York, McGraw-Hill, 1962. 337 p.

An introduction to probability and statistics requiring only high school algebra.

c. Library Management

Allen, K. S. "Management Methods in Libraries: A Symposium. Administrative Viewpoint," Medical Library Association Bulletin, 49:514-16, 1961.

Primarily limited to library literature.

Battles, D. D., H. Davis, and W. Harms. "A Motion and Time Study of a Library Routine," The Library Quarterly, 13:241-44, July, 1943.

Results of a motion and time study at Bradley Polytechnic Institute Library. Describes step-by-step routine of loaning a book. Concludes with recommendations.

Bolles, S. W. "The Use of Flow Charts in the Analysis of Library Operations," Special Libraries, 58:95-98, February, 1967.

Cavender, T. P. "Time and Motion Techniques Related to Costs of Expanding the Card Catalog," Library Resources and Technical Services, 1:104-8, Spring, 1957.

Results of a study at the library of the State University of Iowa.

Dougherty, R. M., and F. J. Heinritz. Scientific Management of Library Operation. New York, Scarecrow Press, 1966. 258 p.

An introductory text on the subject. Materials on basic principles, charting procedures, operations analysis, sampling, performance standards, etc. Some literature written by non-librarians included.

Duyvis, F. D. "Standardization as a Tool of Scientific Management," Library Trends, 2:410-27, January, 1954.

Outlines the aims of standardization and applies them to library materials and procedures. Advocates world-wide effort. Includes bibliography.

Goldhor, H. "Scientific Management in Public Libraries." Library Trends, 2:368-89, January, 1954.

Relates scientific approach to study of management, using process and flow charts, experiments, etc. Includes bibliography.

Hausdorfer, W. "Guidance for Administrators," Library Trends, 7:481-491, January, 1959.

A bibliographic essay.

Hayes, R. M. "The Development of a Methodology for System Design and Its Role in Library Education," Library Quarterly, 34:339-51, October, 1964.

The following areas are discussed: use studies, vocabulary development, data processing, file organization, screening processes, organization relationship.

Howard, P. "Consequences of Management Surveys," Library Trends, 2:428-36, January, 1954.

Briefly discusses the use and application of survey results, pointing out the pitfalls, and advocating use of scientific management techniques. Includes bibliography.

Immelman, R. F. M. The Foundation of Library Management. Organization From the Administrative Angle. Cape Town, University of Cape Town, 1947. 61 p.

Written from the British point of view.

John Hopkins University. Program Report on an Operations Research and Systems Engineering Study of a University Library. Baltimore, Md., Milton S. Eisenhower Library. John Hopkins University, 1965. 110 p.

Kingery, R. E. "A Management Engineering Look at Cataloging," College and Research Libraries, 14:52-56, January, 1953.

After a firm of management engineers made a survey of the preparation procedures of the Reference Department of the New York Public Library, they suggested seventy-five changes in the procedure. A number of the recommendations, which are of wide interest and applications, are discussed here.

Kingery, R. E. "What Happens When the Management Engineers Leave?" College and Research Libraries, 15: 202-4, April, 1954.

An informative article on how to follow-up the conclusions and recommendations of the management engineer.

Kipp, L. J. "Scientific Management in Research Libraries," Library Trends, 2:390-400, January, 1954.

Points out that literature on the subject does not reflect the actual growth in the area. Stresses humane practices. Includes bibliography.

Leimkuhler, F. F. "Systems Analysis in University Libraries," College and Research Libraries, 27:13-18, January 1966.

Based on research undertaken by librarians and industrial engineers at Purdue University.

__________. "Operations Research in the Purdue Libraries" In: Meeting on Automation in the Library - when, where and how, Purdue University, 1964. Papers. Edited by T. Andrews. Lafayette, Ind., Purdue University, 1965. Pp. 82-89.

Lock, R. N. Library Administration. London, Crosby Lockwood, 1961.

Logsdon, R. H. "Time and Motion Studies in Libraries," Library Trends, 2:401-9, January, 1954.

Suggests systematic study of industrial practices and application to library operations. Includes bibliography.

McDiarmid, E. W. "Scientific Method and Library Administration," Library Trends, 2:361-67, January, 1954.

Outlines procedure of scientific method and advocates it as an aid in library administration.

Miles, Arnold, and Lowell Martin. Public Administration and the Library. Chicago, University of Chicago Press, 1941. 313p.

Deals primarily with the economic and social functions of the library, including political considerations.

Morris, T. D. "Techniques of Appraising the Administrative Strength of an Organization," College and Research Libraries, 13:111-16, April, 1952.

The theory of effective management of technical services, with some comments on evaluation of the organization of the NYPL Acquisition Division.

Morsch, L. M. "Scientific Management in Cataloging," Library Trends, 2:470-83, January, 1954.

Cites a number of investigations which brought about improved efficiency, and points out the need for sound personnel practices. Includes bibliography.

Mumford, L. Q., and R. D. Rogers. "Library Administration and Its Current Development," Library Trends, 7:357-367, January, 1959.

Oh, T. K. "New Dimensions of Management Theory," College and Research Libraries, 27:431-8, November, 1966.

Ottemiller, J. H. "The Management Engineer," Library Trends, 2:437-51, January, 1954.

Points out the advantages of hiring a management engineer to analyze library operations. Includes bibliography.

Pierce, Watson O. D. Work Measurement in Public Libraries. A Review and Manual on Time Studies and Work Units with a Statistical Analysis and an Evaluation of Administrative and Management procedures in Certain Public Libraries. New York, Social Science Research Council, 1949. 238p.

Poage, S. T. "Work Sampling in Library Administration," The Library Quarterly, 30:213-18, July, 1960.

An industrial engineer's brief description of work sampling techniques as applied to library operations.

Reichmann, F. "Management and Operation," Library Trends, 3:462-70, April, 1955.

Summarizes the results of a survey of thirty-one university libraries regarding their management and operation. Includes bibliography.

Shaw, R. R. "Scientific Management in the Library," Louisiana Library Association Bulletin, 19:97-101, Fall, 1956.

Urges librarians to consider the values to be gained by the employment of scientific management. Uses examples to stress the cardinal point that there is one best way to do any job under the conditions with which it must be done, and that scientific management may be used to determine this.

Shaw, R. R., ed. "Scientific Management in Libraries," Library Trends, 2:359-483, January, 1954.

The entire issue is devoted to the management problems in several types of libraries.

St. John, F. R. "Management Improvements in Libraries," College and Research Libraries, 14:174-77, April, 1953.

Emphasizes the need in most libraries for careful management analysis, and the application of sound management improvements. Describes the development of management improvements in the Brooklyn Public Library.

Schultheiss, L., D. S. Culbertson, and E. M. Heiliger. Advanced Data Processing in the University Library. New York, Scarecrow Press, 1962.

Swenson, S. "Flow Chart of Library Searching Techniques," Special Libraries, 56:239-242, April, 1965.

Van Pelt, J. D. "Time and Motion Study in a Catalogue Room," Australian Library Journal, 5:55-63, April, 1956.

Weed, K. K. "A Tool for Management Evaluation of Library Services," Special Libraries, 48:378-82, October, 1957.

> The adaptation of time and motion studies in evaluating library service. Some recommendations for initiating work measurements are listed.

Wight, E. A. "Research in Organization and Administration," Library Trends, 6:141-46, October, 1957.

> Discusses the meanings of terms and mentions a few research efforts in the areas of administrative organization and management. Includes bibliography.

Wilson, E. H. "Future of Library Administration," Library Trends, 7:472-480, January, 1959.

Woodruff, E. "Work Measurement Applied to Libraries," Special Libraries, 48:139-44, April, 1957.

> Explains in detail the objectives, procedures, and terminology of a work measurement program as applied in the library of the United States Civil Service Commission, Washington, D. C.

Wynar, B. S. Manual for Time and Motion Studies; Division of Technical Services, University of Denver Libraries. Denver: University of Denver Libraries, 1960. 61 p.

d. Systems Approach

Becker, J. "System Analysis--Prelude to Library Data Processing," A. L. A. Bulletin, 59:293-296, April, 1965.

Bolles, S. W. "The Use of Flow Charts in the Analysis of Library Operations," Special Libraries, 58:95-98, February, 1967.

Chapman, E. A., and P. L. St. Pierre. Systems Analysis and Design as Related to Library Operations. Troy, N. Y., Rensselaer Libraries, Rensselaer Polytechnic Institute, 1966. 78p.

Cornell University. Libraries. System Requirements. Ithaca, N. Y., 1965. 12p.

Covill, G. W. "Librarian + Systems Analyst = Teamwork," Special Libraries, 58:99-101, February, 1967.

Flood, M. M. "The Systems Approach to Library Planning," In: Intellectual Foundations of Library Education; the Twenty-Ninth Annual Conference of the Graduate Library School, July 6-8, 1964. Edited by D. R. Swanson. Chicago, University of Chicago Press, 1965. Pp. 38-50.

Haas, W. J. "Computer Simulations at the Columbia University Libraries," In: Clinic on Library Applications of Data Processing, University of Illinois, 2d, 1964. Proceedings. Edited by H. Goldhor. Champaign, Ill., Distributed by the Illini Union Bookstore, 1965. Pp. 36-46.

__________. "A Description of a Project to Study the Research Library as an Economic System," In: Association of Research Libraries. Minutes of the Sixty-third Meeting, January 26, 1964. Pp. 40-46.

Hammer, D. P. "Scheduling Conversion," In: Harvey, J., ed. Data Processing in Public and University Libraries. Washington: Spartan Books, 1966. Pp. 5-20. (Drexel Information Science Series, v. 3).

Hayes, R. M. "The Development of a Methodology for System Design and Its Role in Library Education," In: Chicago. University. Graduate Library School. The Intellectual Foundations of Library Education; the Twenty-ninth Annual Conference, July 6-8, 1964. Edited by D. R. Swanson. Chicago, University of Chicago Press, 1965. Pp. 51-63.

Jackson, I. F. "An Approach to Library Automation Problems," College and Research Libraries, 28:133-137, March, 1967.

Kilgour, F. "Basic Systems Assumptions of the Columbia-Harvard-Yale Medical Libraries Computerization Project," In: Institute on Information Storage and Retrieval, 2d, University of Minnesota, 1965. Minneapolis, 1966. Pp. 145-154.

__________. "Comprehensive Modern Library Systems," In: Brasenose Conference on the Automation of Libraries, Oxford, England, 1966. Proceedings of the Anglo-American Conference of Library Services. Edited by J. Harrison and P. Laslett. London and Chicago, Mansell, 1967. Pp. 46-56.

Kraft, D. H. "Total Systems Approach to Library Mechanization," In: Texas Conference on Library Mechanization, 1st, Austin, 1966. Proceedings. Edited by J. B. Corbin. Austin, Texas Library and Historical Commission, 1966. (Texas State Library Monograph No. 6.)

Lamkin, B. E. "Systems Analysis in Top Management Communication," Special Libraries, 58:90-94, February, 1967.

Leimkuhler, F. F. "System Analysis in University Libraries," College and Research Libraries, 27:13-18, January, 1966.

Markieson, B. E. "A System Development Study for the Library of Congress Automation Program," Library Quarterly, 36:197-273, July, 1966.

Moore, E. "Systems Analysis: an Overview," Special Libraries, 58:87-90, February, 1967.

Morelock, M., and F. F. Leimkuhler. "Library Operations Research and Systems Engineering Studies," College and Research Libraries, 25:501-503, November, 1964.

Morse, P. M. "Probabilistic Models for Library Operations; with Some Comments on Library Automation," In: Association of Research Libraries. Minutes of the Sixty-third Meeting, January, 1964. Pp. 9-19.

Parker, R. H. "Concept and Scope of Total Systems in Library Records," In: Harvey, J., ed. Data Processing in Public and University Libraries. Washington, Spartan Books, 1966. Pp. 67-77. (Drexel Information Science Series, v. 3.)

Schultheiss, L. A. "Systems Analysis and Planning," In: Harvey, J., ed. Data Processing in Public and University Libraries. Washington, Spartan Books, 1966. Pp. 92-102. (Drexel Information Science Series, v. 3.)

Sparks, D. E., M. M. Chodrow, and G. M. Walsh. A Methodology for the Analysis in Information Systems. Final Report to National Science Foundation. Wakefield, Mass., Information Dynamics, 1965. 1v. (various paging).

Taylor, R. S., and C. E. Hieber. Manual for the Analysis of Library Systems. Bethlehem, Pa., Center for Information Sciences, Lehigh University, 1965. 44p + appendices. (Library Systems Analysis, Report No. 3.)

3. Technical Services in General

a. Survey Articles

Cohen, J. H., ed. "The Technical Services Division in Libraries: A Symposium," College and Research Libraries, 10:46-68, January, 1949.

Colburn, E. B. "The Value to the Modern Library of a Technical Services Department," College and Research Libraries, 11:47-53, January, 1950.

DeHart, F. "Faculty-Oriented Technical Services, A Checklist for Evaluation," Catholic Library World, 34: 146-171, November, 1962.

Discusses the problem of orders initiated by faculty versus order librarian responsibility.

Frieze, W. S. "The Administrator Looks at Technical Processing: The Public Library," Library Resources and Technical Services, 1:203-206, Fall, 1957.

Marvin, J. C. "Administrator Looks at Technical Services and Asks ... Target or Taurus?" Illinois Libraries, 43: 329-334, May, 1961.

Shachtman, B. E., ed. "Technical Services: Policy, Organization, and Coordination," Journal of Cataloging and Classification, 11:59-114, January, 1955.

Tauber, M. F. "Technical Services and the Library Building," The Southeastern Librarian, 10:82-91, Summer, 1960.

Discusses physical arrangement of technical processes area in relation to functions performed.

__________, and I. R. Stephens. "Surveys of Technical Services in Libraries," In: Conference on Library Surveys, Columbia University, 1965. Library Surveys, New York, Columbia University Press, 1967. Pp. 46-70.

A review of major surveys in this area with numerous bibliographic references.

Wright, W. E. "Some Aspects of Technical Processes," Library Trends, 1:73-82, July, 1952.

b. Personnel

American Library Association. Board of Personnel Administration. Descriptive List of Professional and Non-Professional Duties in Libraries. Chicago, American Library Association, 1948. 75 p.

Thirteen broad activities of library work are briefly examined, listing various professional and non-professional duties performed in each.

__________. __________. Personnel Administration for Libraries; a Bibliographical Essay. Chicago, American Library Association, 1953.

__________. __________. Personnel Organization and Procedure. A Manual Suggested for the use in College and University Libraries. Chicago, American Library Association, 1952.

__________. __________. A Manual Suggested for use in Public Libraries. Chicago, American Library Association, 1952.

Ashley, E. M. "Clerical Automation," Library Journal, 82:1725-1729, July, 1957.

Bassam, B. "Training for Technical Services," Library Resources and Technical Services, 8:35-46, Winter, 1964.

Davison, G. H. "Desirable Ratio of Professional and Non-Professional Staff," Aslib Proceedings, 14:361-379, November, 1962.

Dunkin, P. S. "The Development of Technical Services Training," Journal of Education for Librarianship, 2:123-131, Winter, 1962.

Fay, A. M. Supervising Library Personnel. Chicago, American Library Association, 1950.

Field, F. B., and J. H. Treyz. "The Technical Services Librarian and the Profession," Library Resources and Technical Services, 9:200-204, Spring, 1965.

Frarey, C. J. "Implications of Present Trends in Technical Services for Library Instruction," Journal of Education for Librarianship, 2:132-143, Winter, 1962.

Herner, S., and M. K. Heatwole. The Establishment of Staff Requirements in a Small Research Library. Chicago, Association of College and Reference Libraries, 1952. (ACRL Monograph, No. 3).

Howard, P. Library Staff Manuals and a Theory of Library Management. Chicago, University of Chicago, 1939. (University of Chicago. M. A. Thesis).

Jesse, W. H. "Interpersonal Relations in Libraries," College and Research Libraries, 21:149-155, March, 1960.

Library Association. Membership Committee. Professional and Non-Professional Duties in Libraries: A Descriptive List Compiled by Subcommittee. London, Library Association, 1962.

McCoy, R. E. Personnel Administration in Libraries. Chicago, American Library Association, 1953.

McDiarmid, E. W. "Training for Clerical and Subprofessional Workers," In: Berelson, B. R., ed. Education for Librarianship. Chicago, American Library Association, 1949. Pp. 232-248.

McNeal, A. L. "Ratio of Professional to Clerical Staff," College and Research Libraries, 17:219-223, May, 1956.

Martin, L., ed. Personnel Administration in Libraries, Papers Presented Before the Library Institute at the University of Chicago, August 27-September 1, 1945. Chicago, University of Chicago Press, 1946. 168 p.

A collection of twelve papers which examine the personnel problem within the framework of library services.

Poage, S. T. "Work Sampling in Library Administration," Library Quarterly, 30:213-218, July, 1960.

Shaffer, K. R. Library Personnel Administration and Supervision. 2d ed. Hamden, Conn., Shoe String Press, 1963. 214 p.

__________. Twenty-Five Short Cases in Library Personnel Administration. Hamden, Conn., Shoe String Press, 1959. 135 p.

A collection of cases drawn from public and academic libraries. Each situation is followed by a series of questions. 2d edition published in 1963 contains nine new cases.

Sollenberger, J. K. In-Service Training: A Bibliographic Essay. Chicago, American Library Association, 1965. 25 p.

A selective bibliography of writings published since 1955.

"Staff Manuals: A Selected Bibliography on Their Preparation and Use," News Notes of California Libraries, 50:389-392, April, 1955.

Stebbins, K. B. Personnel Administration in Libraries. New York, Scarecrow Press, 1966. 373 p.

Covers modern personnel practices. Final half of book contains forms used in various libraries and specific personnel practices and salaries in 43 of them.

Van Horne, B., ed. "Current Trends in Personnel Administration," Library Trends, 3:1-94, July, 1954.

Voos, H. "Standard Times for Certain Clerical Activities in Technical Processing," Library Resources and Technical Services, 10:223-227, Spring, 1966.

Weber, D. "The Clerical Staff," Library Trends, 3:52-58, April, 1955.

Wilson, E. H. "The Preparation and Use of the Professional Staff," The Library Quarterly, 31:104-114, January, 1961.

Winslow, A. "Supervision and Morale," Library Trends, 3:39-51, April, 1955.

Wisconsin. Free Library Commission. Proceedings of the Seventh Institute on Public Library Management: Personnel Management, Madison, April 11-12, 1960, Madison, Wisconsin, 1960.

c. Budget, Work Measurements, and Cost Accounting

See also pp. 101-107, "Budgeting and Funds."

American Association of Law Libraries. Cutting Costs in Acquisitions and Cataloging. South Hackensack, N. J., F. B. Rothman, 1960. (AALL Publications Series, No. 1).

Armstrong, C. M. Money for Libraries: A Report on Library Finance. New York, Social Science Research Council, for the Public Library Inquiry, 1951.

Baldwin, Erma V., and William E. Marcus. Library Costs and Budgets. New York, Bowker, 1941. 201 p.

Bouman, G. P. "Cost Accounting in Special Libraries," Bibliotheekleven, 36:281-290, October, 1951.

Bray, H. E. The Library's Financial Records: A Manual for Small and Medium-Sized Public Libraries. Ann Arbor, Mich., Edwards Brothers, 1943. 58p.

Discussion and illustration of types of financial accounts and records needed in library management.

Brownlow, J. L. "Cost Analysis for Libraries," District of Columbia Libraries, 31:54-60, October, 1960.

Brutcher, C., et. al. "Cost Accounting for the Library," Library Resources and Technical Services, 8:413-431, Fall, 1964.

Bryan, W.W., and B.W. Carroll, "Public Library Budgeting and Accounting," Illinois Libraries, 42:384-391, June, 1960.

Budington, W.S. "Cost of Information Services," In: Illinois University. Graduate School of Library Science. Library as a Community Information Center. Urbana, Illini Union Bookstore, 1950. Pp. 51-60.

Corbett, Edmund V. Public Library Finance and Accounting. London, Library Association, 1960. 212 p.

Elftmann, R.A. "Library Cost Studies; Industrial Engineering Versus Cost Accounting Techniques," Unpublished Master thesis, University of Minnesota, Minneapolis, 1953. 101 p.

Fasana, P.J., and J.E. Fall. "Processing Costs for Science Monographs in the Columbia University Libraries," Library Resources and Technical Services, 11:97-114, Winter, 1967.

Hirayama, K. "Time Required, Cost and Personnel for Documentation," American Documentation, 13:313-319, July, 1962.

Laich, K. "Preparing the Library's Performance Budget," California Librarian, 20:180-186, July, 1959.

Lingk, B.G., comp. Public Library Costs, Budgets, Finance: A Selected List of Books and Periodical Articles Prepared for an Institute on the Public Library Finance and Budgets. Minneapolis, University of Minnesota Library School, 1957.

Littleton, I.T. "The Distribution and Cost of Library Service," College and Research Libraries, 17:474-482, November, 1956.

Logsdon, R. H. "Time and Motion Studies in Libraries," Library Trends, 2:401-9, 1954.

Los Angeles. Bureau of Budget and Efficiency. Organization, Administration and Management of the Los Angeles Public Library. Los Angeles, 1948-1951. 12v.

Volumes: 3, 4, 7, 11 discuss work measurements and cost accounting.

McAnally, A. M. "Budgets by Formula," Library Quarterly, 33:159-171, April, 1963.

McCormick, E. J. Human Factors Engineering. New York, McGraw-Hill, 1964.

MacQuarrie, Catherine. "Cost Survey: Cost of Ordering, Cataloging, and Preparation in Southern California Libraries," Library Resources and Technical Services, 6: 337-350, Fall, 1962.

Maybury, C. "Performance Budgeting for Libraries," ALA Bulletin, 55:46-53, January, 1961.

Miller, R. A. "Cost Accounting for Libraries: A Technique for Determining the Labor Costs of Acquisitions and Cataloging Work." Unpublished Doctoral thesis, University of Chicago, 1936. 193 p.

Mixer, C. W., "New Developments in Insurance and Protection of Library Contents," Library Trends, 11:427-435, April, 1963.

Nitecki, A. and others. "Cost Accounting Forms. Guides to Aid Libraries to Determine the Unit Cost of Technical Services of a Library." Michigan Librarian, 29:19-21, December, 1963.

Olive, B. A. Management. A Subject Listing of Recommended Books, Pamphlets, and Journals. Ithaca, N. Y., Cornell University. Graduate School of Business and Public Administration, 1965. 222 p.

Parker, Ralph H. "Operating Costs of College and University Libraries," Library Trends, 11:376-383, April, 1963.

__________, and P. P. Price, eds. "Aspects of the Financial Administration of Libraries," Library Trends, April, 1963.

The entire issue is devoted to this problem.

Peterson, H. N. "Performance Budgeting, Work Measurement and the Public Library," Wilson Library Bulletin, 27:620-23, 1953.

A literature survey, now of historical interest.

Pickett, A. S. "San Francisco State College Library Technical Services Time Study," Library Resources and Technical Services, 4:45-58, Winter, 1960.

Pierce, W. O. Work Measurement in Public Libraries: Report to the Director of the Public Library Inquiry. Chicago, Social Science Research Council, 1949. 238 p.

A manual on time study programs with measurement data from three representative libraries included and analyzed.

Pilton, J. W., and S. Cooper. "Cost of Purchasing, Cataloging and Processing a Book at the Edmonton Public Library, A Preliminary Study," Edmonton Public Library News Notes, 6:22-26, March, 1961.

Rider, F. "Library Cost Accounting," Library Quarterly, 6:331-381, October, 1936.

Voos, H. Standard Times for Certain Clerical Activities in Technical Processing. Dover, N. J., Technical Information Branch, Picatinny Arsenal, 1964. 137 p. Based on Ph. D. dissertation, Graduate School, Rutgers State University.

Vroom, V. N. Work and Motivation. New York, Wiley, 1964.

One of the standard texts on human engineering and related subjects.

Welch, H. M. Technical Service Costs, Statistics and Standards, " Library Resources and Technical Services, 11:436-442, Fall, 1967.

Wight, E. A. Public Library Finance and Accounting. Chicago, American Library Association, 1943. 137 p.

Williams, R. L. The Administration of Academic Affairs in Higher Education. Ann Arbor, University of Michigan Press, 1965. 182 p.

Wilson, E. W. R. "Cost of Purchasing, Cataloging, and Processing a Book in the Edmonton Public Library, " Edmonton Public Library News Notes, 8:74-78, November, 1963.

Woodruff, E. L. "Work Measurement Applied to Libraries, " Special Libraries, 48:139-144, April, 1957.

Wynar, B. "Cost Analysis in a Technical Services Division, ' Library Resources and Technical Services, 7:312-326, Fall, 1963.

Wynar, B., and H. R. Malinowsky, eds. Cost Analysis Study of Technical Services Division, University of Denver Libraries. Denver, Graduate School of Librarianship, University of Denver, 1965. 118 p. (Studies in Librarianship, No. 4).

> During 1960-61 the Technical Services Division of the University of Denver Libraries made a cost analysis of processing costs. Topics discussed include in-print and out-of-print materials, gifts, discounts, cataloging procedures and preparation costs.

4. ORGANIZATION OF TECHNICAL SERVICES

a. College and University Libraries

See also pp. 87-91.

Bach, H. "Evaluation of the University Library," Library Resources and Technical Services, 2:24-29, Winter, 1958.

"Centralization and Decentralization in Academic Libraries: Symposium," College and Research Libraries, 22:327-340, 398, September, 1961.

Coney, D. "Management in College and University Libraries," Library Trends, 1:83-94, July, 1952.

Downs, R. B., and R. F. Delzell. "Price Tag on a University Library," College and Research Libraries, 21:359-361, 404, September, 1960.

Farley, E. "Combined Procedures for Technical Processes," Library Resources and Technical Services, 8:257-265, Summer, 1964.

University of Kansas experience.

Harrer, G. A. "Library Expenditures: An Examination of Their Distribution," College and Research Libraries, 18: 210-212, May, 1957.

Kaser, D. E. "Outside Funding of Academic Libraries," Library Trends, 11:353-361, April, 1963.

Kilpatrick, N. L. "The Administrator Looks at Technical Processing," Library Resources and Technical Services, 1:198-200, Fall, 1957.

A few tips on how to make technical processing more effective and efficient.

Kipp, L. J. "Scientific Management in Research Libraries," Library Trends, 2:390-400, January, 1954.

Points out that literature on the subject does not reflect the actual growth in the area. Stresses human practices. Includes bibliography.

Krueger, H. E. "Acquisition and Cataloging; and Integral Part of Reader Services," Library Resources and Technical Services, 3:192-197, Summer, 1959.

Describes the divisional plan in use at the Washington State University Libraries. Includes bibliography.

Logsdon, Richard H. "Administrative Organization of Columbia University Libraries," College and Research Libraries, 24:219-222, May, 1963.

Charts, with explanatory notes. Of interest to this study is the fact that the acquisitions department is directly under the director of libraries, and not formally connected with a technical services division.

Lyle, Guy R. The Administration of the College Library. 3d ed. New York: H. W. Wilson, 1961. 419 p.

Designed as an introductory text for all aspects of college library administration.

McAnnally, A. M. "Organization of College and University Libraries," Library Trends, 1:20-36, July, 1952.

Discusses organization and practices of some of the larger university libraries. Includes bibliography.

Marshall, John David, ed. The Library in the University; the University of Tennessee Library Lectures, 1949-1966. Hamden, Conn., Shoe String Press, 1967. 304 p.

Various aspects of history and changing problems of the research library.

Meier, R. L. "Efficiency Criteria for the Operation of Large Libraries," Library Quarterly, 31:215-234, July, 1961.

Describes a number of questionnaires and their findings in ". . . a large library for research and higher education in the Middle West. The item-use day is proposed as a catch-all unit for measuring the service provided." Statistical results are based on this unit.

Parker, R. H. "Operating Costs of College and University Libraries," Library Trends, 11:376-383, April, 1963.

Pickett, A. S. "San Francisco State College Library Technical Services Time Study," Library Resources and Technical Services, 4:45-46, Winter, 1960.

Tabulated results of a seven-year survey.

Reichmann, F. "Management and Operation," Library Trends, 3:462-470, April, 1955.

Summarizes the results of a survey of 31 university libraries regarding their management and operation. Includes bibliography.

Slama, M. "Technical Services and the Division Plan at Idaho," Library Resources and Technical Services, 3:198-201, Summer, 1959.

Discusses changes resulting from a move to a new building, with resulting economies. Includes bibliography.

Swank, Raymond C. "Report on Selected Problems of the Technical Department of the University of Illinois." In: Illinois University. Library School. Occasional Papers No. 42. Urbana, 1955.

Tauber, M. F. Technical Services in the Libraries of the University of New Mexico. Albuquerque, University of New Mexico, 1964.

Walker, L. "The Technical Processes in Small College Libraries of the Southeast," Journal of Cataloging and Classification, 9:108-111, June, 1953.

Report based on 110 replies to questionnaires (1952) sent out to libraries in four-year colleges, having total collections of 50,000 volumes or less.

Wilson, Louis Round, and Maurice F. Tauber. The University Library: The Organization, Administration, and Functions of Academic Libraries. 2d ed. New York, Columbia University Press, 1956. 641 p.

A systematic consideration of the principles and methods of university library administration and its unique role in higher education.

b. Public Libraries

See also pp. 91-93.

Bowler, R., ed. Local Public Library Administration. Chicago, International City Manager's Association, 1965.

Frarey, C. J. The Processing Services of the Dallas Public Library. Dallas, The Library, 1959. 235 p.

The results of an eight week survey during the summer of 1959 conducted by a technical services consultant.

Goldhor, H. "Scientific Management in Public Libraries," Library Trends, 2:368-389, January, 1954.

Relates scientific approach to study of library management, using process and flow charts, controlled experiments, etc. Includes bibliography.

Humphrey, J. A. "Pratt Reshapes Its Processing," Library Journal, 73:1345-1350, 1404, October 1, 1948.

A detailed account of how the above library combined acquisitions, cataloging and preparations into one division.

McDiarmid, E. W., and J. McDiarmid. Administration of the American Public Library. Chicago, American Library Association and University of Illinois Press, 1943.

Comparison and analysis of methods of organization and management.

Morris, T. D. "Techniques of Appraising the Administrative Strength of an Organization," College and Research Libraries, 13:111-116, April, 1952.

The theory of effective management of technical services, with some comments on evaluation of the organization of the NYPL Acquisition Division.

St. John, F. R. "Management Improvements in Libraries," College and Research Libraries, 14:174-177, April, 1953.

Emphasizes the need in most libraries for careful management analysis, and the application of sound management improvements. Describes the development of management improvements in the Brooklyn Public Library.

Sinclair, D. Administration of the Small Public Library. Chicago, American Library Association, 1965. 173 p.

Addressed primarily to the administrator of a library with fewer than three professional people on the staff.

Snow, J. B. "Comparison of Time Spent on Technical Processes by Two Separate Library Units Within one County With That Spent on Similar Operations in a Regional Library." Unpublished Master's thesis, University of Washington, Seattle, 1952.

Sommerville, C. "Short Cuts in Processing at the Public Library of Des Moines, Iowa," Library Resources and Technical Services, 1:95-103, Spring, 1957.

Time savers in acquisition and cataloging.

Wheeler, J. L., and H. Goldhor. Practical Administration of Public Libraries. New York, Harper, 1962. 571 p.

A guide for those involved directly with public library management. Intended primarily for libraries in communities of 10, 000-500, 000 population.

c. Special Libraries

See also pp. 93-94.

Ashworth, W., ed. Handbook of Special Librarianship and Information Work. 2d ed. London, Aslib, 1962. 508 p.

Includes concisely written chapter on administration.

Graham, E. C. "Administrative Policies for the Special Library: An Inventory," Special Libraries, 45:367-370, November, 1954.

"Management Methods in Libraries; A Symposium," Medical Library Association Bulletin, 49:514-540, October, 1961.

Shachtman, B. E. "Simplification Pays Off," Library Journal, 7:1254-1258, August, 1952.

Describes a process form developed in the Division of Technical Processes of the Department of Agriculture Library.

Smith, D. L., and E. G. Baxter. College Library Administration in Colleges of Technology, Art, Commerce, and Further Education. London, Oxford University Press, 1965. 185 p.

Written from a British frame of reference.

Special Libraries Association. Social Science Division. Public Administration Libraries; A Manual of Practice. Chicago, Public Administration Service, 1948. 91 p.

Includes chapters on acquisitions, classification, administration, finance, and service.

Strable, E. G., ed. *Special Libraries: A Guide for Management.* New York, Special Libraries Association, 1966.

Straus, L. J., et. al. *Scientific and Technical Libraries: Their Organization and Administration.* New York, Interscience, 1964. 398p.

Introductory guide to present practices.

Tauber, M. F. "Some Problems of Technical Services in Special Libraries," *Special Libraries,* 49:241-246, July-August, 1958.

Discussion of current trends in administration, with some comments on the developments in machine applications.

d. School Libraries

See also pp. 94-100.

American Association of School Libraries. *Standards for School Library Programs.* Chicago, American Library Association, 1960. 132p.

Revised qualitative and quantitative standards established by School Library Standards Committee.

Fargo, L. F. *The Library in the School.* 4th ed. Chicago, American Library Association, 1947. 405p.

A text dealing with library work at secondary school level.

Gardiner, Jewel. *Administering Library Service in the Elementary School.* Chicago, American Library Association, 1954. 160p.

Includes several chapters on acquisitions.

Gaver, M. V. *Patterns of Development in Elementary School Libraries Today.* 2d ed. Chicago, Encyclopedia Britannica, 1965.

Jones, Milbrey L. "Technical Services in School Libraries, An Analysis of the Literature, 1951-1961," Library Resources and Technical Services, 7:189-196, Spring, 1963.

Lowrie, J. E. Elementary School Libraries. New York, Scarecrow Press, 1960.

Moss, Margaret. "Problems and Policies; Librarians Describe the Services Their Central Departments Provide and Discuss the Problems to be Solved," Junior Libraries, 3:5-8, February, 1957.

Discusses method of ordering, detailed processing and routing through various operations including delivery to individual schools.

Whittier, C. T. "The Administrator Looks at Technical Processing: School Libraries," Library Resources and Technical Services, 1:201-203, Fall, 1957.

A few thoughts on school library efficiency.

Wisconsin. University. Second Annual School Library Institute. Planning Technical Services for School Libraries. Madison, University of Wisconsin, July 21-23, 1965. (Mimeographed).

5. Centralized and Cooperative Processing

See also pp. 258-265, "Cooperative Acquisitions."

Bebbington, J. "Library Cooperation, with Special Reference to Co-operative Acquisition and Storage," Library Association. Proceedings of the Public Libraries Conference, 1964, Pp. 43-50.

Bendix, D. "Regional Processing for Public Libraries, a Survey," Library Resources and Technical Services, 2:155-70, Summer, 1958.

Discusses, in detail, the various aspects of the above, with numerous examples cited. Includes bibliography.

Bonsall, George. "The Story of ALANAR," California School Libraries, 36:9-11, March, 1965.

Discusses ALANAR'S ROLE --- to supply books cataloged and processed, ready to shelve and read in accordance with school library requirements. Elaborates on ALANAR Elementary Program and The Elementary School Library Catalog, a listing of ready-to-shelve books for all titles available in publishers' library bindings.

"Book Processing Services," California School Libraries, 36:1-48, March, 1965.

Bundy, M. L. "Behind Central Processing," Library Journal, 88:3539-3543, October 1, 1963.

__________. Missouri Processing Cooperatives. A Report. Urbana, Ill., 1961.

__________. Public Library Processing Centers: A Report of a Nationwide Survey. Troy, N. Y., 1962.

Carhart, F. D. Southwest Missouri Library Service Inc.; A Study in Cooperative Centralized Technical Services. Chicago, American Library Association, 1962. 78p.

Presents organizational plan, fiscal structure, processing procedures, and results of three years operation of first independent library processing center.

Carroll, John F. "ALESCO--the Newest of the Commercial Book Processors," California School Libraries, 36:17-26, March, 1965.

Discusses their service. Pursues subject of complete time-dollar cost study of expense involving putting books on shelves. ALESCO will supply librarians with copies of their Elementary Catalog, Junior-Senior High School Catalog, and Young Adult Catalog as well as monthly supplements.

"Cooperation Between Washington State University Library and The University of Idaho Library, November 29, 1960," Bookmark. University of Idaho, 14:102-106, March, 1962.

Cronin, J. "The Library of Congress National Program for Acquisitions and Cataloging," Libri, 16:113-17, 1966.

Culbertson, K. "Public and College Libraries - Cooperative Services," Kentucky Library Association Bulletin, 26:12-18, July, 1962.

Curley, W. W. "Suffolk Cooperative Library System, New York's 21st," Bookmark, 23:285-289, July, 1964.

Dane, Chase. "Commercial Processing Centers for Elementary School Libraries," California School Libraries, 36:32-36, March, 1965.

Offers experiences of Santa Monica Unified School District to help school districts make a wise choice regarding the advisability of doing their own processing or sending it out to be done commercially. Suggests as more companies offer processing services, the picture will change.

Darling, K. L. "School Library Processing Centers," Library Trends, 16:58-66, July, 1967.

Dawson, J. M. "The Acquisitions and Cataloging of Research Libraries; A Study of the Possibilities for Centralized Processing," Library Quarterly, 27:1-22, January, 1957.

__________. "The Library of Congress: Its Role in Cooperative and Centralized Cataloging," Library Trends, 16:85-96, July, 1967.

Downs, R. B. "The Cooperative Program for Kansas City Area Libraries," Missouri Library Association Quarterly, 25:34-37, June, 1964.

Drennan, H. T. "Centralized Technical Services in Idaho," Pacific Northwest Library Association Quarterly, 26:150-158, April, 1962.

Eckford, Mary. "Library Service Center of Eastern Ohio, An Experiment in Centralized Processing," Library Resources and Technical Services, 5:5-33, Winter, 1961.

Esterquest, R. T. "Co-operation in Library Services," In: Chicago. University. Graduate Library School. Persistent Issues in American Librarianship. Chicago, University of Chicago Press, 1961. Pp. 71-89.

__________ Same. Library Quarterly, 31:71-89, January, 1961.

Farley, E. "Combined Procedures for Technical Processes," Library Resources and Technical Services, 8:257-265, Summer, 1964.

Fedder, Alice N. "Research in the School Library Field," Library Trends, 6:29-33, October, 1957.

Flannery, Anne. "Processing En Masse," California School Libraries, 36:29-32, March, 1965.

> Explains Library Processing Systems, a commercial processor. Offers advantages of commercial processing over centralized or cooperative ventures.

Follett, Robert J. R. "A Publisher Looks at Pre-Processing," California School Libraries, 36:5-8, March, 1965.

> Suggests librarians purchase pre-processing services including prebound books; catalog cards; "Ready-process Packet" containing title, author, subject, shelf list cards, book pocket, book card, call number label-all 25¢; custom pre-processing of books; and the ultimate service--supplies shelves, card file, pre-selected basic collection of completely processed books, card catalog, chairs, tables, plus all equipment and materials needed to start a small library.

Galloway, R. D. "Cooperative Acquisitions for California's Libraries," California Libraries, 24:183-187, July, 1963.

Greer, Phyllis. "Small System Elementary School Materials Center," School Libraries, 12:39-42, May, 1963.

"Guidelines for Centralized Technical Services," Library Resources and Technical Services, 10:233-240, Spring, 1966.

Hanley, M. Centralized Processing. Recent Trends and Current Status; A Review and Syntheses of the Literature. Urbana, Ill., Illinois University. Graduate School of Library Science, 1964. (Occasional Papers No. 71).

Henderson, James W. Centralized Processing of Library Materials in West Virginia and Other Matters. A Survey. Charleston, West Virginia Library Commission, 1959.

Hoffman, H. H. "Cooperative Acquisitions in German Research Libraries, 1800-1930," Library Quarterly. 34: 249-257, July, 1964.

Holloway, A. H. "Price of Co-operation (With Discussion)," Aslib Proceedings, 13:15-25, January, 1961.

Humphry, J. A. Library Cooperation; The Brown University Study of University - School - Community Library Coordination in the State of Rhode Island. Providence, Brown University Press, 1963. 213 p.

Hunt, James R. "The Historical Development of Processing Centers in the U. S.," Library Resources and Technical Services, 8:54-62, Winter, 1964.

Shows rapid growth in the last ten years in idea of centralized processing centers. Discusses painful growth and whether centers are necessary, Library Service Act of 1956, varying patterns for centers, and the catalog card as a book pocket. Three-page table lists alphabetically centers throughout the U. S. noting date established, number of participating libraries, basis for participation, book ordering included and type of card reproduction.

Jasper, Harold S. "Professional Library Service," California School Libraries, 36:26-29, March, 1965.

PLS offers a Cards with Books Program---complete set of catalog cards, processed according to rules and standards maintained in Authority Files (abridged copy of rules available from Processing Department on request), with each book purchased; PLS Standard Plan provides books ready for immediate shelving for smaller library units; Custom Processing. Full descriptive information upon request. Offers recommended titles for school library collections---5700 elementary, 5200 junior high, 9400 senior high.

Kenney, B. L. Cooperative Centralized Processing: A Report of the Establishment and First Year of Operation of the Southwest Missouri Library Service, Inc. Chicago, American Library Association, 1959. 98p.

Attempts to ascertain whether new Center achieved its aims: to save time for member libraries, to permit more efficient use of personnel, and to save money.

Ketkar, N. M. "Acquisitions through Legal Deposit," Library Herald, 8:34-50, April and July, 1965.

Describes the history of legal deposits beginning with the state acquisitions in France.

Liebel, Carl J. "A Lure for Librarians," California School Libraries, 36:8-9, March, 1965.

Comments on alluring promise of "cataloged and processed, ready for immediate shelving and circulation" of books. Suggests a refined standard of processing by libraries to enable commercial processors to reduce production costs.

Lively, Gladys M. "The Creative Elementary School Library and Centralized Processing," Wilson Library Bulletin, 36:753-757, May, 1962.

Discusses: why centralized processing?; setting up a processing center; detailed description of specific routines at Madison, Wisconsin; and five recommendations for someone starting from "scratch."

McCain, P. M. "Library Cooperation in Arkansas," Liberal Education, 48:21-25, March, 1962.

MacEachern, J. "Cooperation Between the Libraries of Washington State University and the University of Idaho," Pacific Northwest Library Association Quarterly, 26:90-97, January, 1962.

McJenkin, Virginia. "Streamlining Essential Routines," Wilson Library Bulletin, 37:680-681, April, 1963.

Pursues idea that streamlining routines including centralized processing of books can facilitate service and relieve librarian to maintain creative elementary school library.

Mahoney, O. "Centralized Processing Centers," Library Resources and Technical Services, 5:40-47, Winter, 1961.

Surveys the activities of fourteen centers in the U. S. Includes tabulated summary.

Moody, M. A. "Opportunities for Library Cooperation," Law Library Journal, 54:223-226, August, 1961.

Moore, E. L. "Processing Center for California Junior College Libraries--A Preliminary Study," Library Resources and Technical Services, 9:303-317, November, 1965.

Mullen, Evelyn Day. "Guidelines for Establishing a Centralized Library Processing Center," Library Resources and Technical Services, 2:171-175, Summer, 1958.

Defines centralized processing center as a single agency which processes materials for a wider group of libraries. Discusses: aims; anticipated results; background data needed from prospective members, statistical and administrative; questions on ordering; questions on cataloging; questions on physical preparation methods; and decisions to be made and procedures to be established.

__________. "Regional Processing for Public Libraries," Library Resources and Technical Services, 5:34-40, Winter, 1961.

Nelson Associates, Inc. Centralized Processing for the Public Libraries of New York State. New York, Nelson Associates, 1966.

A survey conducted in collaboration with the Theodore Stein Co.

Oehlerts, D. E. Study to Determine the Feasibility of Establishing a Cooperative Technical Processing Program and Direct Transmission of Inter-library Loans. Denver, Association of State Institutions of Higher Education in Colorado, 1962.

Oellrich, Gertrude L. "ALANAR Book Processing Center," California School Libraries, 36:12-17, March, 1965.

Discusses their technical services department serving libraries ranging in type from elementary, public, college and university, special to overseas, including cataloging, editing and processing sections, and how they meet the problems of subject headings, classification, cataloging and adopting long-range policies at ALANAR to meet individual library differences.

Pettit, Edna M. "How Did We Ever Get Along Without Central Processing?" New York Library Association Bulletin, 3:12-14, February, 1955.

Although this is about public libraries, it offers discussion of many advantages of central processing.

"Processing Centers for Public Libraries: A Tentative List," Library Resources and Technical Services, 10: 489-492, Fall, 1966.

Rather, J. C. "Library Cooperation: A Bibliographical Essay Prepared for the California State Library and the California Library Association," California Librarian, 16:299-310, October, 1955.

Sabsay, D. "North Bay Cooperative Library System," News Notes of California Libraries, 58:335-347, Summer, 1963.

Skipper, J. E. "Library Cooperation in Metropolitan New York," In: Rutgers University. Graduate School of Library Service. Studies in Library Administrative Problems. New Brunswick, N. J., Rutgers University Press, 1960. Pp. 77-94.

Tauber, M. F., and R. E. Kingery. The Central Technical Processing of the Nassau Library System. Hempstead, N. Y., The Nassau Library System, 1962. 103 p.

A report on the organization, facilities, operations, and problems.

__________, and I. R. Stephens. "Southern California Library Study: Centralized Technical Processing," In: Boaz, M., ed. Strength Through Cooperation in Southern California Libraries. Los Angeles, Los Angeles Public Library, 1965.

Vann, S. "Evaluation of Centers: The Views of Members," Library Trends, 16:23-45, July, 1967.

The views of autonomous public libraries which have agreed to participate in centralized processing programs.

Weiss, R. "The State of Automation? A Survey of Machinery Used in Technical Services Departments in New York State Libraries," Library Resources and Technical Services, 9:289-302, Summer, 1965.

An analysis of the results of a questionnaire sent to 25 school, 23 public and 36 college libraries.

Wendel, C. E. "Book Processing Center, Orlando, Florida: A Case Study," Library Resources and Technical Services, 8:71-76, Winter, 1964.

Whitehorn, Catherine. "Central Systems in Operation," Library Journal, 82:562-565, February 15, 1957.

__________, and M. Bernice Wiese. "Central Systems in Operation; the Results of a Survey Conducted by the Baltimore School Library Department as a Basis for Setting Up Its Own System," Junior Libraries, 3:2-5, February, 1957.

Covers ordering, classification, cataloging, processing, statistics, staff, advantages and disadvantages and suggestions and states its conclusions.

6. LIBRARIES AND AUTOMATION

See also pp. 153-163.

Adkinson, B. W. Trends in Library Application of Data Processing. Urbana, Ill., University of Illinois Graduate School of Library Science, 1963.

Anglo-American Conference on the Mechanization of Library Services. Chicago, Mansell, 1967.

The papers of the Brasenose Conference on the automation of libraries.

Bay Area Library Working Committee. Bay Area Libraries Associated Network for Cooperative Exchange. A Report on Computerized Procedures. San Jose, Calif., 1966. 78 p.

Becker, J., and R. M. Hayes. Information Storage and Retrieval: Tools, Elements, Theories. New York, Wiley, 1963.

An overview of the field concentrating on the different specialties which must be interrelated. Also includes a final section on theories.

Becker, J. "Using Computers in a New University Library," ALA Bulletin, 59:823-826, October, 1965.

Besselman, J. A. New Advances in Information Retrieval. New York, Wiley, 1963.

Black, D., and E. A. Farley. "Library Automation," In: Annual Review of Information Science and Technology. 1:273-303. New York, Interscience, Wiley, 1966.

Black, Donald V. "Library Mechanization," Sci-Tech News, 16:115-117, Fall, 1962.

Boaz, M., ed. Modern Trends in Documentation. New York, Pergamon, 1959.

Bourne, C. P. Methods of Information Handling. New York, Wiley, 1963.

Bregzis, R. "The Ontario New Universities Library Project: An Automated Bibliographic Data Control System," College and University Libraries, 26:495-516, November, 1965.

Bryan, H. "American Automation in Action," Library Journal, 92:189-196, January 15, 1967.

Burns, L. R. "Automation in the Public Libraries of Lake County, Indiana," In: Clinic on Library Applications of Data Processing, University of Illinois, 1st, 1963. Proceedings. Edited by H. Goldhor. Champaign, Ill., Distributed by the Illini Union Bookstore, 1964. Pp. 9-17.

Bush, Vannevar. Report to the Secretary of Commerce by the Advisory Committee on Application of Machine to Patent Office Operations. Washington, D. C., U. S. Department of Commerce, December 22, 1954.

Callander, T. E. "Punched Cards Systems: Their Application to Library Technique," Library Association Record, 48:171-174, July, 1946.

Carroll, Kenneth D., and Roger K. Summit. MATICO: Machine Applications to Technical Information Center Operations. Sunnyvale, Calif., Lockheed Missiles & Space Company, September, 1962.

Casey, Robert S., et. al. Punched Cards: Their Application to Science and Industry. 2d ed. New York, Reinhold Publishing Corp., 1958. 697 p.

One chapter covers applications to library routines.

Clapp, V. W. "Closing the Circuit: Automation and Data Processing for Libraries," Library Journal, 91:1165-1171, March, 1966.

__________. "The Computer in the Library," In: Proceedings of the 1960 Computer Applications Symposium, New York, Macmillan, 1961. Pp. 35-44.

__________. The Future of the Research Library. Urbana, Ill., University of Illinois Press, 1964.

__________. "Implications for Documentation and the Organization of Knowledge," Library Quarterly, 25:356-362, October, 1955.

__________. "Mechanization and Automation in American Libraries," Libri, 14:369-375, 1964.

Coblans, H. Use of Mechanized Methods in Documentation Work. London, ASLIB, 1966.

Computer Usage Company. Specifications for an Automated Library System. Prepared for University of California at Santa Cruz. Palo Alto, 1965. 122 p.

Conference on Libraries and Automation, Airlie Foundation, 1963. Libraries and Automation: Proceedings. Edited by B. E. Markieson. Washington, Library of Congress, 1964.

Connor, J. M. "Management Methods in Libraries; A Symposium--Office Machines and Appliances," Bulletin of the Medical Library Association, 49:534-540, October, 1961.

Corbin, J. B. "Automatic Data Processing in the Texas State Library," Texas Library Journal, 41:12-14, Spring, 1965.

"The Cost of Data Processing in University Libraries," College and University Libraries, 24:487-495, November, 1963.

Cox, N. S. M., J. D. Dews, and J. L. Dolby. The Computer and the Library: The Role of the Computer in the Organization and Handling of Information in Libraries. Hamden, Conn., Archon Books, 1967.

Dillon, H. W. Program for the Utilization of Automatic Data Processing Equipment. Columbus, Ohio State University, 1965.

Dubester, H. J. "The Librarian and the Machine," In: Institute on Information Storage and Fetrieval, 1st, University of Minnesota, 1962. Information Retrieval Today. Minneapolis, 1966. Pp. 167-176.

EDP Systems Development Services. Report of the Survey of Data Processing Feasibility for the Prince Georges County Memorial Library System. Hyattsville, Md., 1965. 48 p.

Geddes, A. "Data Processing in a Cooperative System --- Opportunities for Service," In: Harvey, J., ed. Data Processing in Public and University Libraries. Washington, Spartan Books, 1966. Pp. 25-35. (Drexel Information Science Services, v. 3.)

Nassau Library System.

General Electric Company. A Final Report on Improving Information Flow in a University Library. Washington, General Electric Company, Information Systems Operation, July, 1961. (Prepared under contract with the University of Illinois, Chicago Undergraduate Division.)

Goldhor, H. "New Technology; Promise and Reality," Library Quarterly, 33:102-114, January, 1963.

Gordon, G. E. "Columbus Conversion to Data Processing," Wilson Library Bulletin, 41:414-417, December, 1966.

Greiner, W. E. "Data Processing Equipment and the Library," In: Clinic on Library Applications of Data Processing, University of Illinois, 3d, 1965. Proceedings. Edited by F. B. Jenkins. Champaign, Ill., Distributed by the Illini Union Bookstore, 1966. Pp. 175-192.

Griffin, H. L. EDP Procedures in Technical Library Operations. Atomic Energy Division, Idaho Operations Office, U. S. Atomic Energy Commission, 1963.

Library procedures employing electronic data processing.

Gull, C. D. "The Hardware of Data Processing," Library Resources and Technical Services, 9:6-19, Winter, 1965.

__________. "The Present State of Library Automation; A Study in Reluctant Leadership," In: Clinic on Library Applications of Data Processing, University of Illinois, 3d, 1965. Proceedings. Edited by F. B. Jenkins. Champaign, Ill., Distributed by the Illini Union Bookstore, 1966. Pp. 1-14.

Harvey, J., ed. Data Processing in Public and University Libraries. Washington, Spartan Books, 1966. (Drexel Information Science Series, v. 3.)

Hayes, R. M. "The Concept of an Online, Total System," In: American Library Association. Library Technology Project. Library Technology Reports. Chicago, May, 1965.

__________. "Implications for Librarianship of Computer Technology," In: Clinic on Library Applications of Data Processing, University of Illinois, 2d, 1966. Edited by H. Goldhor. Champaign, Ill., Distributed by the Illini Union Bookstore, 1965. Pp. 1-6.

Heiliger, Edward M. "Application of Advanced Data Processing Techniques to University Library Procedures," Special Libraries, 53:472-475, October, 1962.

Heiliger, E. M. "Staffing a Computer Based Library," Library Journal, 89:2738-2739, July, 1964.

Heilprin, Laurence B. "On the Information Problem Ahead," American Documentation, 12:6-14, January, 1961.

Heller, E. W., and C. D. Hobbs. A Survey of Information Retrieval Equipment. Santa Monica, Calif., Systems Development Corp., 1961.

Howe, M. T. "The Establishment and Growth of the Data Processing Department in the Decatur Public Library," In: Harvey, J., ed. Data Processing in Public and University Libraries. Washington, Spartan Books, 1966. Pp. 37-52. (Drexel Information Science Series, v. 3.)

__________, and Mary K. Weidner. "Mechanization in Public Libraries; Data Processing Department in the Decatur Public Library," UNESCO Bulletin for Libraries, 15:317-321, November, 1961.

Howe, M. T. "Mechanization in the Decatur Public Library," In: IBM Library Mechanization Symposium, Endicott, N. Y., 1964. Proceedings. White Plains, N. Y., International Business Machines Corp., 1965. Pp. 1-13.

Howerton, P. W., ed. Information Handling: First Principles. Washington, Spartan Books, 1963.

International Business Machine Coporation. General Information Manual. Mechanical Library Procedures. White Plains, N. Y., IBM Corp., 1962.

__________. IBM Advanced Systems Development and Research Library Procedure Manual. San Jose, Calif., IBM Corp., Advanced Systems Development Division, 1959. (Subsequently including March 19, 1963.)

Jacobs, J. W. "Present and Future Applications of Data Processing Equipment for School Libraries," In: Clinic on Library Applications of Data Processing. Edited by Herbert Goldhor. Champaign, Ill., Distributed by the Illini Union Bookstore, 1964. Pp. 37-42.

Jahoda, G., and F. A. Accola. "Library Records Prepared with the Aid of Data Processing Equipment," College and Research Libraries, 26:129-137, March, 1965.

Kemeny, John G. "A Library for 2000 A. D.," In: Greenberger, Martin, ed. Management and the Computer of the Future. Cambridge, MIT Press, 1962.

Kent, A. Electronic Information Handling. Washington, Spartan Books, 1965. 355 p.

> Papers presented at a national conference with speakers from such diverse fields as government, industry, and education.

Kent, A. Library Planning for Automation. Washington, Spartan Books, 1965. 195 p.

Based on a conference at the University of Pittsburgh which discussed the proposed National Science Library System.

Kent, A. Specialized Information Centers. Washington, Spartan Books, 1965. 290p.

A study of specialized information centers in order to discern similarities and differences.

__________. Textbook on Mechanized Information Retrieval. New York, Interscience, 1966.

Koriagin, Gretchen W. Experience in Man Machine Relationships in Library Mechanization. Santa Monica, Douglas Missiles and Space Division, November, 1962. (Engineering Paper No. 1495.)

__________, and L. R. Bunnow. Mechanized Information Retrieval System for Douglas Aircraft Company, Inc.; Status Report. Santa Monica, Douglas Aircraft Company, Inc., January, 1962. (SM-39167).

Kraft, D. H. "Data Processing Equipment for Library Use in Clerical Tasks and Dissemination of Information," Illinois Libraries, 44:587-592, November, 1962.

__________. "The Influence and Impact of Mechanization on Libraries and Society Today and Tomorrow," In: Texas Conference on Library Mechanization, 1st, Austin, 1966. Proceedings. Edited by J. B. Corbin. Austin, Texas Library and Historical Commission, 1966. Pp. 31-63. (Texas State Library Monograph, No. 6.)

Laughlin, Mildred. "Automation; Implications for Elementary Libraries," School Libraries, 7:19-21, October, 1957.

Lazorick, Gerald J., and Hugh C. Atkinson. Gift and Exchange Department Automation Study. Buffalo, State University of New York at Buffalo, 1965.

Libraries and Automation. Washington, Library of Congress, 1964. 268 p.

> Seven major topics presented with discussion from the Conference on Libraries and Automation in 1963 under the sponsorship of the Library of Congress, National Science Foundation, and the Council on Library Resources.

Library Systems Study for Public Libraries of Santa Clara, Alameda, and Contra Costa Counties. Palo Alto, Freeman Co., 1965.

Licklinder, J. C. R. Libraries of the Future. Cambridge, Mass., M. I. T. Press, 1965. 219 p.

> A summary report from a study of "concepts and problems of libraries of the future."

Lockheed Georgia Company. Mechanization of Library Procedures (Project 163). Marietta, Ga., Lockheed Georgia Co., 1962.

McCormick, E. M. Bibliography on Mechanized Library Processes. Washington, National Science Foundation, 1963.

McCune, L. C., and S. R. Salmon. "Bibliography of Library Automation," A. L. A. Bulletin, 61:674-694, June, 1967.

Markieson, B. E. "A System Development Study for the Library of Congress Automation Program," The Library Quarterly, 36:197-273, July, 1966.

Mayeda, T. A., et. al. Joint College/Industry Library with Automation: The Report of the Study of the Bases, Including the Use of the Techniques of Automation, for Providing the Capability for a Science Library for Academic-Industry Use. Washington, Council on Library Resources, 1964. (Prepared for the Harvey Mudd College.)

Meise, N. R. Conceptual Design of an Automated National Library System, Hartford, 1966. (M. A. Thesis).

Melin, J. S. Libraries and Data Processing: Where Do We Stand? Urbana, University of Illinois, Graduate School of Library Science, 1964. (Occasional Papers, No. 72.)

Mohrhardt, Foster E. "Critique on Developments in the Mechanization of Information Systems," College and Research Libraries, 19:395-397, September, 1958.

Morse, Philip M. "The Prospects for Mechanization," College and Research Libraries, 25:115-119, March, 1964.

Myers, J. E. "Automation, What It Is and What It Is Not," Special Libraries, 46:308-313, September, 1955.

Parker, R. H. Library Applications of Punched Cards; A Description of Mechanical Systems. Chicago, American Library Association, 1952.

Perry, J. W., and Kent, A. Documentation and Information Retrieval. An Introduction to Basic Principles and Cost Analysis. Cleveland, Western Reserve University Press, 1957.

Pflug, G. "Problems of Electronic Data Processing in Libraries," Libri, 15:35-49, 1965.

Proceedings of the 1963 Clinic on Library Applications of Data Processing. Champaign, Ill., University of Illinois, Graduate School of Library Science, 1964.

Roach, John P., Jr. SATIRE: The Technical Librarian's EAM Application of Semi-automatic Technical Information Retrieval. Paramus, N. J., System Development Corporation, December 28, 1961. (SP-595).

Ruggles, Melville J. Mechanization and Automation in Russian Libraries. Washington, Council on Library Resources, 1961.

Schultheiss, Louis A. "Automation of Library Operations," In: Proceedings of the 1961 Computer Applications Symposium. New York, Macmillan, 1962. Pp. 35-44.

Schultheiss, Louis A., et. al. Advanced Data Processing in the University Library. New York, Scarecrow Press, 1962. 388p.

A report on the information system project at the University of Illinois.

Sharp, J. R. Some Fundamentals of Information Retrieval. London, Deutsch, 1965. 224p.

Study of the principles of the several kinds of retrieval systems.

Shaw, Ralph R. "Implications for Library Services," Library Quarterly, 25:344-355, October, 1955.

Shaw, Ralph R. "Management, Machines and the Bibliographic Problems of the 20th Century," In: Shera, Jesse H., and Margaret E. Egan, eds. Bibliographic Organization. Chicago, University of Chicago Press, 1951. Pp. 220-225.

Shera, J. H. "Automation Without Fear," ALA Bulletin, 55:787-794, October, 1961.

Recent developments in automation and its psychological implications upon librarianship.

__________. "Effect of Machine Methods on the Organization of knowledge," American Documentation, 3:15-20, Winter, 1952.

Simonton, W., ed. Information Retrieval Today. Minneapolis, University of Minnesota, 1963.

Slamecka, Vladimir, ed. Studies in Technical Data Management. Atlanta, School of Information Science, Georgia Institute of Technology, 1965.

Spagler, M. R., ed. General Bibliography: Information Storage and Retrieval. Phoenix, Ariz., General Electric Co., 1962.

Stein, T. "Automation and Library Systems," Library Journal, 89:2723-2734, July, 1964.

Stewart, B. W. "Data Processing in an Academic Library," Wilson Library Bulletin, 41:388-395, December, 1966.

Texas A & M University.

Stone, C. W., et. al. A Library Program for Columbia, Md. Pittsburgh, 1965. 54 p.

Swanson, Don R. "Library Goals and the Role of Automation," Special Libraries, 54:466-471, October, 1962.

__________. Library Service With or Without Automation. Ottawa, Canadian Library Association, 1965. (Occasional Paper, No. 61).

Tams, M. P. "Libraries and Computers, the State of the Art," Southeastern Librarian, 13:229-234, Winter, 1963.

Trotier, Arnold H., ed. "Mechanization in Libraries," Library Trends, 5:191-308, October, 1956.

Turner, Lester D., and James H. Kennedy. System of Automatic Processing and Indexing of Reports. Livermore, Calif., University of California Radiation Laboratory, July 12, 1961. (UCRL-6510).

U. S. Library of Congress, Automation and the Library of Congress, Washington, U. S. Library of Congress, 1963. 88 p.

A survey of the possibilities of automation in the Library of Congress which shows feasibility.

U. S. Library of Congress. A Preliminary Report on the MARC (Machine Readable Cataloging) Pilot Project. Prepared by the Information Systems Office. Washington, October, 1966. 101 p.

Vertanes, C. A. "Automating the School Library; An Advanced Report," <u>Wilson Library Bulletin</u>, 37:864-867, June, 1963.

Vickery, B. C. "The Future of Libraries," <u>The Library Association Record</u>, 68:252-260, July, 1966.

__________. <u>On Retrieval System Theory</u>. 2d ed. London, Butterworth, 1965.

Waldron, R. K. "Implications of Technological Progress for Libraries," <u>College and Research Libraries</u>, 19:118-123, March, 1958.

Walker, R. D., and M. L. Bundy. "Use of Machines in College and University Libraries in Illinois," <u>Illinois Libraries</u>, 43:653-666, November, 1961.

Warheit, I. A. "Machines and Systems for the Modern Library," <u>Special Libraries</u>, 48:357-363, October, 1957.

> The mechanization of many mechanical and even intellectual library activities is not only possible but practical. Special attention is given to such problems as document and index storage possibilities, cataloging with machines, and systems which can manipulate entries for subject headings.

Wasserman, P. <u>The Librarian and the Machine</u>. Detroit, Gale, 1965. 170p.

> Observations on the applications of machines in administration of college and research libraries.

Weiss, R. "The State of Automation? A Survey of Machinery Used in Technical Services Departments in New York State Libraries," <u>Library Resources and Technical Services</u>, 9:289-302, Summer, 1965.

White, Herbert S. <u>Mechanized Information Processing and the Librarian</u>. Kingston, N. Y., IBM Corp., Data Systems Division, April 10, 1962. (TP 62-1241).

CHAPTER II

ORGANIZATION AND ADMINISTRATION OF ACQUISITIONS

---

1. HISTORICAL BACKGROUND

a. Bibliographies

See also pp. 66-78, "Libraries and Automation."

McCormick, E. M. Bibliography on Mechanized Library Processes. Washington, National Science Foundation, 1963.

A selective bibliography limited mostly to periodical articles, now somewhat outdated.

Schultze, G. Documentation Source Book. New York, The Scarecrow Press, 1965. Pp. 103-122.

A selective bibliography emphasizing the practical aspects of acquisitions.

Wynar, B. Syllabus for Technical Processes in Libraries. Denver, University of Denver Graduate School of Librarianship, 1962. Pp. 13-32.

b. Reviews of Literature

Bevis, Dorothy L. "Acquisitions and Resources; Highlights of 1962," Library Resources and Technical Services, 7: 142-155, Spring, 1963.

A survey of the work on cooperation, exchange and publication in the U. S. S. R., Latin America, Africa, rare books, distribution costs and figures, and grants. Emphasizes the effort being made to make available the book resources of the country to every citizen.

Bevis, Dorothy L. "A Sampling of the Year's Work in Acquisitions and Resources," Library Resources and Technical Services, 6:110-112, Spring, 1962.

> 1961 is characterized as a year of cooperative effort. Discusses rare books, cooperation, acquisitions and resources, and costs and figures.

__________. "The Year's Work in Acquisitions and Resources," Library Resources and Technical Services, 5: 105-115, Spring, 1961.

> Reviews acquisitions progress on national and international scale. Includes bibliography.

Chicorel, M. "Highlights in Acquisitions," Library Resources and Technical Services, 8:112-125, Spring, 1964.

> Trend in 1963 was toward continued efforts at cooperation and coordination. Discusses work on budgets, cost patterns, statistics and standardization, mechanization, library cooperation, area acquisitions, selection aids, international trends in cooperation, and research.

Dougherty, Richard M. "Acquisitions--1965 in Review," Library Resources and Technical Services, 10:165-172, Spring, 1966.

> The most significant highlights in 1965 included progress toward a national centralized acquisitions and cataloging program. Reviews automation, Public Law 480, book dealer-library relations, the antiquarian market and reprint publishing, and price indexes.

__________. "Year's Work in Acquisitions," Library Resources and Technical Services, 9:149-156, Spring, 1965.

> 1964 is characterized as a year of continuation. Emphasis is on centralization and cooperation. Discusses publishers and jobbers, blanket acquisitions plans, resources, USBE, statistics, price indexes, paper deterioration, central processing centers, and automation.

Dougherty, R. M., and A. McKinney. "Ten Years of Progress in Acquisitions: 1956-1966," Library Resources and Technical Services, 11:289-300, Summer, 1967.

Welch, H. M. "The Year's Work in Acquisitions and Resources," Library Resources and Technical Services, 4:101-108, Spring, 1960.

Reviews the past year's developments, including general reference to publications in the field. Includes bibliography.

__________. "The Year's Work in Acquisitions and Resources," Library Resources and Technical Services, 3: 78-83, Spring, 1959.

Briefly reviews the past year's developments and quotes articles. Includes bibliography.

__________. "The Year's Work in Acquisitions," Library Resources and Technical Services, 2:75-82, Spring, 1958.

Briefly reviews the past year's major developments in acquisitions. Includes bibliography.

c. Textbooks and Manuals

Acquisition of Special Materials. Calif., S. L. A. Bay Region Chapter, 1966.

A recent text on the subject, with numerous bibliographical references.

American Association of Law Librarians. Order Procedures Presented at 1959 AALL Institute for Law Librarians. A Manual. South Hackensack, N. J., F. B. Rothman, 1960. (AALL Publications Series, No. 2).

Bird, V., et al. Order Processes: A Manual. South Hackensack, N. J., F. B. Rothman, 1960.

Carter, M. D., and W. J. Bonk. Building Library Collections. 2d ed. New York, Scarecrow Press, 1964.

Corbin, J. B. A Technical Services Manual for Small Libraries. Austin, Texas, Library and Historical Commission, 1965. (Monograph No. 3, Texas State Library).

Drury, Francis K. W. Order Work for Libraries. Chicago, American Library Association, 1930.

Written as a textbook for a course in acquisitions. Dated.

__________. The Selection and Acquisition of Books for Libraries. Chicago, American Library Association, 1928.

George, V. "Acquisitions." In: Ashworth, W., ed. Handbook of Special Librarianship and Information Work. 2d ed. London, Aslib, 1962. Pp. 32-69.

Discussion of general principles.

Strauss, L. J., et. al. "Books and Their Publications: Selection and Acquisition," In: Scientific and Technical Libraries: Their Organization and Administration. New York, Interscience, 1964, Pp. 90-123.

Wulfekoetter, Gertrude. Acquisition Work Processes Involved in Building Library Collections. Seattle, University of Washington Press, 1961. 268p.

Discussion of the practices involved in all phases of acquisition work --- organization of the department, order work, serials, binding, etc.

2. DEVELOPING ACQUISITION PROGRAMS

a. Acquisition Policy in General

Chicorel, Marietta. "Acquisitions in an Age of Plenty," Library Resources and Technical Services, 10:19-27, Winter, 1966.

Coney, D. "The Administration of Technical Processes," In: Joeckel, C. B. Current Issues in Library Administration. Chicago, University of Chicago Press, 1939. Pp. 163-180.

Functional vs. material organization; divisional vs. department administration.

Dougherty, R. M., et. al. Policies and Programs Designed to Improve Cooperation and Coordination Among Technical Service Operating Units. Urbana, University of Illinois Graduate School of Library Science, 1967. 45 p. (Occasional Papers, No. 86.)

Updating of a technical services practices study made in 1955 based on reports of 70 research libraries.

Fussler, H. H., et. al. "Acquisition Policy: A Symposium," College and Research Libraries, 14:363-372, October, 1953.

Metcalf, K. D. "The Essentials of an Acquisition Program," In: Randall, W. M., ed. The Acquisition and Cataloging of Books. Chicago, University of Chicago Press, 1940. Pp. 76-94.

Price, M. O. "Acquisition and Technical Processing," Library Trends, 6:430-458, April, 1958.

Deals with laws governing libraries, principally copyright laws.

Reichmann, F. "Management and Operation," Library Trends, 3:462-469, April, 1955.

Shaffer, K. R. The Book Collection: Policy Case Studies in Public and Academic Libraries. Hamden, Conn., Shoestring Press, 1961. 147 p.

A presentation of twenty-five cases dealing with book selection, acquisitions, and service problems at the administrative level.

Sprod, T. D. "Framing an Acquisition Policy," In: Raymond, I. D., ed. Seminar on Technical Services, Baillieu Library, University of Melbourne, 17th-18th August, 1961; directed by Maurice F. Tauber (working papers). Canberra, Australian Advisory Council on Bibliographic Services, 1962.

Vosper, R. G. "Current Acquisition Trends in American Libraries," Library Trends, 3:333-336, April, 1955.

The introduction to an issue devoted entirely to the acquisition problems in American libraries.

b. Selection of Materials for Purchase

American Library Association. Freedom of Book Selection. Chicago, American Library Association, 1954. 132 p.

Problems of censorship as seen at Conference on Intellectual Freedom in 1953.

Asheim, L. "Facets of Book Selection," Mountain-Plains Library Quarterly, 5:3-4, Spring, 1960.

Presents an interesting analogy drawn between the librarian and the responsible book publisher in the matter of book selection.

__________. "Problems of Censorship in Book Selection," Bay State Librarian, 52:5-9 , Winter, 1962.

Ashmore, W. S. H. "Book Selection Team; With Discussion," In: Library Association Conference, 1961, Hastings. Proceedings. The Association, 1961. Pp. 40-47.

"Book Selection or Censorship; Summary of a Panel Discussion Which Took Place at the APLA Conference, May 20, 1960," Atlantic Provinces Library Association Bulletin, 25:17-22, Fall, 1960.

Broderick, D. M. "I May, I Might, I Must; Some Philosophical Observations on Book Selection Policies and Practices and the Freedom to Read," Library Journal, 88:507-510, February 1, 1963.

Budington, W. S. "Problems of Selection in Science," In: Illinois. University. Graduate School of Library Science. Collecting Science Literature for General Reading. Champaign, Illini Union Bookstore, 1961. Pp. 138-149.

Carlson, W. H. "Mobilization of Existing Library Resources," Library Trends, 6:272-295, January, 1958.

Cave, R. "Translations and the Book-Selection Problems," Library World, 62:32-35, August, 1960.

Danton, J. Periam. Book Selection and Collections: A Comparison of German and American University Libraries. New York, Columbia University Press, 1963. 188 p.

Concerned primarily with philosophies and policies of book selection in the eighteen West German university libraries as compared to their American counterparts.

Dimalanta, C. "Selection and Acquisition of Library Materials in Pure and Applied Sciences," Association of Special Libraries of the Philippines Bulletin, 6:74-78, June-September, 1960.

Eaton, E. M., and M. H. Mahar. "Selection and Organization of Library Materials for Modern Language Programs," School Life, 42:14-17, May, 1960.

Goldhor, H., ed. Selection and Acquisition Procedures in Medium-Sized and Larger Libraries. Papers Presented at an Institute Conducted by University of Illinois Graduate School of Library Science, November 11-14, 1962. Champaign, Ill., Illini Bookstore, 1963. 139 p. (Allerton Park Institute Publications, No. 9).

Eleven papers covering practical aspects of acquisition work.

Gregory, R. W., "Readings on Book Selection and Intellectual Freedom, 1954-1961," American Library Association, 56:145-149, February, 1962.

Haight, A. L. Banned Books. Rev. by E. J. Gaines. 3d ed. New York, Bowker, 1958.

Selective listing with comments of books banned throughout world from 850 B. C. to present.

Haines, H. E. Living with Books. The Art of Book Selection. 2d ed. New York, Columbia University Press, 1950.

Standard textbook, now outdated.

Haviland, V. "Building the Foundation: The Book Collection, Library Trends, 12:14-23, July, 1963.

Hawes, M. E., and D. Sinclair, eds. Book Selection Policies. 2d ed. Baltimore, Md., Enoch Pratt Free Library, 1961.

Hirsch, R. "Evaluation of the Book Collection," In: Yenawine, W. S., ed. Library Evaluation. Syracuse, Syracuse University Press, 1959. (Frontiers of Librarianship, No. 2).

Lake, A. C., and J. S. Dunn. "Book Selection Standards: Education or Communication?" Wilson Library Bulletin, 37:672-676, April, 1963.

McClellan, A. W. "Accessibility and Other Problems of Book Provision," Library World, 63:275-281, May, 1962.

Merritt, L. C., et. al. Reviews in Library Book Selection. Detroit, Wayne State University Press, 1958. 188p. (Wayne State University Studies, No. 3).

Three separate studies on the status of book reviewing in the United States, with special emphasis on its relation to library acquisitions.

Moon, E., ed. Book Selection and Censorship. New York, Bowker, 1968.

An anthology of articles that have appeared in Library Journal.

Pickett, A. S. "Faculty Participation in Book Selection," Indiana Librarian, 15:32-35, June, 1960.

Reid, D. "Drafting a Written Book Selection Policy," Wilson Library Bulletin, 35:48-49, September, 1960.

Rowell, J. "A Total Book Selection Process," Wilson Library Bulletin, 41:190-197, October, 1966.

Sattley, H. R. "Problem Areas in Book Selection: What They Imply for All Librarians," Library Journal, 87:3120-3123, September, 1962.

Weinstein, F. D. "Book Selection in the Sciences," ALA Bulletin, 52:509-519, July, 1958.

c. University and College Libraries

"Acquisition Policy: A Symposium," College and Research Libraries, 14:363-372, October, 1953.

Underlying problems and characteristics of acquisition policy in a large university library and a small college library.

Archer, Horace Richard. "Some Aspects of the Acquisition Program of the University of Chicago Library 1892-1928," Unpublished Doctoral thesis, The University of Chicago, 1954.

Ault, Nelson. "A Faculty Look at the Library," PNLA Quarterly, 21:21-23, October, 1956.

Bach, H. "Acquisition Policy in the American Academic Library," College and Research Libraries, 18:441-451, November, 1957.

Responsibility rests primarily with the librarian. Cooperative specialization between libraries is recommended.

Chen, W. C. "Small College Library Acquisition Problems," Library Journal, 84:1762-1765, June 1, 1959.

Summarizes results of three questionnaires dealing with small college libraries, university presses and dealers in university press publications.

Christ, Robert W. "Acquisition Work in College Libraries," College and Research Libraries, 10:17-23, January, 1949.

__________. "Acquisition Work in Ten College Libraries," Unpublished Master's thesis, Columbia University, New York, 1948.

Cox, M. A. G. "Acquisition Policies in Academic and Public Libraries." Unpublished Master's thesis, University of Mississippi, 1963.

Dawson, J. M. "Acquisitions of University Libraries." Unpublished Doctoral thesis, University of Chicago, 1956.

Dunlap, Connie. "Automated Acquisitions Procedures at the University of Michigan Library," Library Resources and Technical Services, 11:192-202, Spring, 1967.

Fussler, H. H. "Acquisitions Policy; Larger University Libraries," College and Research Libraries, 14:363-367, October, 1953.

Gorchels, C. "Acquisitions Policy Statements in Colleges of Education," Library Resources and Technical Services, 5:157-159, Spring, 1961.

Grieder, E. M. "The Foundations of Acquisition Policy in the Small University Library," College and Research Libraries, 10:208-214, July, 1949.

Hamlin, A. T. "Impact of College Enrollments on Acquisition Policy," Ohio Library Association Bulletin, 35:4, October, 1965.

Institutions are placing too much emphasis on research collections and not giving sufficient consideration to the number of undergraduates. Recommends heavy duplication of important, recent books.

Harlow, N. R. "Improving Faculty-Library Relations: The Administrator's View," PNLA Quarterly, 21:24-26, October, 1956.

Haro, R. "Book Selection in Academic Libraries," College and Research Libraries, 28:104-106, March, 1967.

Helen, Sister, S. N. D. "Book Purchasing for Small College Library," Catholic Library World, 29:147-152, December, 1957.

A detailed outline of acquisition techniques used in Trinity College, Washington, D. C. The guiding principles given would prove helpful to any librarian in a small college library. Especially good are sections relating to foreign and out-of-print books and to record keeping in order department.

Henderson, W. T. "Acquisitions Policies of Academic and Research Libraries." Unpublished Master's thesis, University of Chicago, 1960.

Knapp, P. B. College Teaching and the College Library. Chicago, American Library Association, 1951. (ACRL Monograph, No. 2.)

McCrum, B. P. "Book Selection in Relation to the Optimum Size of a College Library," College and Research Libraries, 11:138-142, April, 1950.

Matthews, S. E. "Simplifying Library Acquisitions with University Purchasing," College and Research Libraries, 18:331-334, July, 1957.

Describes a system worked out at Ohio State University between the Acquisitions and Purchasing Departments.

Metcalf, K. D. "Problems of Acquisitions Policy in a University Library," Harvard Library Bulletin, 4:293-303, Autumn, 1950.

Osborn, A. D. "Development of Library Resources at Harvard," Harvard Library Bulletin, 9:197-212, Spring, 1955.

Ottmers, S. W. "Southwest Texas State College Library: An Exploratory Study with Implications for a Library Acquisition Program." Unpublished Master's thesis, University of Texas, 1961.

Pafford, J. H. P. "Book Selection in the University Library, UNESCO Bulletin for Libraries, 17:12-16, January, 1963.

Pullen, W. R. "Selective Acquisitions at Yale," In: Rutgers University. Graduate School of Library Service. Studies in Library Administrative Problems. New Brunswick, N. J., Rutgers University Press, 1960. Pp. 23-40.

Ralston, Edna Rachel. "Bibliographical Problems in the Order Department of a Large University Library." Unpublished Master's thesis, University of Illinois, Urbana, 1939.

Simpson, M. L. "Experiment in Acquisition with the Lamont Library List," College and Research Libraries, 15:430-433, October, 1954.

Skipper, J. E. "The Continuing Program of Book Selection and Acquisition," Library Resources and Technical Services, 2:265-271, Fall, 1958.

Stiffler, S. A. "A Philosophy of Book Selection for Smaller Academic Libraries," College and Research Libraries, 24:204-208, May, 1963.

Tauber, M. F. "Faculty and the Development of Library Collections," Journal of Higher Education, 32:454-458, November 8, 1961.

Thakore, A. V. "Practice of Book Selection in a University Library," Indian Librarian, 15:71-75, September, 1960.

Thompson, Lawrence S. "The Dogma of Book Selection in

University Libraries," *College and Research Libraries*, 21:442-445, November, 1960.

Book selection problems, responsibility of the university library; divided by fields: sciences, social sciences, humanities.

Trump, A. G. "Book Selection in a College Library," *South Dakota Library Bulletin*, 46:156-158, October, 1962.

Veit, Fritz. "Book Order Procedures in the Publicly Controlled Colleges and Universities of the Midwest," *College and Research Libraries*, 23:33-40, January, 1962.

Evaluates the library order procedure of 107 midwestern institutions. Reports definite trends such as, one fund and continuous ordering.

Vosper, R. G. "Acquisition Policy: Fact or Fancy?" *College and Research Libraries*, 14:367-370, October, 1953.

Weitzel, W. T. "Why and How of a Book Selection Policy," *North Country Libraries*, 6:1-4, March, 1963.

Wilson, Doris E. "Faculty-Library Relations from the Standpoint of the Staff Member," *PNLA Quarterly*, 2:22-28, October, 1956.

Wolf, H. C. "Library Board's Responsibility for Book Selection," *Library Journal*, 85:209, January 15, 1960.

d. Public Libraries

"Acquisition Policy of the Illinois State Library," *Illinois Libraries*, 43:362-366, May, 1961.

Bendix, D. *Some Problems in Book Selection Policies and Practices in Medium Sized Public Libraries*. Urbana, University of Illinois Library School, 1959. (University of Illinois Library School Occasional Papers, No. 55).

Carter, Frances Jeannette. "Science in the Public Library: A Study in Acquisition and Use." Unpublished Master's thesis, University of Chicago, 1948.

Frarey, C. J. Processing Services of the Dallas Public Library. Dallas, Dallas Public Library, 1959. 235p.

The results of an eight week survey during the summer of 1959 conducted by a technical services consultant.

Garceau, O. The Public Library in the Political Process. New York, Columbia University Press, 1949. 254p.

A study of the government of the American public library with a chapter on acquisitions.

Hagler, Ronald Albert. "Selection and Acquisition of Books in Six Ontario Public Libraries in Relation to the Canadian Publishing System." Unpublished Doctoral Thesis, University of Michigan, 1961.

Henderson, J. D. "The Public Library Acquisitions Program," Library Trends, 3:448-454, April, 1955.

Discusses problems of book selection, as determined from returns of questionnaire sent to 105 libraries of various sizes. Includes bibliography.

Jenkins, F. B., ed. Collecting Science Literature for General Reading. Papers Presented at the Institute Conducted by the University of Illinois Graduate School of Library Science, November 6-9, 1960. Champaign, Ill., Illini Union Bookstore, 1961. (Allerton Park Institute, No. 7).

Morris, T. D. "Techniques of Appraising the Administrative Strength of an Organization," College and Research Libraries, 13:111-116, April, 1952.

A survey of the acquisition department of the New York Public Library.

Thompson, Evelyn, and G. Forrester. "The Automatic Ordering of Replacement Titles for Libraries in Metropolitan Toronto," Library Resources and Technical Services, 11:215-220, Spring, 1967.

Wheeler, J. L., and H. Goldhor. Practical Administration of Public Libraries. New York, Harper, 1962.

Developing the book collection and administration of order work is discussed in chapter four.

Wisconsin. Free Library Commission. "Acquisition Policy," Wisconsin Library Bulletin, 57:69-74, March, 1961.

Zimmerman, W. E. "Technical Book Selection and Survey of Practice in Public Libraries-- A Bibliographic Essay." Unpublished Master's thesis, Western Reserve University, 1957.

e. Special Libraries

Anderson, I. T. "Acquisition and Preservation," In: Doe, J., and M. L. Marshall, eds. Handbook of Medical Library Practice. 2d ed. Chicago, American Library Association, 1956. Pp. 67-88.

Cabatu-Agcaoili, C. "Selection and Acquisition of Materials on the Social Sciences," ASLP Bulletin, 6:46-51, June-September, 1960.

Dimalanta, C. "Selection and Acquisition of Library Materials in Pure and Applied Sciences," ASLP Bulletin, 6:74-78, June-September, 1960.

Foy, B. L. "Order Work in a Special Library," Special Libraries, 32:312-313, October, 1941.

George, V. "Acquisitions," In: Ashworth, W., ed. Handbook of Special Librarianship and Information Work. 2d ed. London, Aslib, 1962. Pp. 32-69.

Jenkins, F. S. "Acquisition of Scientific and Technological Material," Library Trends, 3:414-422, April, 1955.

Johnson, R. K. "Some Facets of Acquisition Work in Selected Military Libraries," Library Resources and Technical Services, 2:16-24, Winter, 1958.

Lunn, B. "Acquisitions in Special Libraries," South African Libraries, 29:57-64, October, 1961.

Phelps, R. H. "Selecting Materials for Science-Technology Libraries," Special Libraries, 44:89-92, March, 1953.

Saul, M. "The Business of Book Buying - As Special Librarians See It," Library Journal, 88:2636-2639, July, 1963.

Strauss, L. S., et. al. "Books and Other Publications: Selection and Acquisition," In: Scientific and Technical Libraries: Their Organization and Administration. New York, Interscience, 1964. Pp. 90-123.

Thibault, Charles D. "Survey of Specialized Acquisitions Procedures in a Technical Documents Center; A Survey Conducted at the Engineering Research and Development Laboratories." Unpublished Master's thesis, Catholic University of America, 1956.

Wilkerson, M. "Library Purchasing Practices," Special Libraries, 42:19-22, January, 1951.

f. School Libraries

"AASL Urges Organized and Wide Use of Trade Book Examination Centers," Library Journal, 88:1308-09, March 15, 1963.

Adler, Irving. "On Writing Science Books for Children," Horn Book, 41:524-29, October, 1965.

Allison, Mary L., et. al. A Manual for Evaluators of Films and Filmstrips. Washington, U. S. Educational, Scientific and Cultural Organization, 1956. 23 p.

Procedures for committee selection, evaluation and recommendations for purchasing educational films and filmstrips.

Alm, Richard S. "The Glitter and the Gold," English Journal, 44:315-22, September, 1955.

Evaluation of junior and adult novels for teenage readers.

American Association of School Librarians. "Policies and Procedures for Selection of School Library Materials," School Libraries, 11:37-38, October, 1961.

Policies approved by AASL Board of Directors on February 3, 1961.

__________. Standards for School Library Programs. Chicago, American Library Association, 1960. Pp. 73-86.

Arbuthnot, May Hill. Children and Books. 3d ed. Chicago, Scott, Foresman, 1964.

A standard textbook with much information on selection of childrens books.

Asheim, Lester. "The Librarian's Responsibility: Not Censorship but Selection," In: F. J. Moshier, ed. Freedom of Book Selection, Chicago, American Library Association, 1954. Pp. 90-99.

Auld, L. W. S. "Compiling School Library Orders with Punched Cards in Centralizing Processing," Hawaii Library Association Journal, 20:14-25, Spring, 1964.

Bagshaw, M. "Enter Computer," Top of the News, 23:39-42, November, 1966.

Use of computer for book ordering of replacement copies of children's books at the Toronto Public Library.

Baur, Esther. "The Fader Plan: Detroit Style," Library Journal, 92:3119-21, September 15, 1967.

Magazine and paperbacks in a high school library.

Behn, Harry. "Poetry for Children," Horn Book, 42:163-75, April, 1966.

Broderick, Dorothy. Introduction to Children's Work in Public Libraries. New York, Wilson, 1965.

Brown, James W., et. al. A-V Instruction; Materials and Methods. 2d ed. New York, McGraw-Hill, 1964. 592 p.

Standard textbook presenting basic information for selection of a-v materials.

Burton, Dwight L. Literature Study in the High School. 2d rev. ed. New York, Holt, 1964.

California Association of School Librarians. Instructional Materials: Selection Policies and Procedures. Daly City, Calif., The Association, 1965.

California Schools State Their Book Selection Policies: How One State Achieved This Objective," School Libraries, 6:18, 21, March, 1957.

Carlsen, G. Robert. Books and the Teen-age Reader. New York, Harper, 1967. 218 p.

Traces development of reading tastes of modern teenagers from comic books to Catcher in the Rye. 9 of 14 chapters deal with types of books: biography, classics, modern literature, etc; bibliographies. Sponsored by National Book Committee and endorsed by ALA, IRA, NCTE.

__________. "For Everything There is a Season," Top of the News, 21:103-110, January, 1965.

Young adults need to choose reading suited to their "season"; required adult books designed to "expose" readers to the classics, etc., tend to cause reader rejection.

Carlsen, G. Robert. "The Right Size," Top of the News, 23:55-62, November, 1966.

Discusses adolescents' reading patterns as they move toward adult literature.

Conklin, Graff. "What is Good Science Fiction?" Library Journal, 83:1256-57, April 15, 1958.

Colby, Jean P. Children's Book Field. New York, Pellegrini, 1952.

__________. "How to Present the Negro in Children's Books," Top of the News, 21:191-96, April, 1965.

__________. Writing, Illustrating and Editing Children's Books. New York, Hastings House, 1966.

Daigon, Arthur C. "The Novel of Adolescent Romance," Library Journal, 91:2152-56, April 15, 1966.

Dane, Chase. "Recent Trends in Book-Buying," School Library Association of California Bulletin, 33:11-13, November, 1961.

__________. "Selection and Reference Use in the School Library," Library Trends, 15:87-92, July, 1966.

Selection and use of government publications in school libraries.

Doughty, Frances W. "Selection Criteria: Science Books for Children," Horn Book, 41:195-200, April, 1965.

Egoff, Shila A. "Tomorrow Plus X; Some Thoughts on Science Fiction," Top of the News, 19:31-35, December, 1962.

Reprinted from Ontario Library Review, May, 1962.

Enoch Pratt Free Library. Book Selection Policies. Rev. ed. Baltimore, The Library, 1961.

Fiske, Marjorie. Book Selection and Censorhsip; A Study of School and Public Libraries in California. Berkeley, University of California Press, 1959. 145 p.

Ford, Nick Aaron. "What High School Students Say About Good Books," English Journal, 50:539-45, November, 1961.

Fay, Ray M. "Some Recent Trends in Books for Young Adults," Top of the News, 17:30-35, May, 1960.

Fuller, Muriel. "Youth Magazines in the United States, Horn Book, 42:110, February, 1966.

Hanna, Geneva R., and Marianna K. McAllister. Books, Young People and Reading Guidance. New York, Harper & Row, 1960. 219 p.

General introductory textbook for young adult reading guidance. Includes special aspects of book selection for young people and book selection tools.

Hatch, L. "The Book Order Deadline," Library Journal, 78:1986-88, November 15, 1953.

Haviland, Virginia. "Book Selection, Problem? Pleasure? Privilege?" Illinois Libraries, 47:310-17, April, 1965.

Heffernan, Virginia, and Esther Helfand. "The Blurred Boundary." Top of the News, 21:39-42, November, 1964.

Problems in selecting books for the young adults, ages 13 (grade eight) and up. The transition between ages 12 and 13 is discussed.

Hodge, Elizabeth. "Book Selection Practices in the Nation's Schools," School Libraries, 6:11-15, March, 1957.

Jordan, R. T. "Eliminate the Middlemen in Book Ordering," Library Journal, 86:327-29, January 15, 1961.

Krarup, Agnes. "Book Selection Policies in the Pittsburgh Public Schools," School Libraries, 6:24-28, March, 1957.

Lembo, Diana. "A Stepchild Comes of Age," Library Journal, 92:3122-23, September 15, 1967.

Introduction to filmstrips; brief basic list of bibliographic tools. Prepared by reviewer of filmstrips for Library Journal.

Leonard, Virginia. "Book Selection in Grosse Points: Where School Librarians Advise the Public Library," ALA Bulletin, 6:627-29, June, 1966.

Lohrer, Alice. "A Spotlight on Reviewing Books for Children," Illinois Libraries. 46:851-53, December, 1964.

Mahar, Mary H. "Determining Values in Instructional Materials," Illinois Libraries, 46:286-90, April, 1964.

"The Media Librarian and A/V," Library Journal, 92: 1683, April 15, 1967.

National Council of Teachers of English. The Student's Right to Read. Champaign, Ill., the Council, 1962. 21 p.

NCTE's position on censorship and book selection. Suggested procedures for book adoptions.

New York City. Board of Education. Division of Curriculum Development. Improving the Professional Library in the School. New York, New York City Board of Education, 1965.

Nicholsen, M. E. "The Professional Library," Bulletin of the National Association of Secondary School Principals, 50:96-106, January, 1966.

Paige, N. "Goals for Service: A Survey of School Library Ordering," Library Journal, 90:937-41, February 15, 1965.

__________. "Is It Habit or Law? Cutting the Red Tape of Library Book Buying," Library Journal, 89:909-13, February 15, 1964.

"Periodicals for Children and Young People," _School Libraries_, 11:33-35, October, 1961; 11:31-32, January, 1962.

Peterson, Dorothy G. "Teachers' Professional Reading," _Library Journal_, 88:1730-33, April 15, 1963.

Public Library Association. _Young Adult Services in the Public Library_. Chicago, American Library Association, 1960.

Rausen, Ruth G. "The Junior High School Reader," _Top of the News_, 23:19-22, November, 1966.

Rice, Helen J. "Periodicals, Pictures and Pamphlets," _Illinois Libraries_, 46:878-80, December, 1965.

Rowell, John. "A Total Book Selection Process," _Wilson Library Bulletin_, 41:190-96, October, 1966.

Saunders, Leila B. "Mysteries for Young Adults," _Top of the News_, 16:34-35, May, 1960.

Selection and Use of Programed Materials; A Handbook for Teachers. Washington, National Education Association, 1964. 71p.

Appendix contains article, "Criteria for assessing programed instructional materials" and an annotated bibliography; of interest to IMC librarians who work with teachers on curriculum problems.

Shadick, R. C. "School Librarian: Key to Curriculum Development," _Elementary School Journal_, 62:298-303, March, 1962.

Smith, Lillian H. _The Unreluctant Years: A Critical Approach to Children's Literature_. Chicago, American Library Association, 1953. 200p.

A classic on the subject; stresses the function of book selection in making known the best in children's literature.

Spain, F. L. "Selection and Acquisition of Books for Children," Library Trends, 3:455-61, April, 1955.

White, D. L. "Government Publication: Much for Little," School Libraries, 13:43-46, May, 1964.

Wiese, M. Bernice. "Cooperative Book Reviewing," School Libraries, 6:28-34, March, 1957.

Organization of an elementary school reviewing committee; procedures of reviewing used in Baltimore Public Schools.

Williams, Catharine M. Learning from Pictures. Washington, Department of Audiovisual Instruction, National Education Association, 1963. 163 p.

A guide to selection and use of pictures for schools; lists sources and producers.

Wooford, Azile. Book Selection for School Libraries. New York, Wilson, 1962. 318 p.

A general introduction to practical aspects of book selection. Emphasis is on elementary schools.

Yungmeyer, Elinor. "School Libraries, the Institutional Market," Wilson Library Bulletin, 38:577, March, 1964.

3. BUDGETING AND FUNDS

a. Principles of Managerial Budgeting

See also pp. 45-49.

Aspley, J. C., ed. The Dartnell Office Manager's Handbook, 3d ed. Chicago, Dartnell, 1964.

Beranek, William. Analysis for Financial Decisions. Homewood, Ill., Irwin, 1962.

Cooke, Gilbert W., and Edwin Bomeli. Business Financial Management. Boston, Houghton Mifflin, 1967. 465 p.

Gerstenberg, Charles W. Financial Organization and Management of Business, 3d rev. ed., New York, Prentice Hall, 1951.

Guthmann, Harry G. Analysis of Financial Statements, 4th ed. New York, Prentice Hall, 1953.

Heiser, Herman C. Budgeting Principles and Practice. New York, Ronald Press, 1959.

Kennedy, Ralph D. Financial Statements. Honewood, Ill., Irwin, 1962.

Knight, W. D., and E. H. Weinwrum. Managerial Budgeting. New York, Macmillan, 1964.

Shultz, W. J., and Harris, C. Lowell. American Public Finance. 7th ed. Englewood Cliffs, N. Y., Prentice-Hall, 1959.

Smithies, A. The Budgeting Process in the United States. New York, McGraw-Hill, 1955.

Sord, B. H., and G. A. Welsch. Business Budgeting; A Survey of Management Planning and Control Practices. New York, Controllership Foundation, 1958.

Stedry, A. C. Budget Control and Cost Behavioral. Englewood Cliffs, N. J., Prentice-Hall, 1960.

Tucker, S. A. Successful Managerial Control by Ratio-Analysis. New York, McGraw-Hill, 1961.

Villers, R. Research and Development: Planning and Control. New York, Financial Executives Research Foundation, 1964.

Wall, Alexander. Ratio Analysis of Financial Statements. New York, Harper, 1928.

Welsch, G. A. Budgeting and Profit Planning and Control. Englewood Cliffs, N. J., Prentice-Hall, 1963.

Wright, W. Direct Standard Costs for Decision Making and Control. New York, McGraw-Hill, 1962.

b. Accounting Principles and Practice

Bauer, R. D. M., and P. H. Darby. Elementary Accounting. 3d ed. New York, Barnes and Noble, 1962.

Crawingshield, Gerald R. Cost Accounting: Principles and Managerial Applications. Boston, Houghton Mifflin, 1962.

Dixon, R. L., and W. A. Paton. Essentials of Accounting. New York, Macmillan, 1958.

Grant, E. L., and L. F. Bell. Basic Accounting and Cost Accounting. 2d ed. New York, McGraw, 1964.

Hall, S. Accounting Principles and Practice. New York, Pergamon, 1964.

Horngreen, C. T. Cost Accounting: A Managerial Emphasis. Englewood Cliffs, N. J., Prentice-Hall, 1962.

Knox, F. M. Integrated Cost Control in the Office. New York, McGraw-Hill, 1958.

Lasser, J. K. Standard Handbook for Accountants. New York, McGraw, 1956.

MacKenzie, D. H. Fundamentals of Accounting. Rev. ed. New York, Macmillan, 1956.

Mason, Perry, Sidney Davidson, and James S. Schindler, Fundamentals of Accounting, 4th ed. New York, Holt, 1959.

Milroy, Robert R., E. Walden, and L. Vann Seawell. Accounting Theory and Practice, Advanced. Boston, Houghton Mifflin, 1961.

Minrath, W. Simplified Accounting. New York, Van Nostrand, 1959.

Wade, H. M. Fundamentals of Accounting. 3d ed. New York, Wiley, 1951.

c. Library Finances and Budget

American Library Association. Cost of Public Library Service in 1959. Chicago, American Library Association, 1960.

American Library Association. Protecting the Library and its Resources: A Guide to Physical Protection and Insurance. Chicago, 1963. (LTD Publications, No. 7).

Armstrong, C. M. Money for Libraries. A Report on Library Finance. New York, Social Science Research Council, 1951.

Report to the director of Public Library Inquiry.

Baldwin, Emma V., and William E. Marcus. Library Costs and Budgets. New York, Bowker, 1941. 201 p.

Many statistics and charts. Practical suggestions for cost analysis of the period the libraries were surveyed.

Bray, Helen E. The Library's Financial Records. New York, Bowker, 1943.

Corbett, E. V. Public Library Finance and Accounting. London, Library Association, 1960. 212 p.

Drennan, H. T. "The Costs of Public Library Service," Library Trends, 11:362-375, April, 1963.

"Extra University Sources of Financial Support for Libraries A Symposium," College and Research Libraries, 23:509-21, November, 1962.

Gipson, J. S. "Total Cost of Acquisitions in a Community College," College and Research Libraries, 28:273-276, July, 1967.

A Macomb County Community College costs are determined at $4.85 per book for use.

Hamlin, A. T. "The Financial and Economic Status of Research Libraries," The Library Quarterly, 23:190-98, July, 1953.

Examines various factors which affect the economic status of research libraries: inflation, cost-size relationship, taxes, interest on endowments, philanthropy, tuition, etc.

"The Higher Education Act of 1965: A Symposium," College and Research Libraries, 27:335-353, September, 1966.

Includes "Implications for Resources and Technical Services," by H. M. Welch.

Hopp, R. H. "Private and Industrial Funds for University Libraries," College and Research Libraries, 23:509-513, November, 1962.

Kaiser, J. B. "Problems of Library Finance," In: Joeckel, C. B., ed. Current Issues in Library Administration. Chicago, University of Chicago Press, 1939. Pp. 216-39.

Kaser, D. "Outside Funding of Academic Libraries," Library Trends, 11:353-361, April, 1963.

Maybury, C. "Performance Budgeting for the Library," ALA Bulletin, 55:46-53, January, 1961.

Orlans, H. The Effects of Federal Programs on Higher Education. Washington, The Brookings Institution, 1962.

Parker, R. H. "Operating Costs of College and University Libraries," Library Trends, 11:376-383, April, 1963.

Peterson, H. N. "Performance Budgeting, Work Measurement, and the Public Library," Wilson Library Bulletin, 27:620-23, April, 1953.

Price, P. P. "Budgeting and Budget Control in Public Libraries," Library Trends, 11:402-414, April, 1963.

Price, P. P. "Performance Budgeting in Practice," Library Journal, 84:797-800, March 15, 1959.

Rather, J. C. "Library Personnel Costs," Library Trends, 11:395-401, April, 1963.

Richard, E. W., and T. J. Orsagh, "Holdings and Expenditures of U. S. Academic Libraries: An Evaluative Technique," College and Research Libraries, 27:478-487, November, 1966.

> The current acquisitions expenditures and holdings of the nation's academic libraries as a whole are examined relative to the numbers of students and faculty for the period 1952-62 by the use of random sampling and multivariate analysis.

Richards, J. H. "Academic Budgets and Their Administration - 1962," Library Trends, 11:415-426, April, 1963.

Shank, R. "Federal Funds for University Libraries," College and Research Libraries, 23:514-518, November, 1962.

Sherman, C. F. "The Library Budget," In: Vitz, C., ed. Current Problems in Public Library Finance. Chicago, American Library Association, 1933.

Welch, H. "Cost of Library Materials," Library Trends, 11:384-394, April, 1963.

Wight, E. A. "Financial Support of Public Libraries," Library Trends, 11:343-352, April, 1963.

__________. Public Library Finance and Accounting. Chicago, American Library Association, 1943.

Williams, G. "The Librarian's Role in the Development of Library Book Collection," Library Quarterly, 34:374-86, October, 1964.

d. The Book Budget

Bach, H. "Why Allocate?" Library Resources and Technical Services, 8:161-165, Spring, 1964.

Broestl, J. A. "Revised Index for the Allocation of the University Library Book Fund to the Various Subject Departments of the College of Arts and Sciences and of the Graduate School of Western Reserve University." Unpublished Master's thesis, Western Reserve University, Cleveland, 1951.

Coney, D. "An Experimental Index for Apportioning Departmental Book Funds for a University Library," The Library Quarterly, 12:422-428, July, 1942.

Considers the following factors: registrations, courses offered, faculty, graduate majors, "non-quantitative" elements, and cost of material. Statistical discussion relating to the University of Texas library.

Elias, A. W., ed. Third Conference on Technical Information Center Administration. Philadelphia, Pa., August 29-Sept. 1, 1966. New York, Spartan Books, 1966. 135p. (Drexel Information Science Series, v. 4.)

Contains information about budget allocations for acquisition of materials.

Ellsworth, R. E. "Some Aspects of the Problem of Allocating Book Funds Among Departments in Universities," Library Quarterly, 12:486-494, July, 1942.

Lists the factors which govern departmental allocation of book funds at the University of Colorado. Based on data compiled in 1940-1941.

Hamlin, A. T. "Book Fund and Book Orders," Bookmark, University of Idaho, 16:14 15, September, 1963.

Headings, B. E. "The Formulation of a Book Budget Policy for a Small College Library," Wilson Library Bulletin, 26:389-391, 393, January, 1952.

Ladenson, A. "Budget Control of Book Purchases and Binding Expenditures in Large Public Libraries," Library Resources and Technical Services, 4:47-58, Winter, 1960.

Muller, Hans I. "Administration of Book Funds in College Libraries," Unpublished Master's thesis, University of Chicago Graduate Library School, 1941.

__________. "Management of College Library Book Budgets," College and Research Libraries, 2:320-326, September, 1941.

McCarthy, S. A. "Centralization and Decentralization at Cornell," College and Research Libraries, 22:334-38, September, 1961.

McGrath, W. E. "Determining and Allocating Book Funds for Current Domestic Buying," College and Research Libraries, 28:269-72, July, 1967.

According to the author - courses described in the catalog are matched with the books listed in BPR, Cumulative 1965.

Pike, M. H. "Distribution of the Book Budget within the Library System and between the Main Library and Branches," ALA Bulletin, 36:108-110, September 15, 1942.

Reeves, F. W. "The Administration of the Library Book Budget," Library Quarterly, 2:268-278, July, 1932.

Richards, J. H., Jr. "Academic Budgets and Their Administration, 1962," Library Trends, 11:415-426, April, 1963.

__________. Allocation of Book Funds in College Libraries,"

College and Research Libraries, 14:379-380, October, 1953.

A Study of twelve colleges at the end of the year 1951-1952.

Shaw, R. R. "Control of Book Funds at the University of Hawaii Library," Library Resources and Technical Services, 11:380-382, Summer, 1967.

Simms, M. "Allocating the Book Fund to Departments and Branch Libraries," Library Journal, 71:1302-1308, October, 1, 1946.

Steffey, D. "The Librarian Considers the School Library Budget," Illinois Libraries, 34:97-100, March, 1952.

Tanis, N. E. "The Departmental Allocation of Library Book Funds in the Junior College: Developing Criteria," Library Resources and Technical Services, 5:321-327, Fall, 1961.

Vosper, R. "Allocation of the Book Budget," College and Research Libraries, 10:215-218, 259, July, 1949.

A survey conducted at the University of California at Los Angeles.

CHAPTER III

PUBLISHING

---

1. HISTORICAL BACKGROUND

a. Bibliographies

Astbury, R. Bibliography and Book Production. London, Pergamon, 1967. 260 p.

> Discussion of publishing, copyright, censorship and authorship in Great Britain, including book production technique. The second half of the book deals with universal, national and special bibliographies.

Classified Catalogue of a Collection of Books on Publishing and Bookselling in the British Library of Political and Economic Science. London, British Library of Political and Economic Science, 1961. 186 p.

Freer, Percy. Bibliography and Modern Book Production. Johannesburg: Witwatersrand University Press, 1954.

> Intended primarily as a guide to sources, rather than as a textbook, this work is based on the Correspondence Course in Final Bibliography and Modern Book Production conducted for many years by Mr. Freer for the South African Library Association. Contains an annotated list of about 700 books and periodicals on bibliography and book production.

Handbuch der Technischen Dokumentation und Bibliograpie. Bd. 2. Die Fachliteratur zum Buch-und Bibliothekswesen. 6th ed. München, Verlag Dokumentationen der Technik, 1966.

> The second volume and its supplement includes a comprehensive bibliography of book trade in classified arrangement.

Klieman, Horst, and P. Meyer-Dohm. *Buchhandel. Eine Bibliographie*. Gütersloh, Bertelsmann, 1963. 160 p. (Schriften zur Buchmarkt-Forschung, No. 1.)

b. General Treatises

Barnes, J. J. *Free Trade in Books: A Study of the London Book Trade*. Oxford, Clarendon Press, 1964.

Barker, R. E. and G. R. Davies, eds. *Books are Different. An Account of the Defense of the Net Book Agreement Before the Restrictive Practices Court in 1962*. London, St. Martin's Press, 1966. 938 p.

Bowker Lectures on Book Publishing. New York, R. R. Bowker, 1957. 389 p.

Chapters on history of publishing, subscription books, text books, children's books, book clubs, paperbound books.

Butler, Pierce. *Librarians, Scholars, and Booksellers at Mid-Century*. Chicago, University of Chicago Press, 1953. 107 p.

Carlson, Pearl Gertrude. *Choice of Editions*. Chicago, American Library Association, 1942. 69 p.

Escarpit, R. *The Book Revolution*. New York, UNESCO, 1966. 160 p.

An overview report of world book publishing activities.

Grannis, C. B., ed. *What Happens in Book Publishing*. New York, Columbia University Press, 1957.

Gross, G. *Publishers on Publishing*. New York, Grosset and Dunlap, 1961.

An anthology of writings about publishing by thirty-six American and British publishers.

Guinzburg, H. K., et. al. *Books and the Mass Market.*

Urbana, University of Illinois Press, 1953.

Hackett, A. P. Sixty Years of Best Sellers, 1895-1955. New York, R. R. Bowker, 1956. 260 p.

Facts and figures about American best sellers accompanied by some comment and interpretation.

James, S. Association Press: The First Fifty Years, 1907-1957. New York, Association Press, 1957.

Jennet, Sean. The Making of Books. 4th ed. New York, Praeger, 1967. 512 p.

The standard reference book on book design.

Jennison, P. S., and W. H. Kurth. Books in the Americas: A Study of the Principle Barriers to the Book Trade in the Americas. Washington, Pan American Union, 1960.

Joy, T. The Truth about Bookselling. London, Pitman, 1965. 206 p.

Kalhöfer, K. H., and H. Rötzsch. Beiträge zur Geschichte des Buchwesens. Leipzig, VEB Bibl. Institut, 1965-66, 2 v.

A comprehensive historical treatise including the history of book trade.

Langdon-Davies, B. M. The Practice of Bookselling. With Some Opinions on Its Nature, Status, and Future. London, Phoenix House, 1951.

Lee, Marshall. Bookmaking: The Illustrated Guide to Design and Production. New York, Bowker, 1965. 416 p.

Lehmann-Haupt, H., et al. The Book in America: A History of the Making and Selling of Books in the United States. 2d ed. New York, Bowker, 1951. 493 p.

Comprehensive account of printing, bookselling, and publishing from colonial times to the present.

Lehmann-Haupt, H. The Life of the Book: How the Book is Written, Published, Printed, Sold, and Read. London. Aberlard-Schuman, 1962. 240 p.

Lewis, J. The Twentieth Century Book. New York, Reinhold, 1967. 272 p.

The development of book design in Europe and U. S., well illustrated.

Madison, Charles A. Book Publishing in America. New York, McGraw-Hill, 1966. 628 p.

History from colonial beginnings to the present.

Melcher, D., and N. Larrick. Printing and Promotion Handbook. New York, McGraw-Hill, 1966. 451 p.

Alphabetical approach to information about planning, producing, and using printing and advertising services.

Miller, W. The Book Industry. New York, Columbia University Press, 1949.

Melinat, C. H. Librarianship and Publishing. Syracuse, Syracuse University School of Library Science, 1963.

Mumby, Frank Arthur. Publishing and Bookselling: A History from the Earliest Times to the Present Day. 4th ed. London, Cape, 1956. 442 p.

A history with primary emphasis on Great Britain.

Peterson, T. Magazines in the Twentieth Century. Urbana, University of Illinois Press, 1964.

A history of the commercial popular magazines from their beginnings in the late 1800's to the present.

Plant, M. The English Book Trade. An Economic History of the Making and Sale of Books. 2d ed. London, Allen and Unwin, 1965. 500 p.

Roberts, W. Book Hunters in London. Chicago, McClurg, 1895. 333 p.

Historical studies of collectors and collecting.

Roberts, W. Earlier History of English Bookselling. London, 1889. 341 p. (Gale reprint).

The pioneer study in the history of English bookselling.

Rosenberg, L. Literary, Political, Scientific, Religious and Legal Publishing, Printing, and Bookselling in England, 1551-1700. Twelve Studies. New York, Donald G. Wing, 1965. 2v.

Schullian, D. M. "Adams Jewett and John Shaw Billings, Partners in Acquisition," Medical Library Association Bulletin, 49:443-449, July, 1961.

Sheehan, D. This Was Publishing: A Chronicle of the Book Trade in the Gilded Age. Bloomington, Indiana University Press, 1952. 288 p.

Covers publishing industry in years between Civil War and World War I.

Smith, D. C. A Guide to Book Publishing. New York, Bowker, 1966.

Discussion of problems of book production and distribution.

Smith, R. H., ed. The American Reading Public: A Symposium. New York, Bowker, 1964. 268 p. (From Winter 1962 issue of Daedalus).

Twenty articles on the nature of the current reading public from both the educator's and the publisher's view.

Strauss, Victor. The Printing Industry: an Introduction to Its Many Branches, Processes and Products. New

York, Printing Industries of America in association with Bowker, 1967. 814p.

The most comprehensive encyclopedia manual of modern printing, including printing processes, presses, composition, graphic arts, photography, paper, inks and other aspects of printing. Includes bibliography.

The Times, London. *Printing in the 20th Century. A Survey*. London, The Times, 1930.

Covers history of printing, typography, book making with a short chapter on printing abroad.

Underwood, Edward G. *Production and Manufacturing Problems of American University Presses*. New York, Association of University Presses, 1960.

Unwin, S. *The Truth About Publishing*. 7th ed. New York, Macmillan, 1961. 348p.

A classic textbook with interesting chapters on the pricing of books, agreements and royalties, selling and distribution, publicity and other aspects.

Walter, F.K. *The Library's Own Printing*. Chicago, American Library Association, 1934. 116p.

Discussion of several principles on which effective printing for libraries is based and which are at the same time practicable for small jobs and limited appropriations.

Welter, R. *Problems of Scholarly Publications in the Humanities and Social Sciences*. New York, American Council of Learned Societies, 1959. 81p.

Publishing experience of scholars with information on scholarly journals and university presses.

Yard, R.S. *The Publisher*. Boston and New York, Houghton Mifflin, 1913.

Informal discussion about what makes a book sell.

c. Reference Works

See also lists of reference works in Chapter IV, e.g. pp. 147-150, 167-169.

Bennett, W. Practical Guide to Book Collecting, 1663-1940. New York, Bennett Book Studies, 1941.

Carter, J. ABC for Book-Collectors. 2d rev. ed. New York, Knopf, 1953. 196p.

A dictionary of terms commonly used in book-collecting.

Glaister, G. A. Encyclopedia of the Book. Cleveland, World Publishing Co., 1960. 484p.

Alphabetical arrangement of terms used in paper-making, printing, bookbinding and publishing.

Landau, T., ed. Encyclopedia of Librarianship. 3d ed. New York, Hafner, 1966. 484p.

Orne, J. The Language of the Foreign Book Trade: Abbreviations, Terms, Phrases. 2d ed. Chicago, American Library Association, 1962.

Dictionary of foreign terms used in the book trade. Each of eight languages is presented separately.

Taubert, S. Bibliopola: Pictures and Texts about the Book Trade. New York, Bowker, 1966. 2v.

Text in English, French, and German.

Turner, M. C. The Bookman's Glossary. 4th ed. Rev. and enl. New York, Bowker, 1961. 212p.

Provides short definitions of terms in such areas as printing, typography, publishing, editing and bookselling. Purely technical terms are omitted. Short biographical notes about some booksellers, publishers and book collectors.

2. BOOKS AND BOOK TRADE

See also pp. 111-115, "General Treatises."

Ahn, H. K. "Increasing International Understanding: An Introduction to the Publishers of International Organization," *California Librarian*, 21:29-36, January, 1960.

Archer, H. R. "Private Presses and Collector's Edition," *Library Trends*, 7:57-65, July, 1958.

Baker, J. "Book Clubs," In: Hampden, J., ed. *The Book World Today*. London, Allen and Unwin, 1957. Pp. 120-127.

Bowker Lectures on Book Publishing. New York, Bowker, 1957. 389 p.

Chapters on history of publishing, subscription books, textbooks, children's books, book clubs, paperbound books.

Brown, George Berdine. "Practices of Law Publishers as They Affect Law Libraries." Unpublished Master's thesis, University of Illinois, Urbana, 1940.

Chèney, O. H. *Economic Survey of the Book Industry, 1930-1931*. Reprint ed. New York, Bowker, 1960. 356 p.

A general survey of conditions in the book industry with practical suggestions for strengthening it.

Colby, J. P. *Children's Book Field*. New York, Farrar, Straus, and Cudahy, 1952. 246 p.

Non technical material divided into four sections: editing and writing, illustration and book design, production, and publishing.

Dalton, P. I., and C. E. Lee, and B. Mumm. "Government and Foundation Publishing," *Library Trends*, 7:116-133, July, 1958.

Describes publishing policies and practices by government agencies and by various U. S. foundations. Includes bibliography.

Dane, C. "Recent Trends in Book Buying," School Library Association of California Bulletin, 33:11-13, November, 1961.

DeAngelo, R. W. "Children's Book Publishing," Library Trends, 7:220-233, July, 1958.

Gives a brief historical sketch and surveys the current field to date of writing.

Dolmatch, T. B. "Association Publishing," Library Trends, 7:134-138, July, 1958.

Briefly discusses the publishing activities of such organization as the Y. M. C. A., A. M. A., A. A. U. N., etc. Includes bibliography.

Fisher, D. C. Book Clubs. New York, New York Public Library, 1947. (R. R. Bowker Memorial Lectures, No. 11.)

Fleming, T. P., and R. Shank. "Scientific and Technical Book Publishing," Library Trends, 7:197-209, July, 1958.

Gives a brief historical account of scientific book publishing in the U. S. and discusses present trends.

Grannis, C. B. "Trade Book Publishing," Library Trends, 7:29-37, July, 1958.

Summarizes developments in the book publishing industry since the end of World War II.

__________., ed. What Happens in Book Publishing. New York, Columbia University Press, 1957. 414 p.

A picture of the industry for the layman with special emphasis on steps in publishing a trade book. Additional chapters on major problem areas for the publisher and other phases of publishing, e. g. children's books, textbooks, etc.

Johnson, B. C. "Medical Book Publishing," Library Trends, 7:210-219, July, 1958.

Jovanovich, William. The Structure of Publishing. New York, American Book Publisher's Council, 1957.

Kerr, C. "University Press Publishing," Library Trends, 7:38-49, July, 1958.

Kilgour, R. L. "Reference and Subscription Book Publishing," Library Trends, 7:139-152, July, 1958.

Reviews the products of the major U. S. publishers of encyclopedias, dictionaries, atlases, etc.

King, L. W., and M. R. Redding. "Textbook Publishing," Library Trends, 7:50-56, July, 1958.

Surveys the ten years from 1946 to 1956 in the textbook publishing business.

Lehmann-Haupt, H., ed. "Current Trends in Antiquarian Books," Library Trends, 9:387-499, April, 1961.

The organization and structure of the American antiquarian market is discussed in this issue of Library Trends. The reader will find the references to individual articles in the next chapter.

Myers, K. "Music Book Publishing," Library Trends, 169-180, July, 1958.

Pargellis, S. "Book Supply and the Book Market," Library Quarterly, 23:199-204, April, 1953.

Plant, A. S. "Art and Architecture Publishing," Library Trends, 7:162-168, July, 1958.

Robinson, Eleanor. "Paper-Bound Book Publishing 1939-1953," Unpublished Master's thesis, Carnegie Institute of Technology, Pittsburgh, 1954.

Schick, F. L. "British Paperbacks," Library Journal, 83:1149-1152, April 15, 1958.

Schick, F. L. *The Paperbound Book in America: The History of Paperbacks and Their European Background.* New York, Bowker, 1958. 262 p.

________. "Paperback Publishing," *Library Trends,* 7:93-104, July, 1958.

Traces development of paperbacks from the incunabula period through dime novels to the current multimillion dollar business. Includes bibliography.

Shaw, R. R. "Publication and Distribution of Scientific Literature," *College and Research Libraries,* 17:293-303, July, 1956.

Deals with the economics of publishing in the science field, copying processes and copyright laws.

Shaw, T. S., ed. "Federal, State and Local Government Publications," *Library Trends,* 15:3-194, July, 1966.

The problems of bibliographic control, cataloging, selection and reference use are discussed in this issue. The reader will find references to individual articles in the next chapter, under government publications.

Sheppard, E. L. "Religious Book and Bible Publishing," *Library Trends,* 7:153-161, July, 1958.

Strout, D. E. "Book Club Publishing," *Library Trends,* 7:66-81, July, 1958.

Sullivan, H. A. "Vanity Press Publishing," *Library Trends,* 7:105-115, July, 1958.

"Technical Books and Their Sale. Examined at Denver ABA (American Booksellers' Association) Meeting," *Publisher's Weekly,* 184:30-31, November 11, 1963.

Underwood, Edward G. *Production and Manufacturing Problems of American University Presses.* New York, Association of University Presses, 1960.

"U. S. Book Exports and Imports, 1962," Publishers' Weekly, 184:25-26, December 2, 1963.

Weber, D. C. "Introductions to the Intricacies, Facilities, and Complications in the Recent International Book Trade of the U. S." Unpublished Master's thesis, Harvard University, Cambridge, 1953.

Welch, H., and M. F. Tauber, eds. "Current Trends in U. S. Periodical Publishing," Library Trends, 10:289-446, January, 1962.

Several aspects of publishing and types of periodicals are discussed in this issue of Library Trends. The reader will find references to individual articles in the next chapter, under periodicals.

West, N. D. "Law Book Publishing," Library Trends, 7:181-196, July, 1958.

Whitten, J. N., and A. L. Fessler. "Hard-Cover Reprint Publishing," Library Trends, 7:82-92, July, 1958.

Zeitlin, J. "Bookselling Among the Sciences," College and Research Libraries, 21:453-57, November, 1960.

3. STATISTICAL SURVEYS

a. Descriptive Material

American Book Publishers Council. The Buck Hill Falls - The Changing Nature and Scope of the School and Library Market. New York, The Council, 1967. 125 p.

American Book Publishers Council. The Situation and Outlook for the Book Trade. New York, The Council, 1951.

Bennett, F. "The Current Bookmarket," Library Trends, 3:376-84, April, 1955.

Briefly describes the book publishing industry and

reports on the results of a questionnaire survey (1954), with librarians of twenty-five public and forty-two college or university libraries replying. Includes bibliography.

"Book Industry Profit Ailment Diagnosed in New BMI (Book Manufacturers' Institute) Study," Library Journal, 88: 3478-3479, October 1, 1963.

Discussion of the profit decrease suffered by book manufacturers when they provide free warehousing.

Chicorel, M. "Cost Indexes for Library Materials," Wilson Library Bulletin, 39:896-900, June, 1965.

Traces the history of the development of cost indexes for books, serials, and periodicals. Includes the following charts: U. S. book price indexes, foreign book price indexes, U. S. periodical indexes, and U. S. serial services price indexes. For each index the chart states the years covered, sources of information, and number of subject categories.

__________. "Trends in Book Prices and Related Fields in West Germany, 1954-1960," Library Resources and Technical Services, 7:47-56, Winter, 1963.

Buch und Buchhandel was the price information source for a cost study of book production. Article includes tables of West German book prices selected by categories, 1954-1960; increase in total title production, 1951-1960; and a cost of living and book price index.

__________. "West German and U. S. Book Costs as Comparative Factors in Book Budgets," Library Resources and Technical Services, 7:328-333, Fall, 1963.

Comparison of the increases in the costs of books in the two countries for the years 1954-1961.

Donaldson, M. "Book Prices Surveyed," Library Journal, 83:2388-2389, September 15, 1958.

Frase, R. W. "Economic Development in Publishing," Library Trends, 7:7-15, July, 1958.

Statistical discussion of U. S. book production, sales, exports and imports, 1946-1957.

Huff, W. H., and N. B. Brown. "Serial Services Cost Indexes," Library Resources and Technical Services, 4: 158-160, Spring, 1960.

"Index of Book Prices by Category, Selected Years," Library Journal, 89:578, February 1, 1964.

Kelley, Mary E. "A Book is Not a Bargain," North County Libraries, 6:3-4, November, 1961.

The rise in book prices since 1949, with reference to the ALA Cost of Library Materials Index, and the need for increased book budgets.

Kurth, William H. "Additional Price Indexes for U. S. Books," Library Journal, 85:1496, April 15, 1960.

Two tables of statistics of price increased in "medicine and biography" books from 1947-1958.

__________. "U. S. Book and Periodical Prices -- A Preliminary Report," Library Journal, 85:54-57, January 1, 1960.

Summary of the ALA Committee on Cost of Library Materials Index report. Tables give book prices by subject field.

Ludington, F. B. "The Increased Cost of Books," Library Journal, 84:151, January 15, 1959.

Tabulated average book costs, by subject, covering 1931-1958.

Maxwell, I. R. "Cost of Scientific Periodical Publications," Nature, 187:1052, September 17, 1960.

Comments on the price per page of scientific periodicals handled by the Pergamon Press in relation to the cost of other journals.

Miller, William. The Book Industry: A Report of the Public Library Inquiry. New York, Columbia University Press, 1949, 156 p.

Analyzes present conditions and trends in the trade-book industry with a section on its relationship to the public library.

"Price Indexes for 1967. U. S. Periodicals and Serial Services," Library Journal, 92:2526-28, July, 1967.

Publishers' World, 1966. 2d ed. Comp. and ed. by S. Weckler. New York, Bowker, 1966. 349 p.

A general survey of international book production including statistics of 1964 book production.

Schick, F. "The National and International Standardization of Book and Periodical Publishing Statistics," Library Resources and Technical Services, 11:221-229, Spring, 1967.

Tree, R. A. L. "Fashions in Collecting and Changing Prices Library Trends, 5:476-82, April, 1957.

"Trends in Retail Sales of Books, 1957-1962," Publishers' Weekly, 184:14-15, December 16, 1963.

Trimble, J. W. "Survey of Canadian English Language Trade Book Publishing, 1953-1957," Unpublished Master's thesis, University of Washington, Seattle, 1960.

U. S. Office of Education. Library Services Branch. The Cost of Library Materials: Price Trends of Publications. Washington: Govt. Print. Off., 1961. 20 p.

Provides information on the quantity of United States trade books published over the last thirty years, and on the prices of books, periodicals, and serial services.

Welch, H. M. "Cost Indexes for U. S. Periodicals: A Progress Report," Library Resources and Technical Services, 4:150-157, Spring, 1960.

b. Periodicals and Serial Publications

There are several basic sources of statistics on book publishing and distribution, e.g. annual statistics compiled by Publishers' Weekly, Bowker Annual of Library and Book Trade Information, the periodic Federal Census of Manufacturers and Census of Business, the annual foreign trade reports of the Bureau of the Census, and the internal industry surveys conducted for the American Textbook Publishers Institute and the American Book Publishers Council. In addition information on book trade, distribution, book prices, and book market in general are frequently found in library periodicals and book trade journals. The following, highly selective list, provides only a sample of such periodical literature.

Antiquarian Bookman; The Specialist Book Trade Weekly. Newark, N.J., Ed. and Pub. by Sol M. Malkin, 1948—.

> A weekly journal of book trade information of special interest to librarians interested in O.P. market. Contains valuable information on book trade and related subjects.

The A.B. Bookman's Yearbook, v.1—. Newark, N.J., Antiquarian Bookman, 1954.

Antiquariat. Zeitschrift für Alle Fachgebiete des Buch- und Kunstantiquariats. Wien, Walter Krieg Verlag, 1945—.

> Published irregularly (monthly and bi-monthly) this German book trade journal is of special importance to librarians interested in European O.P. market.

Book Production Industry; Incorporating Book Industry and Book Production. Cleveland, Penton Publ. Co., 1965—. Monthly.

> One of the leading American journals providing valuable information on the subject.

Bookseller: The Organ of the Book Trade. London,

J. Whitaker, 1858—. Weekly.

A leading journal of British book trade. In addition to information of current interest, the last issue of each month contains a cumulated monthly list of publications which in turn cumulates into Whitaker's Cumulative Book List.

Bowker Annual of Library and Book Trade Information, v. 1—. New York, Bowker, 1923—.

Annual publication of essential information on libraries book trade statistics, library activities, etc. Includes book publishing prices, legislation of library and book trade interest, information on library professional organizations, public library salaries, library and book awards, selective bibliography of year's best books on library science and other topics of current interest.

British Books; Incorporating the Publishers' Circular and Booksellers' Record. London, Publishers' Circular, 1959—

This trade journal is British counterpart of Publishers' Weekly.

Buchmarkt. Zeitschrift für den Buchhandel. Düsseldorf, Junge Ed. K. Werner Gmbh, 1963—. Quarterly.

A leading journal of commercial German book trade covering primarily Western Germany.

Library Journal. New York, Bowker, 1876—. S-Monthly.

In addition to articles and book reviews, provides occasional information on book trade.

Library Bookseller. The American Antiquarian Bookseller' Weekly. Philadelphia, Albert Saifer, ed. and publ., 1945— Weekly.

Publishers' Weekly. The Book Industry Journal. New York, Bowker, 1872—. Weekly.

Publishers' Weekly year-end statistics of American book production are based upon an analysis of all books listed in the Weekly Record during the calendar year. Not included are government publications, books sold only by subscription (except encyclopedias) and pamphlets under 49 pages.

Quill and Quire. The Magazine of the Canadian Book Trade. Toronto, Ed. N. Dereck Lewis, 1935—. Monthly.

Recent French Books. A Quarterly Review of Publications in the French Language Extracted from the Bulletin Critique du Livre Française. Paris, Association Nationale du Livre Française a l'Etranger, 1953—. Quarterly.

Scholarly Books in America. A Quarterly Bibliography of University Press Publications. Chicago, University of Chicago, 1959—. Quarterly.

Stechert-Hafner Book News. New York, Stechert-Hafner, 1946—. 9 times a year.

U. S. Bureau of the Census. Census of Manufactures, 1963. Industry Statistics; Newspapers, Periodicals, Books, and Miscellaneous Publishing. Washington, Govt. Print. Off., 1966.

One of the most important primary sources of information on the subject.

Winckler, P. A., Comp. Library Periodicals Directory. A Selected List of Periodicals Currently Published Throughout the World Relating to Library Work. Brookville, N. Y., Graduate Library School of Long Island University, 1967. 76 p.

Annotated list of some 300 periodicals.

4. COPYRIGHT

Bogsch, A. The Law of Copyright Under the Universal Convention. New York, Bowker, 1964. 591 p.

Contains the text of the international copyright documents which went into effect in 1955, along with a commentary on each article, and an exposition of the copyright laws of each of the participating countries.

Bogsch, A. Universal Copyright Convention. An Analysis and Commentary. New York, Bowker, 1958. 279p.

Budington, W. C. "Using Copyrighted Material," Special Libraries, 52:510-13, November, 1961.

Brown, A. L. "Summary of Copyright Positions," Special Libraries, 52:499-505, November, 1961.

Berne Convention for the Protection of Literary and Artistic Works, 1948. Berne, International Union for the Protection of Literary Works, 1948. 24p.

Clapp, V. W. "Library Photocopying and Copyright: Recent Developments," Law Library Journal, 55:10-15, 1962.

A discussion of copying in libraries from early times to the present.

Clark, A. J. The Movement for International Copyright in Nineteenth Century America. Washington, Catholic University Press, 1960. 215p.

Clarke, R. F. "The Impact of Photocopying on Scholarly Publishing," Library Journal, 88:2625-29, July, 1963.

A study of the volume of journal and theses photocopying, based upon a doctoral thesis.

Copyright Law Symposium, No. 15. Sponsored by American Society of Composers, Authors and Publishers. New York, Columbia University Press, 1967. 239p. (Nathan Barkan Memorial Competition).

Includes chapter on the effect of the Copyright Act and the proposed revisions on educators as users of copyright material.

Freehafer, E. G., et al. "Joint Libraries Committee on Fair Use in Photocopying: Report on Single Copies," Special Libraries, 52:251-55, May-June, 1961.

Gipe, G. A. Nearer to the Dust: Copyright and the Machine. Baltimore, Md., Williams and Wilkins, 1967. 290 p.

Hattery, L. H., and G. P. Bresh. Reprography and Copyright Law. Washington, American Institute of Biological Sciences, 1964. 204 p.

Based on symposium in 1963 sponsored by The American University.

Kaplan, B. "Copyright, Libraries, the Public Interest," College and Research Libraries, 21:213-216, May, 1960.

Koepke, J. C. "Implications of the Copyright Law on the Dissemination of Scientific and Technical Information," Special Libraries, 54:553-556, November, 1963.

Latman, A. "Copyright Office Recommendations for a New Copyright Law," Special Libraries, 52:514-521, November, 1961.

Nicholson, M. Manual of Copyright Practice for Writers, Publishers, and Agents. 2d ed. New York, Oxford University Press, 1956. 273 p.

A handbook for the layman in the literary world who wants information about a specific copyright question.

Pilpel, H. F. Copyright Guide. 2d ed. New York, Bowker, 1966. 40 p.

General background information for copyright questions about literary works. Presented in question-answer form.

Price, M. O. "Photocopying by Libraries and Copyright," Library Trends, 8:432-447, January, 1960.

Rogers, J. W. U. S. National Bibliography and the Copyright Law. New York, Bowker, 1960. 115 p.

A historical review of the U. S. copyright law and the growth of bibliographical activity as it relates to it.

Shaw, R. R. *Literary Property in the United States*. New York, Scarecrow Press, 1950. 277p.

Basic text on the philosophy underlying literary property in U. S. and other countries.

U. S. Copyright Office. Copyright Law Revision. *Supplementary Report of the Register of Copyrights on the General Revision of the U. S. Copyright Law: 1965 Revision Bill*. Washington, Govt. Print. Off., 1965. 338p.

Wincor, R. *How to Secure Copyright. The Law of Literary Property*. New York, Oceana Publications, 1957. 96p.

Wittenberg, P. *Law of Literary Property*. Boston, The Writer, Inc., 1964.

An explanation for the layman of the legal aspects of literary property and how they have developed and changed.

CHAPTER IV

PURCHASES

---

1. ORDER ROUTINES

a. Streamlining Essential Routines

"ALA and National League of Cities to Study Book Bidding Practices," Library Journal, 91:5566-67, November 15, 1966.

Batts, N. C. "Data Analysis of Science Monograph Order-Cataloging Forms," Special Libraries 57:583-86, October, 1966.

Bennett, Fleming. "Prompt Payment of Bookdealers' Invoices: An Approach to Standards," College and Research Libraries, 14:387-392, October, 1953.

> Case study conducted at Columbia University to determine whether university libraries pay as promptly as they should and whether standards acceptable to both dealer and librarian can be constructed.

Bryan, H. "Order in Ordering," Australian Library Journal, 6:120-126, July, 1957.

__________. "Streamlining Order and Accession Routines," Australian Library Journal, 3:121-126, October, 1954.

Chamberlain, D. E. "In-Process Records," College and Research Libraries, 7:335-338, October, 1946.

Colburn, E. B. Multiple Order Forms Used By American Libraries. Chicago, American Library Association, 1949.

> A collection of order forms and description of their use.

"Comparative Desiderata. Choice's List from Volumes I and II," Choice, 3:389-92, July-August, 1966.

Coppola, D. "Library---Book Trade Relations in the Field of Current Books," College and Research Libraries, 17:330-333, July, 1956.

Pleads for closer communication between librarian and bookseller, including standardization of order forms.

Dougherty, R., and Samuel M. Boone. "An Ordering Procedure Utilizing the Xerox 914 Electrostatic Process," Library Resources and Technical Services, 10:43-45, Winter, 1966.

Describes the application of the Xerox 914 Electrostatic Process at the Louis Round Wilson Library at the University of North Carolina at Chapel Hill. Includes an analysis of the original and revised ordering procedures.

Flannery, A. "A Routine for Checking Book Orders by the Cataloging Department," Journal of Cataloging and Classification, 8:98-102, September, 1952.

Discusses steps used at Lehigh University Library, resulting in improved efficiency and accuracy.

Fristoe, Ashby J. "The Bitter End," Library Resources and Technical Services, 10:91-95, Winter, 1966.

A study of bibliographic tools used for verification demonstrated that the LC proof slip file, Publishers' Weekly Announcements, and Cumulative Book Index arranged in that sequence offer the optimum searching depth for current American imprints ordered for a large university library.

Kebabian, J. S. "Book Appraisals," Library Trends, 9:466-470, April, 1961.

Briefly discusses practical, legal, and ethical aspects of book appraisal.

Kenny, L. A. "Multiple Forms: How They Smooth Technical Processes," Catholic Library World, 24:39-42, November, 1952.

Kritzer, H. W. "Effect of the Introduction of a Multiple-Copy Order Form on the Technical Processing of Books in a Medium-Sized University Library," Unpublished Master's thesis, Catholic University of America, 1958.

Lazorick, G. J., and T. L. Minder. "A Least Cost Searching Sequence," College and Research Libraries, 25:85-90, March, 1964.

The cost of searching information to order a book at Pennsylvania State University was found to be $.73.

Lowy, G. A Searcher's Manual. Hamden, Conn., Shoe String Press, 1965. 104 p.

A description of desirable practices involved in searching for information about titles under consideration for library purchase.

McJenkin, V. "Streamlining Essential Routines," Wilson Library Bulletin, 37:680-681, April, 1963.

Matthews, S. E. "Multiple Order Form Slips," Library Journal, 82:635-638, March, 1957.

Describes multiple order forms used by Ohio State University Libraries. Includes bibliography.

New York. State Library. Albany. "Acquisitions Policy of the New York State Library," Bookmark, 22:95-100, December, 1965.

Overmyer, LaVahn. "An Analysis of Output Costs and Procedures for an Operational Searching Service," American Documentation, 14:123-142, April, 1963.

"Plan to Speed Pre Viewing and Ordering of Books," Library Journal, 84:2018-2020, June 15, 1959.

Randall, F. S. "Economics in Order Work," Illinois Library Association Record, 8:71-75, April, 1955.

Southern California University, School of Library Science. "Order Records and Methods: A Workshop," Library Resources and Technical Services, 3:278-288, Fall, 1959.

Several libraries in Southern California report on various aspects of their order department routines, forms, and procedures.

Statham, M. H. "Desiderata Lists," Library World, 62: 108-109, November, 1960.

Sweet, A. P. "Forms in Acquisitions Work," College and Research Libraries, 14:396-401, 452, October, 1953.

The design and use of forms in library acquisition work.

"Systems Development Corporation Develops New Book Purchasing System," Special Libraries, 55:703-705, December, 1964.

Tauber, M. "Desiderata Files," Stechert-Hafner Book News, 5:17-19, October, 1950.

Discussion about desiderata files by means of reviewing a study by Lena Biancardo on what they contained, how they are arranged, and their usefulness. Also discussed was the policy used at Cornell in using second hand dealers catalogs to obtain out-of-print books.

Teeple, H. M. "Acquisition Form Letter," Illinois Libraries, 48:323-26, April, 1966.

"Uniterm Code for Invoices Proposed by ABPC," Library Journal, 86:4147-4148, December 1, 1961.

Van Pelt, J. D. "Duplication of Books: Causes and Remedies," Australian Library Journal, 3:42-46, April, 1954.

Veit, F. "Book Order Procedures in the Publicly Controlled Colleges and Universities of the Midwest," College and Research Libraries, 23:33-40, January, 1962.

Wulfekoetter, G. "Background for Acquisition Work," Library Journal, 86:522-526, February 1, 1961.

Discusses prerequisites and tools for the acquisition librarian.

b. Placing Orders with Publishers

Angoff, Allan. "Know Your Publishers," Wilson Library Bulletin, 37:156-158, October, 1962.

Davidson, J. S. "Direct from the Publisher," Publishers' Weekly, 178:40-41, July 11, 1960.

Discussion of inconsistent policies of publishers regarding discounts, handling charges, invoices.

"The Future of the Library Market Explored by Publishers' Council," Publishers' Weekly, 171:24-33, June 17, 1957.

Relationship between librarians and publishers discussed at the annual meeting of American Book Publisher's Council, May 19-21, 1957.

Hirsch, F. E. "The Librarian Looks at the Publisher," College and Research Libraries, 12:321-327, October, 1951.

Jordan, R. T. "Eliminate the Middlemen in Book Ordering," Library Journal, 86:327-329, January 15, 1961.

Discusses problems of school libraries in ordering books.

"TABS --- McGraw-Hill Offers Book Selection Assistance," Library Journal, 85:2898-2899, September 1, 1960.

Veenstra, J., and L. L. Mai. "When Do You Use a Jobber?" College and Research Libraries, 23:522-524, November, 1962.

Purdue University Libraries' decision to bypass the jobbers and buy directly from publishers.

Waller, T. "Problems of American Book Publishers," College and Research Libraries, 13:147-150, April, 1952.

c. Placing Orders with Jobbers

Alford, H. W. "A New Concept in Serial Dealers," Library Resources and Technical Services, 7:259-263, Summer, 1963.

Banerjea, P. K. "Librarian and the Bookseller," Indian Librarian, 19:114-118, December, 1964.

Bennett, F. "The Current Bookmarket," Library Trends, 3:376-384, April, 1958.

Discusses the buying habits of libraries, indicating an apparent preference for buying through jobbers. Includes bibliography.

"The Bookseller and the Librarian," ALA Bulletin, 42: 509-515, November, 1948.

This series of six articles by persons in various phases of the book business is an attempt to present the situation from its various points of view. Writer of each article is person who would see the situation differently because of the aspect of the work with which he is connected. Writers point out services libraries and dealers expect from each other and the extent to which the services are effectively rendered. Suggestions are listed for providing better services in handling scientific and technical material.

Busse, D. "The Role of the Wholesaler," In: Illinois. University. Library School. The Nature and Development of Library Collection. Champaign, Ill., Illini Book Store, 1957. Pp. 104-116.

Coppola, D. The International Bookseller Looks at Acquisitions," _Library Resources and Technical Services_, 11:203-206, Spring, 1967.

Henshaw, R. H., and W. H. Kurth. "Dealer Rating System at L. C.," _Library Resources and Technical Services_, 1:131-136, Summer, 1957.

Describes a rating system used by the Order Division, Library of Congress, for evaluating bookdealers throughout the world.

Hitchen, H. S. "Bookseller and the Libraries," _Library World_, 63:158-160, January, 1962.

Jackson, C., Jr. "Bookdealer-Library Relations Committee," _Wilson Library Bulletin_, 37:340, December, 1962.

Kaiser, J. B. "Library Journal's Survey of Wholesale Book Purchasing," _Library Journal_, 84:365-368, February 1, 1959.

Results of a survey (162 replies) of libraries regarding experiences with specific wholesalers.

__________. "What Wholesalers Think of Library Customers," _Library Journal_, 84:369-370, February 1, 1959.

Summarizes oral replies of wholesalers to questions regarding customers.

Mason, Harold J. "Beating the Brush for Books: The Dealers' Sources of Supply," _College and Research Libraries_, 22:21-29, January, 1961.

Pickett, A. S. "Experiment in Book Buying," _Library Journal_, 84:371-372, February 1, 1959.

Report of buying from retail stores in a metropolitan area, San Francisco.

Ruback, M. "We Can Get It for You Wholesale --- with Help," _Library Journal_, 87:730, February 15, 1962.

Scheckter, Stella J. "Study of Book Supply Agencies Employed by Eleven College and University Libraries in the Vicinity of Philadelphia." Unpublished Master's thesis, Drexel Institute of Technology, Philadelphia, 1952.

Strieby, I. M. "Simplified Library-to-Dealer Purchasing," Stechert-Hafner Book News, 9:81-82, March, 1955.

Veenstra, John, and Lois Mai. "When Do You Use a Jobber?" College and Research Libraries, 23:522-524, November, 1962.

> Purdue University Library made a comparison of American jobbers' and publishers' discounts and delivery time. Results showed that a publisher provided faster service at a larger discount. Study questioned value of using a jobber for the majority of its books.

Welch, H. M., ed. "Dealers Look at the LC Rating System," Library Resources and Technical Services, 2:115-120, Spring, 1958.

> Replies by seven bookdealers regarding Henshaw-Kurth article, "Dealer Rating System at LC," (LRTS, 1:131-136, Summer, 1957).

"Wholesaler Profile: Fiction Specialist to Libraries," Publishers' Weekly, 179:25-27, May 1, 1961.

Zeitlin, J. "Bookseller and the Librarian," California Librarian, 23:91-94, April, 1962.

d. Placing Standing Orders

"Collier-Macmillan Standing Order Plan for Libraries," Publishers' Weekly, 183:40, February 25, 1963.

Dick, M. H. "Standing Book Orders," Library World, 58:95-99, January, 1958.

Jacob, E., and B. Salisbury. "Automatic Purchase of University Press Books," Library Journal, 83:707-708, March 1, 1958.

A brief description of a university library's automatic purchase program.

McNiff, P. J. "Harvard's Position on Blanket Orders and En Bloc Purchases," Library Journal, 86:146, January 15, 1961.

Ready, W. B. "Acquisition by Standing Order," Library Resources and Technical Services, 1:85-88, Spring, 1957.

Briefly discusses the Marquette University Libraries' domestic and foreign acquisitions procedures.

e. Serials and Periodicals

Alford, H. Wendell. "A New Concept in Serial Dealers," Library Resources and Technical Services, 7:259-263, Summer, 1963.

Ash, L. "Subsidized Periodical Publishing," Library Trends, 10:302-309, January, 1962.

Ball, Alice Julany. "Costs of Serial Acquisition through USBE," Serial Slants, 4:11-15, April, 1952.

Barry, J. W. "A Study on Long Term Periodical Subscriptions," Library Resources and Technical Services, 3:50-54, Winter, 1959.

A Committee report on the savings available through the use of three-year subscriptions, as compared with shorter term ones.

Bennett, F. "A Multi-Purpose Serials Record," College and Research Libraries, 9:231-237, July, 1948.

A very clear presentation of how West Virginia University evolved into the use of a multi-purpose record.

It discusses types of equipment and card forms. Enumerates the information which can be organized on a multi-purpose record.

Berry, P. "Library of Congress Serial Record Techniques," Serial Slants, 3:14-18, July, 1952.

Bishop, D., et al. "Publication Patterns of Scientific Serials," American Documentation, 16:113-121, April, 1965.

Bishop, D., and L. K. Osborn. "Translation Frequency as a Guide to the Selection of Soviet Biomedical Serials," Medical Library Association Bulletin, 52:557-567, July, 1964.

Bjorkbom, C. "Bibliographical Tools for Control of Current Periodicals," Review of Documentation, 20:19-24, March 31, 1953.

Brady, Sister E. M. "Fine Printing Periodicals," Catholic Library World, 33:551-553, May, 1962.

Brigham, C. S. History and Bibliography of American Newspapers, 1690-1820. Worcester, Mass., American Antiquarian Society, 1947. 2 v.

Brodman, E. "Medical Periodicals," Library Trends, 10:381-389, January, 1962.

Brown, C. H. Scientific Serials. Chicago, Association of College and Research Libraries, 1956. 189 p. (ACRL Monograph, No. 16).

Characteristics and lists of most cited publications in science field.

Brown, D. A. "Agricultural Periodicals," Library Trends, 10:405-413, January, 1962.

Bourne, C. P. "The Worlds Technical Journal Literature: An Estimate of Volume, Origin, Language, Field, Indexing and Abstracting," American Documentation, 13:159-168, April, 1962.

Cabeen, V. A., and D. C. Cook. "Organization of Serials and Documents," Library Trends, 2:199-216, October, 1953.

Clarke, J. A. "Social Science Journals," Library Trends, 10:353-359, January, 1962.

Clasquin, F. F. "Procurement of Periodicals on an Annual Bid Basis," SLA Sci-Tech News, 19:10-12, Spring, 1965.

Curran, A. T. "The Mechanization of the Serial Records for the Moving and Merging of the Boston Medical and Harvard Medical Serials," Library Resources and Technical Services, 10:362-372, Summer, 1966.

Danielson, R. H. "Serials Holdings Information Service in Research Libraries," Library Resources and Technical Services, 10:261-283, Summer, 1966.

Data based on a survey of 74 member libraries of the Association of Research Libraries.

Davinson, D. E. Periodicals: A Manual of Practice for Librarians. London, Deutsch, 1960. 165 p.

A practical approach to serial work.

Elftman, R. A. "Some Simplified Procedures in the Handling of Serials in a Small Library," Serial Slants, 5:89-94, July, 1954.

Eyman, E. G. "Periodicals Automation at Miami-Dade Junior College," Library Resources and Technical Services, 10:341-361, Summer, 1966.

Fabber, E. I. "General Periodicals," Library Trends 10:310-320, January, 1962.

Fowler, M. J. Guide to Scientific Periodicals, London, Library Association, 1966.

Gable, J. H. Manual of Serials Work. Chicago, American Library Association, 1937. 229 p.

Incorporates practical aspects of serial work with results of a questionnaire from 125 representative libraries.

Gellatly, P. "Libraries and Subscription Agencies," PNLA Quarterly, 31:35-40, October, 1966.

Gottschalk, C. M., and W. F. Desmond. "Worldwide Census of Scientific and Technical Serials," American Documentation. 14:188-194, July, 1963.

Compares natural and physical sciences, medicine, agriculture and technology for U. S., Germany, Soviet Union, England, France, and Japan.

Graziano, E. E. "Interlibrary Loan Analysis: Diagnostic for Scientific Serials Backfile Acquisitions," Special Libraries, 53:251-257, May, 1962.

Grenfell, D. Periodicals and Serials, Their Treatment in Libraries. London, Aslib, 1953.

Hand, T. S. "Acquisition and Handling of Periodicals in Ten College Libraries in the Philadelphia Area," Serial Slants, 5:58-61, April, 1954.

Hartje, G. H. Centralized Serial Records in University Libraries. Urbana: University of Illinois Library School, 1951. (Occasional Papers No. 24).

Hitt, S. W. "Evolution of the Serials Department at the University of Missouri Library," Serial Slants, 6:85-88, April, 1955.

Huff, W. H. "Indexing, Abstracting and Translation Services," Library Trends, 10:427-446, January, 1962.

__________. "Periodicals," Library Trends, 15:398-419, January, 1967.

Jacobstein, J. M. "Legal Periodicals," Library Trends, 10:374-380, January, 1962.

Jolley, L. "The Use of Microfilm for Completing Sets," Journal of Documentation, 4:41-44, June, 1948.

Kirchenbaum, F. J. "Periodicals in the Humanities," Library Trends, 10:321-329, January, 1962.

Kilpatrick, N. L. "Serial Records in a University Library," Journal of Cataloging and Classification, 6:33-35, Spring, 1950.

Kuhlman, A. F. "Administration of Serial and Document Acquisition and Preparation," In: Randall, W. M., ed. The Acquisition and Cataloging of Books. Chicago, University of Chicago Press, 1940. Pp. 95-116.

LaHood, C. G. "Newspapers: Directories, Indexes and Union Lists," Library Trends, 15:420-429, January, 1967.

Lewis, S. T. "Periodicals in the Visual Arts," Library Trends, 10:330-352, January, 1962.

Martin, R. C., and W. Jett. Guide to Scientific and Technical Periodicals. Denver, Alan Swallow, 1963.

Mason, H. J. "Beating the Brush for Books: The Dealers' Sources of Supply," College and Research Libraries, 22: 21-29, January, 1961.

Purchase of serial sets.

__________. "Periodical Sets and the World Market; or, Life in a Rubber-Boot Factory," Library Resources and Technical Services, 4:295-302, Fall, 1960.

Acquisition of periodicals, current and back issues, domestic and foreign.

McGrath, W. E., and H. Kolbe. "A Simple, Mechanized, Non-Computerized System for Serials Control in Small Academic Libraries: A Primer," Library Resources and Technical Services, 10:373-382, Summer, 1966.

Orr, R. W. "A Few Aspects of Acquiring Serials," Library Trends, 3:393-402, April, 1955.

Osborn, A. D. "Evaluation of Serial Equipment for Library Purposes," Serial Slants, 6:118-122, July, 1955.

A good article for evaluating the various types of equipment available for a serial record. Discusses the things which must be considered before setting up a multi-purpose serial file.

__________. Serial Publications: Their Place and Treatment in Libraries. Chicago, American Library Association, 1955. 309 p.

Theoretical and practical introduction to library aspects of serial publications.

Payne, K. B. "Procuring Serials by Bid at the USDA Library---Some Experiences and Observations," Serial Slants, 7:71-75, April, 1956.

Peterson, T. Magazines in the Twentieth Century. Urbana, University of Illinois Press, 1956.

Pizer, I. H., et al. "Mechanization of Library Procedures in the Medium-Sized Medical Library: The Serial Record," Medical Library Association Bulletin, 51:313-338, July, 1963.

Sankey, J. "A Survey of Little Magazine Publishing," Trace, 5:1-13, October, 1953.

Schultheiss, L. A. "Two Serial Control Card Files Developed at the University of Illinois, Chicago," Library Resources and Technical Services, 9:271-287, Summer, 1965.

Shachtman, B. E. "Current Serial Records, an Experiment," College and Research Libraries, 14:240-242, 248, July, 1953.

Deals with the conversion back to standard 3x5 inch card trays at the U. S. Department of Agriculture Library serial department.

Shank, R. "Scientific and Technical Periodicals," Library Trends, 10:390-404, January, 1962.

Shaw, K. B. "Periodical Acquisition Policies," Aslib Proceedings, 5:81-86, May, 1953.

Skipper, J. E. "Organizing Serial Records at the Ohio State University Libraries," College and Research Libraries, 14:39-45, January, 1953.

A good discussion of the adoption of a central serial record at Ohio State University. Elaborates on the type equipment, card forms, information consolidated and processing procedures.

Tallman, J. E. "A Survey of Methods of Claiming Serials," Serial Slants, 7:76-85, April, 1956.

Thompson, D. E. "Business and Economics Periodicals," Library Trends, 10:360-373, January, 1962.

Vickery, B. C. "Periodical Sets; What Should You Buy?" Aslib Proceedings, 5:69-74, May, 1953.

Welch, H. M. "Cost Indexes for U. S. Periodicals: A Progress Report," Library Resources and Technical Services, 4:150-157, Spring, 1960.

Classified list based on prices of nearly 2000 periodicals.

Welch, H. M. "The Economics of Periodical Publishing," Library Trends, 10:233-301, January, 1962.

Wessells, H. E. "Bibliographical and Library Science Periodicals," Library Trends, 10:414-426, January, 1962.

Whetstone, G. "Serial Practices in Selected College and University Libraries," Library Resources and Technical Services, 5:284-290, Fall, 1961.

Reviews information obtained from sixteen questionnaires.

Wood, J. P. Magazines in the United States. 2d ed. New York, Ronald Press, 1956.

f. Discounts

Baier, George. "A Study of Book Discounts Received by Mary Reed Library from Special Jobbers during 1960 and 1961." Unpublished Research Paper, University of Denver, June, 1961.

Compares discounts given by four general and two special jobbers.

Conover, Robert Warren. "A Study of Discounts Allowed by Five Major Publishers in Relation to Discounts Received by the University of Denver Libraries." Unpublished Research Paper, University of Denver, 1962.

Comparison of discounts received with those advertised.

Donaldson, M. "Book Prices Surveyed," Library Journal, 83:2388-2389, September 15, 1958.

Grether, E. T. Price Control Under Fair Trade Legislation. New York, Oxford University Press, 1939.

Kaser, D. "Discounts and Service," Missouri Library Quarterly, 19:92-95, September, 1958.

Melcher, D. "Discount Diversity," Library Journal, 86: 960-962, March 1, 1961.

Summarizes reasons for diversity to wholesalers' discounts.

Orman, O. C. Library Discount Control: A Hurried Survey. St. Louis: Washington University, 1940.

Price, M. O. "Lowest Responsible Bidder---A Legal Interpretation," Library Journal, 83:1005-1007, April 1, 1958.

Wynar, B. S., and H. R. Malinowsky, eds. Cost Analysis Study of Technical Services Division, University of Denver Libraries. Denver, Graduate School of Librarianship, University of Denver, 1965.

Discounts are discussed in Chapter VI, pp. 44-53.

g. A Selected List of Directories and Guides

See also pp. 188-191.

American Book Trade Directory, Lists of Publishers, Booksellers, Periodicals, Trade Organizations, Wholesalers, etc. 18th ed. New York, Bowker, 1967. 828 p.

Up-to-date lists for American book market as well as foreign.

Ayer firm, Philadelphia. N. W. Ayer and Son's Directory of Newspapers and Periodicals. Philadelphia, Ayer, 1880—.

Ayer, a comprehensive annual directory, lists some 20, 000 newspapers and periodicals published in the United States, Canada, Bermuda, Panama, and the Philippines with descriptions of the states, provinces, cities, and towns in which they are published. In 1910 the Ayer firm absorbed Rowell's American Newspaper Directory (1869-1908, 40 v.).

Bowker Annual of Library and Book Trade Information, New York, Bowker, 1923—.

Downs, R. B., and F. B. Jenkins. "Bibliography: Current State and Future Trends, Part I and II," Library Trends, 15:337-598, January, 1967 and 15:601-919, April, 1967.

A number of survey articles covering national bibliography, subject bibliography, government publications, serials and periodicals.

Educational Publishers. Paris, UNESCO, 1963. 141 p.

Part 1. International and national publishers' associations.

Part II. Lists of individual educational publishers of teaching materials.

Hoffman, F. J., et al. *The Little Magazine; A History and a Bibliography*. Princeton, N. J., Princeton University Press, 1946.

Index to Little Magazines. Denver, Alan Swallow, 1948—.

International Federation for Documentation. *List of Current Abstracting and Indexing Services.* The Hague, The Federation, 1949.

Koltay, E., ed. *Irregular Serials and Annuals: An International Directory*. New York, Bowker, 1966. 668 p.

14, 500 titles, all of which have been issued after Jan. 1, 1960, are alphabetically listed by subjects resembling the arrangement of *Ulrich's Directory*.

Literary Market Place: The Business Directory of American Book Publishing. New York, Bowker, 1940—.

Directory of publishing and allied fields.

NACS Trade Text Manual. 10th ed. Oberlin, Ohio, National Association of College Stores, 1960.

Provides information on discounts for College and University Bookstores. For additional information see *Publishers Trade List Annual.*

National Directory of Newspapers and Reporting Services, 1st ed. Detroit, Gale, 1966. 240 p.

Includes 1, 500 national, international and selected foreign newsletters, information services, financial services and association bulletins with short description of contents.

Polking, K., ed. *Writer's Market 1966*. 22nd ed. Cincinnati, Ohio, Writer's Digest, 1966. 656 p.

Describes 4000 markets for free-lance writers,

serving at the same time as useful source of description of the contents of all kinds of magazines and in this respect will offer a valuable assistance to the order librarian.

The Printers' Ink Directory of House Organs. New York, Printers' Ink Publishing Company, 1954.

Titles in Series; A Handbook for Librarians and Students. 2d ed. New York, Scarecrow Press, 1964—. 2 v. Suppls.

Alphabetical listing of series published in United States with an author/title index to individual publications. Approximately 45, 000 entries.

Ulrich's International Periodicals Directory. 12th ed. New York, Bowker, 1967-68. 2 v. Suppls.

v. 1. Scientific, Technical, Medical
v. 2. Arts, Humanities, Business and Social Sciences

U. S. Library of Congress. General Reference and Bibliography Division. Union Lists of Serials. A Bibliography prepared by R. A. Freitag. Washington, Govt. Print. Off., 1964.

U. S. Library of Congress. Science and Technology Division. A Guide to the World's Abstracting and Indexing Services in Science and Technology. Washington, 1963. (National Federation of Science Abstracting and Indexing Services. Report No. 102).

The Working Press of the Nation. Volume I: Newspaper and Allied Services Directory. Chicago, National Research Bureau, 1967—. Published annually.

World List of Social Science Periodicals. 3d ed. Prepared by the International Committee for Social Science Documentation. Paris, UNESCO, 1966. 448p.

An example of a subject guide. Lists 1, 312 journals. published in 92 countries.

h. A Selected List of Verification Aids

American National and Trade Bibliographies

Last Week and Prepublications:

Forthcoming Books. New York, Bowker, 1967—.

Publishers' Weekly: the American Book Trade Journal. New York, Bowker, 1872—.

Last Month:

BPR: American Book Publishing Record . . . as Cataloged by the Library of Congress and Annotated by Publishers' Weekly. New York, Bowker, 1960—.

Cumulative Book Index; A World List of Books in the English Language. New York, Wilson, 1929—.

Books in Print:

Publishers' Trade List Annual. New York: Bowker, 1873—.

Books in Print; An Author-Title Index to the Publishers' Trade List Annual. New York, Bowker, 1948—.

Subject Guide to Books in Print; An Index to the Publishers' Trade List Annual. New York, Bowker, 1957—.

Serials and Periodicals:

New Serial Titles; A Union List of Serials Commencing Publication after December 31, 1949. Washington, Library of Congress, 1953—.

Subject Index to New Serial Titles, 1950-1965. Ann Arbor, Mich., Pierian Press, 1968.

Union List of Serials in Libraries of the United States and Canada. 3d ed. New York, Wilson, 1965. 5 v.

Library Catalogs:

U. S. Library of Congress. *Catalog of Books Represented by Library of Congress Printed Cards. . . .* Ann Arbor, Mich., Edwards Brothers, 1942-1955. 191 v. Title varies.

__________. *The National Union Catalog; A Cumulative Author List Representing Library of Congress Printed Cards, and Titles Reported by Other American Libraries.* January, 1956—. Washington, Govt. Print. Off., 1956—. Title varies.

__________. *Library of Congress Catalog. Books: Subjects, 1950-1954.* Ann Arbor, Mich., J. W. Edwards, 1955. 20 v. *1955-1959:* Patterson, N. J., Pageant Books, 1960. 22 v.

i. *General Guides to Reference Books*

Barton, M. N. *Reference Books.* 6th ed. Baltimore, Enoch Pratt Free Library, 1966. 145 p.

Carter, Mary Duncan, and Wallace John Bonk. *Building Library Collections.* 2d ed. New York, Scarecrow Press, 1964. 287 p.

Collison, Robert L. *Bibliographies, Subject and National; A Guide to Their Contents, Arrangement, and Use.* New York, Hafner, 1962. 185 p.

Courtney, William P. *Register of National Bibliography.* London, Constable, 1905-1912, 3 v.

Hirschberg, Herbert S. Subject Guide to Reference Books. Chicago, American Library Association, 1942. 259 p.

Hoffman, Hester R. The Reader's Adviser and Bookman's Manual. 10th ed. New York, Bowker, 1964. 1292 p.

11th ed. edited by W. E. Courtney in 2 volumes is in progress. Volume 1, 1968, Volume 2, 1969.

Hutchins, Margaret. Introduction to Reference Work. Chicago, American Library Association, 1944. 228 p.

Linder, LeRoy Harold. The Rise of Current Complete National Bibliographies. New York, Scarecrow Press, 1959. 300 p.

Malcles, Louise Noelle. Manuel de Bibliographie. Paris, Presses Universitaires de France, 1963. 328 p.

__________. Les Sources du Travail Bibliographique. Geneva, Droz Lille Girard, 1950-58. 3 v. in 4.

Minto, John. Reference Books. A Classified and Annotated Guide to the Principal Works of Reference. London, Library Association, 1929.

__________. Reference Books. A Classified and Annotated Guide to the Principal Works of Reference. Supplement. London, Library Association, 1931.

Mudge, I. G. Guide to Reference Books. 6th ed. Chicago, American Library Association, 1936. 504 p.

Murphy, Robert. How and Where to Look It Up. New York, McGraw-Hill, 1958. 750 p.

Roberts, A. D. Introduction to Reference Books. 3d ed., rev. London, Library Association, 1956. 237 p.

Shores, Louis. Basic Reference Books. Chicago, American Library Association, 1939.

Shores, Louis. Basic Reference Sources. Chicago, American Library Association, 1954. 388 p.

Stein, Henri. Manuel de Bibliographie Generale: Bibliotheca Bibliographica Nova. Paris, Picard, 1897. 895 p.

Totok, Wilhelm, and Rolf Weitzel. Handbuch der Biblioprophischen Nachschlagswerke. 2., stark erweiterte, völlig neu bearb, Auflage. Frankfurt am Main, Klostermann, 1959. 335 p.

Walford, A. J. Guide to Reference Material. London, Library Association, 1959. Supplement, 1963. (New edition in process, v. 1. Science and Technology, 1966).

Winchell, C. M. Guide to Reference Books. 8th ed. Chicago, American Library Association, 1967. 741 p.

Wynar, B. S. Introduction to Bibliography and Reference Work. 4th ed. Rochester, N. Y., Libraries Unlimited, 1967. 310 p.

2. THE USE OF MECHANIZED EQUIPMENT

a. Automated Acquisition Procedures

See also pp. 66-78, "Libraries and Automation."

Ahn, H. K. Computer-assisted Library Mechanization (CALM); Acquisition (ACQ); CALMACQ Project Notebook. Irvine, University of California, 1967.

Alanen, S., D. E. Sparks, and F. G. Kilgour. "A Computer-monitored Library Technical Processing System," In: American Documentation Institute. Proceedings of the Annual Meeting. v. 3; 1966. Woodland Hills, Calif., Adrienne Press, 1966. Pp. 419-426.

Baatz, W. H., and E. H. Maurer. "Machines at Work," Library Journal, 78:1277-1281, August, 1953.

Milwaukee Public Library.

Bagshaw, M. G. "Enter Computer: Bookordering Practices and Procedure of the Toronto Public Library," Top of the News, 23:39-42, November, 1966.

Becker, Joseph. "System Analysis --- Prelude to Library Data Processing," American Library Association Bulletin, 59:293-296, April, 1965.

Systems analysis is a prerequisite to electronic data processing in the library. Describes the system of the acquisitions department at Penn State University Library. In June, 1964, a prototype system was in operation. System reserves professional work for librarians and clerical duties for the machines.

Benkin, J. "Automated Procedures at Purdue University Library: Accounting Procedures," In: Meeting on Automation in the Library --- When, Where, and How, Purdue University, 1964. Papers. Edited by T. Andrews. Lafayette, Ind., Purdue University, 1965. Pp. 36-38.

Brown, G. B. "Use of Punched Cards in Acquisition Work: Experience at Illinois," College and Research Libraries, 10:219-220, 257, July, 1949.

Butcher, S. J. "The Acquisition of Books," Library Association Record, 54:259-262, August, 1952.

Corbin, J. B. "The Acquisition Programs of the Centralized Processing Center of the Texas State Library," In: Texas Conference on Library Mechanization, 1st, Austin, 1966. Proceedings. Edited by J. B. Corbin. Austin, Texas Library and Historical Commission, 1966. (Texas State Library Monograph, No. 6.) Pp. 36-46.

Cox, Carl R. "Mechanized Acquisitions Procedures at the University of Maryland," College and Research Libraries, 26:232-236, May, 1965.

Technical explanation of the mechanization of acquisitions. Order request forms serve as the source documents for key punching. These requests are accumulated and consolidated. The IBM 407 prints the purchase orders weekly.

Culbertson, D. S. "The Costs of Data Processing in University Libraries; In: Book Acquisitions and Cataloging," College and Research Libraries, 24:487-489, November, 1963.

__________. "Data Processing for Technical Procedures at the University of Illinois Library," In: Institute on Information Storage and Retrieval, 1st, University of Minnesota, 1962. Information Retrieval Today. Minneapolis, 1966. Pp. 99-107.

Divett, Robert. "Mechanization in a New Medical School Library; I, Acquisitions and Cataloging," Medical Library Association Bulletin, 53:12-25, January, 1965.

Traces the development of the use of electronic data processing for routine jobs at the University of New Mexico Library of Medical Science. Program utilizes punched card equipment, IBM 407 Model E8 Accounting Machine, IBM 26 Printing Card Punch, IBM 82 Sorter, and IBM 85 Collator.

Dunlap, C. "Automated Acquisition Procedures at the University of Michigan Library," Library Resources and Technical Services, 11:192-202, Spring, 1967.

Felter, J., and D. S. Tjoeng. "A Computer System for a Union Catalog; Theme and Variations," Medical Library Association Bulletin, 53:163-177, April, 1965.

Ferris, H. D. "Automated Procedures at Purdue University Library: Order Department," In: Meeting on Automation in the Library --- When, Where, and How, Purdue University, 1964. Papers. Edited by T. Andrews. Lafayette, Ind., Purdue University, 1965. Pp. 39-42.

Geddes, A. "Data Processing in a Cooperative System --- Opportunities for Service," In: Harvey, J., ed. Data Processing in Public and University Libraries. Washington, Spartan Books, 1966. (Drexel Information Science Series, v. 3.) Pp. 25-35.

Gladstone, J. M. "Marginal Punched Cards as an Order Record," Libri, 5:365-369, 1965.

Hardkopf, J. C. "Office Machines and Appliances," Library Trends, 5:225-238, October, 1956.

Holzbaur, F. W., and E. H. Farris. Library Information Processing Using an On-Line, Real-time Computer System. Poughkeepsie, N. Y., International Business Machines Corp., 1966.

International Business Machines Corporation. Purchase Analysis Procedure---Boston Public Library. New York, IBM Corp., 1964.

Juhlin, Alton P. "Use of IBM Equipment in Order Procedures at Southern Illinois University Library," Illinois Libraries, 44:598-602, November, 1962.

> Describes entire order procedure and the role of IBM. Illinois has used IBM equipment since 1951 for accounting purposes, but not for the actual preparation of purchase orders.

Keller, Alton H. "Book Records on Punched Cards," Library Journal, 71:1785-1786, December 15, 1946.

Kozlow, R. D. Report on a Library Project Conducted on the Chicago Campus of the University of Illinois. Washington, National Science Foundation, 1966. 1 v. (various paging).

Line, M. B. "Automation of Acquisition Records and Routine in the University Library, Newcastle-upon-Tyne," In: Program; News of Computers in British University Libraries, No. 2, June, 1966. 4 p.

McCune, L. C., and Salmon, S. R. "Bibliography of Library Automation," ALA Bulletin, 61:474-75, June, 1967.

McGaw, H. F. Marginal Punch Cards in Colleges and University Libraries. New York, Scarecrow Press, 1952.

A beginning guide for the librarian interested in possibilities of punched cards for his institution. Emphasis is on inexpensive hand operations.

Miller, E. F., et al. "Automated Book Ordering and Receiving," Special Libraries, 57:96-100, February, 1966.

Minder, T. L., and G. J. Lazorick. "Automation of the Penn State University Acquisition Department," (Reprinted from Automation and Scientific Communication. AD1 Proceedings, 1963.)

Moore, E. A., E. Brodman, and G. S. Cohen. "Mechanization of Library Procedures in the Medium-sized Medical Library: III. Acquisitions and Cataloging," Medical Library Association Bulletin, 53:305-328, July, 1965.

Morrissey, E. F. "Mechanized Book Order and Accounting Routine," Southeastern Librarian, 15:143-148, Fall, 1965.

Discussion of the mechanization of acquisitions at the Joint University Libraries, Nashville, Tennessee. This system uses a 526 summary keypunch, an 82 sorter, and a 402 accounting machine to do its purchase order writing.

Optner, S. L., and Associates. Report on the Integral Data Processing System for Library Technical Services to the Public Library, City of Los Angeles. Los Angeles, 1964.

Parker, R. H. "Automatic Records System at the University of Missouri Library," College and Research Libraries, 23:231-232, May, 1962.

IBM equipment was installed in the library of the University in 1957. The IBM cardatype, Type 858, is used for all ordering, paying, and accounting. This is the beginning of an integrated automatic records system.

Parker, R. H. "Development of Automatic Systems at the University of Missouri Library," In: Clinic on Library Applications of Data Processing, University of Illinois, 1st, 1963. Proceedings. Edited by H. Goldhor. Champaign, Ill., Distributed by the Illini Union Bookstore, 1964. Pp. 43-54.

Randall, G. E., and Rogers P. Bristol. "PIL (Processing Information List) or a Computer-Controlled Processing Record," Special Libraries, 55:82-86, February, 1964.

A Study of the Thomas J. Watson Research Library revealed inefficiencies. It was decided that punched cards could be made at the time of ordering and filed in a processing information file. When at item is moved from one step to another; for example, from "ordered" to "ordered but not yet published," the progress would be noted on PIL.

Rift, L. R. Automation of Library Acquisition Procedures at Bowling Green State University. Bowling Green, Ohio, The Library, 1966. 3 p. illus.

__________. Automation of Standing Order Acquisitions Procedures at Bowling Green State University. Bowling Green, Ohio: The Library, 1966. 5 p. illus.

__________. Use of the IBM 1050 System for Library Acquisition Procedures at Bowling Green State University. Bowling Green, Ohio, The Library, 1966. 2 p. illus.

Schultheiss, L. A. "Data Processing Aids in Acquisitions," Library Resources and Technical Services, 9:66-72, Winter, 1965.

Thompson, E. "The Automatic Ordering of Replacement Titles for Libraries in Metropolitan Toronto," Library Resources and Technical Services, 11:215-220, Spring, 1967.

Paperback books were chosen as the medium for this experimental study.

b. Mechanized and Computerized Systems for Serial Control

Anthony, L. J., and J. E. Hailstone. "Use of Punched Cards in Preparation of Lists of Periodicals," Aslib Proceedings, 12:348-360, October, 1960.

Becker, J. "Automating the Serial Record," A. L. A. Bulletin, 58:557-558, June, 1964.

California University. University at Los Angeles. Biomedical Library. Library System Planning Committee. Biomedical Library Computer Project for Serials. Los Angeles, University of California, 1964. 6 p.

Computer Usage Co. Serial Library System. Baltimore, Computer Usage, 1965. 61 p.

U. S. Army Biological Laboratory, Ft. Detrick, Md.

Creager, W. A., and D. E. Sparks. A Serials Data Program for Science and Technology. Final Report to the National Science Foundation. Reading, Mass., Information Dynamics, 1965. 190 p.

Culbertson, D. S. "Computerized Serial Records," Library Resources and Technical Services, 9:53-58, Winter, 1965.

Curran, A. T. "The Mechanization of the Serials Records for the Moving and Merging of the Boston Medical and Harvard Medical Serials," Library Resources and Technical Services, 10:362-372, Summer, 1966.

Eyman, E. G., and others. "Periodicals Automation at Miami-Dade Junior College," Library Resources and Technical Services, 10:341-361, Summer, 1966.

Felter, J. W. "The Union Catalog of Medical Periodicals of New York," In: Institute on Information Storage and Retrieval, 2d, University of Minnesota, 1965. Minneapolis, 1966. Pp. 117-131.

Fetterman, Lois. "Mechanization of Magazine Orders," National Association of Secondary-School Principals Bulletin 43:120-122, November, 1959.

Using of IBM punch cards in ordering magazines by Los Angeles City Schools through a central order department of the library section.

Hammer, D. P. "Automated Procedures at Purdue University Library Serials Department, Including Binding," In: Meeting on Automation in the Library --- When, Where, and How, Purdue University, 1964. Papers. Edited by T. Andrews. Lafayette, Ind., Purdue University, 1965. Pp. 25-35.

__________. "Automated Serials Control in the Purdue University Libraries," In: I. B. M. Library Mechanization Symposium, Endicott, N. Y., 1964. Proceedings. White Plains, N. Y., International Business Machines Corp., 1965. Pp. 133-144.

__________. "Reflections on the Development of an Automated Serials System," Library Resources and Technical Services, 9:225-230, Spring, 1965.

Jones, H. W. "Computerized Subscription and Periodicals Routing in an Aerospace Library," Special Libraries, 58:634-638, November, 1967.

Laucus, C., and S. Russel. Serials Automation Project at Baker Library; Preliminary Report. Boston, Harvard University. Graduate School of Business Administration, 1966. 47 p.

McCann, A. "Applications of Machines to Library Techniques: Periodicals," American Documentation, 12:260-265, October, 1961.

McGrath, W., and H. Kolbe. "A Simple, Mechanized Non-Computerized System for Serials Control in Small Academic Libraries: A Primer," Library Resources and Technical Services, 10:373-382, Summer, 1966.

Moffit, Alexander. "Punched Card Records in Serial Acquisition," College and Research Libraries, 7:10-13, January, 1946.

Moore, E. A., and E. Brodman. "Communications to the Editor; Circulation System Changes, Serial Record Changes," Medical Library Association Bulletin, 53:99-101, January, 1965.

Washington University School of Medicine Library.

Nicholson, D. and W. Thurston, "Serials and Journals in the MIT Libraries," American Documentation, 9:304-307, October, 1958.

Ohio State University, Columbus. Libraries. Committee on Information Science. Subcommittee on Automated Serials Record. Automated Serials Control Project. Report. Columbus, Ohio, The Library, 1964. 13 p.

Payne, L. M., L. Small, and R. T. Divett. "Mechanization in a New Medical School Library: II. Serials and Circulation," Medical Library Association Bulletin, 54:337-350, October, 1966.

Pizer, J. H., D. R. Franz, and E. Brodman. "Mechanization of Library Procedures in the Medium-Sized Library: I. The Serials Record," Medical Library Association Bulletin, 51:313-338, July, 1963.

Rift, L. R. Automation of Subscriptions and Periodicals Records of Bowling Green State University. Bowling Green, Ohio, The Library, 1966. 6 p. Illus.

Roper, F. W. Preparation of Records for the Automated Serials System at the Biomedical Library, University of California at Los Angeles. Los Angeles, University of California, 1964. 6 p.

Schultheiss, L. A. "Two Serial Control Card Files Developed at the University of Illinois, Chicago," Library Resources and Technical Services, 9:271-287, Summer, 1965.

Scoones, M. A. "The Mechanization of Serial Records with Particular Reference to Subscription Control," Aslib Proceedings, 19:45-62, February, 1967.

Srygley, T. F. "Serials Record Instructions for a Computerized Serial System," Library Resources and Technical Services, 8:248-256, Summer, 1964.

Florida Atlantic University.

Stewart, B. W. A Computerized Serials Record for the Texas A & M University Library. College Station, Texas, The Library, Texas A & M University, 1965. 123 p.

__________. "The Serials Mechanization Program of the Texas A & M University Library," In: Texas Conference on Library Mechanization, 1st, Austin, 1966. Proceedings. Edited by J. B. Corbin. Austin, Texas Library & Historical Commission, 1966. (Texas State Library Monograph, No. 6.) Pp. 40-45.

Vdovin, G., et al. "Computer Processing of Serial Records Library Resources and Technical Services, 7:71-80, Winter 1963.

__________., et al. Serials Computer Project; Final Report. LaJolla, University of California, San Diego, 1964. 1 v. (various paging)

Voigt, M. J. "The Costs of Data Processing in University Libraries in Serials Handling," College and Research Libraries, 24:489-491, November, 1963.

Wilkinson, J. P. "Association of Atlantic Universities Mechanized Union List of Serials," Atlantic Provinces Library Association Bulletin, 29:54-59, May, 1965.

Young, H. H. "Use of Punched Cards in the Serials

Acquisition Department of the University of Texas," Special Libraries Association, Texas Chapter. Bulletin, 11:1-3, 1959.

3. SPECIAL PROBLEMS IN ACQUISITIONS

a. Out-of Print Materials

See also pp. 204-214, "Rare Books, Incunabula, Manuscripts."

Placing Orders

Allen, Francis W. "Some Notes on the Acquisition of Old Books," Special Libraries, 38:73-76, March, 1947.

Specific information as to price, use, percentages, and statistics---all in favor of TAAB---are given.

American Library Association. Out-of-Print Books Committee. Report of Out-of-Print Book Survey Conducted by G. William Berquist, under the Auspices of the Out-of-Print Books Committee, Edith A. Busby, Chairman. Chicago, American Library Association, 1951.

Antiquarian Booksellers Association of America. Books and Values. New York, The Association, 1953. (Publication No. 4).

Arden, L. L. "Exit O. P.," Library Association Record, 60:254, August, 1958.

A brief account describing in simple terms the method of reproducing books at Micro Films Inc., Ann Arbor, Michigan.

Burstein, H. M. "Antiquarian Books and Booksellers," Bay State Librarian, 51:12-15, July, 1961.

Carter, J. "Book Auctions," Library Trends, 9:471-482, April, 1961.

Cook, Sarah A. "The Selective Purchase of Out-of-Print Books: A Survey of Practices," Library Resources and Technical Services, 10:31-37, Winter, 1966.

Purdue University Libraries study indicates that the most popular and perhaps the best method of obtaining desiderata was that of circulating and checking dealer catalogs.

Evans, R.W. "O.P. Problems," Choice, 2:285-86, July-August, 1965.

Fessler, Aaron L. "Bring Them Back Alive," American Library Association Bulletin, 50:559-561, October, 1956.

__________. "Facing Problems of the Out of Print Book," Special Libraries, 48:463-465, December, 1957.

A historical sketch of the Reprint Expediting Service which began in May of 1955. The article explains in detail the activities of the service in relationship to libraries and publishers.

Helen, Sister S.N.D. "Book Purchasing for Small College Libraries," Catholic Library World, 29:147-152, December, 1957.

Three methods of obtaining out-of-print materials are discussed: TAAB Weekly, Antiquarian Bookman, and searching services.

Heppell, Shirley G. "A Survey of O. P. Buying Practices," Library Resources and Technical Services, 10:28-30, Winter, 1966.

State University at Cortland, New York surveyed 151 college libraries with an enrollment of 2,000 to 3,000 to see where they were obtaining their out-of-print materials. Most frequently used and providing the largest number of needed books were second-hand catalogs. Schools also used dealer specialists, search services, advertising, microfilm, and xerography.

Jacob, E. "The Use of TAAB in Out-of-Print Book Searching," College and Research Libraries, 17:16-18, 40, January, 1956.

A detailed discussion of the functions and services available to librarians by using TAAB Weekly in the acquisition of out-of-print books.

Leonard, A. "How to Find Out of Print Publications," Special Libraries, 52:22-23, January, 1961.

An outline of the means used by the University of Toronto Library for acquiring out-of-print books. The author suggests four possible ways: by advertising either in TAAB or Antiquarian Bookman; by dealing with second-hand dealers; by exchanging using the U. S. Book Exchange; and by using some method of reproduction; either University Micro Films, Inc. or the Reprint Expediting Service.

MacManus, G. S. "What Librarians Should Know about Book Buying," Library Journal, 85:3394-3397, October 1, 1960.

Discusses the various methods to obtain out-of-print books.

Malkin, S. M. "Organization and Structure of the American Antiquarian Book Trade," Library Trends, 9:483-492, April, 1961.

Describes organizations and publications dealing with antiquarian books. Includes short bibliography and reprint of "Code of Fair Practices for Dealers and Librarians."

Melcher, D. "When is the Book Really O. P.," Library Journal, 91:4576-78, October 1, 1966.

Oboler, E. M. "O. P. and All That," American Library Association Bulletin, 47:433-434, October, 1953.

A discussion of second-hand dealer's catalogs and some business methods.

Pargellis, S. "Book Supply and the Book Market," Library Quarterly, 23:199-204, July, 1953.

"The Perennial OP Problem," Stechert-Hafner Book News, 15:67-68, February, 1961.

Gives practical advice on the preparation of a desiderata list. Rather than arrange book alphabetically by author in one long list, make several classified lists. These classified lists can be sent to people who specialize in the particular field.

Phillips, R. "University and Research Section Out-of-Print Survey," Library Association Record, 68:75-81, March, 1966.

Pickett, A. S. "Experiment in Out-of-Print Book Buying," Indian Librarian, 15:122-123, December, 1960.

"Plan for Reducing Cost of Procuring Out-of-the-Way Books," Library Journal, 84:2894, October 1, 1959.

A report of the searching services offered by Superbooks, White Plains, New York.

Smith, P. "Securing Out-of-Print Books," ALA Bulletin, 42:511-512, November, 1948.

__________. "What Shall We Do about Out-of-Print Books?" Library Journal, 70:479-481, May 15, 1945.

Taylor, A. Book Catalogs: Their Varieties and Uses. Chicago, Newberry Library, 1957.

Tiranti, D. "The Pricing of Books in the Antiquarian Book Trade," Antiquarian Bookman, 3:1261-1263, 1949.

Treyz, Joseph H. "O. P. Market," Choice, 2:283-285, July-August, 1965.

Introduction to the O. P. market. Discusses the out-of-print dealer, the use of advertising in the Antiquarian Bookman and TAAB, exchanges and gifts, and the purchase of collections at an auction.

Wing, D. G., and R. G. Wosper. "Antiquarian Book Market and the Acquisition of Rare Books," Library Trends, 3: 385-392, April, 1955.

Wynar, B. S., and H. R. Malinowsky. Cost Analysis Study Technical Services Division University of Denver Libraries. Denver, Graduate School of Librarianship, University of Denver, 1965.

Chapter on out-of-print materials pp. 28-37.

A Selected List of Directories and Reference Aids

See also pp. 215-18, "Rare Books, Incunabula, Manuscripts."

Adams, Scott. The O. P. Market: a Subject Directory to the Out-of-Print Book Trade, with 1944 Supplement. New York, Bowker, 1944.

American Book Prices Current. A Record of Literary Properties Sold at Auction in the United States and in London. New York, American Book Prices Current, 1895—. Annual.

Includes books, autographs and manuscripts, broadsides, and maps.

The A. B. Bookman's Yearbook. Vol. I—. Newark, N. J., Antiquarian Bookman, 1954—.

Includes list of second hand dealers in subject arrangement.

Book Auction Records. A Priced and Annotated Record of London Book Auctions. New and Rev. ed. by Frank Karlslake. London, Karslake, 1903-19. London, Henry Stevens, 1920—. Annual.

Since 1920 includes also principal American book auctions in New York.

Book Dealers in North America, 1964-1966. London,

Sheppard Press, 1964. 282 p.

A directory of dealers in second-hand and antiquarian books in Canada and the United States.

The Bookman's Glossary. 4th ed. Rev. and enl. by Mary C. Turner. New York, Bowker, 1961. 212 p.

Book-Prices Current. London, Stack, 1886—. Annual.

Subtitle: A Record of the prices at which books have been sold at auction.

Bookman's Price Index. An Annual Guide to the Values of Rare and Other Out-of-Print Books and Sets of Periodicals. Daniel F. McGrath, ed. Detroit, Gale, 1964-1967. 2v.

Lists some 32, 000 quotations from a selected number of dealers' catalogs in the first volume, and 66, 000 entries in the second volume. All entries are in alphabetical arrangement, no indexes.

A Directory of Dealers in Second Hand and Antiquarian Books in the British Isles, 1964-66. London, Sheppard Press, 1964. 222 p.

European Bookdealers. A Directory of Dealers in Second-hand and Antiquarian Books in Europe, 1965-67. London, Sheppard Press, 1965.

Guia de Editores y de Libreros de Espana. Madrid, Inst. Nacional del Libro Espanol, 1961. 744 p.

A guide to publishers, booksellers, and bookstores.

Herzberger, M. Dictionary for the Antiquarian Booktrade. Paris, 1956.

Brief identifications of terminology in French, English, German, Swedish, Danish, Italian, Spanish and Dutch.

International Directory of Antiquarian Booksellers. Brussels, International League of Antiquarian Booksellers, 1965. 633 p.

Geographical listings in French and English.

McKay, G. L. American Book Auction Catalogues, 1713-1934; A Union List. New York, New York Public Library, 1937. 540 p. Suppl., 1-2, 1946-48.

Repertoire des Éditeurs et Liste des Collections. Paris, Cercle de la Librairie, 1963. 294 p. Loose-leaf.

A directory of French publishers, booksellers and non-commercial organizations.

Sijthoff's Adresboek voor den Nederlandse Boekhandel en Aanverwante Vakken. Leiden, Sijthoff, 1885—. Annual.

Includes booksellers.

A Selected List of Verification Aids

American National and Trade Bibliographies

Note: Foreign National and Trade Bibliographies are listed on pp. 192-195.

Evans, Charles. American Bibliography; A Chronological Dictionary of All Books, Pamphlets and Periodical Publications Printed in the United States of America From the Genesis of Printing in 1639 Down to and Including the Year 1820. New York, Peter Smith, 1941. 12 v.

Shipton, Clifford K. The American Bibliography of Charles Evans; A Chronological Dictionary of All Books, Pamphlets and Periodical Publications Printed in the United States of America From the Genesis of Printing in 1639 Down to and Including the Year 1800. Worcester, Mass., American Antiquarian Society, 1955. v. 13.

Bristol, Roger Pattrell. The American Bibliography of Charles Evans; A Chronological Dictionary of All Books, Pamphlets and Periodical Publications Printed in the United States of America From the Genesis of Printing in 1639 Down to and Including the Year 1800. Worcester, Mass., American Antiquarian Society, 1959. v. 14, Index.

Sabin, Joseph. Dictionary of Books Relating to America; from its Discovery to the Present Time. New York, Sabin, 1868-92. Bibliographical Society of America, 1928-36. 29 v.

Shaw, Ralph R. and Richard H. Shoemaker. American Bibliography, 1801-1819. A Preliminary Checklist. New York, Scarecrow Press, 1958-1965. 22 v. Suppls.

Shoemaker, Richard R. Checklist of American Imprints, 1820-1861. New York, Scarecrow Press, 1966—. (In progress.)

Roorbach, Orville Augustus. Bibliotheca Americana, 1820-1861. New York, O. A. Roorbach, 1852-61. 4 v.

Kelly, James. American Catalogue of Books Published in the United States from January 1861 to January 1871. New York, J. Wiley, 1866-71. 2 v.

American Catalogue of Books, 1876-1910. New York, Publishers' Weekly, 1880-1910. 9 v. in 13.

United States Catalog; Books in Print, January 1, 1928. 4th ed. New York, Wilson, 1928. 3164 p.

Earlier editions:

1st, books in print 1899. Minneapolis, 1900.
2d, books in print 1902. Minneapolis, 1903.
3d, books in print 1912. New York, 1912.

Cumulative Book Index; a World List of Books in the English Language. New York, Wilson, 1898—.

Library Catalogs

U. S. Library of Congress. Catalog of Books Represented by Library of Congress Printed Cards. . . . Ann Arbor, Mich., Edwards Brothers, 1942-1955. 191 v. Title varies.

U. S. Library of Congress. The National Union Catalog; a Cumulative Author List Representing Library of Congress

Printed Cards, and Titles Reported by Other American Libraries. January 1956—. Washington, Govt. Print. Off., 1956—. Title varies.

Serials and Periodicals

American Book Collector. Chicago, Ed. and Published by W. B. Thorsen, 1950—. Monthly.

Articles on collected authors and subjects, bibliography.

Antiquarian Bookman. The Specialist Book Trade Weekly. Newark, N. J., Ed. and Published by Sol M. Malkin, 1948—.

Many articles of interest to order librarian, especially in the area of o. p. and related subjects.

Antiquariat. Zeitschrift für Alle Fachgebiete des Buch- und Kunstantiquariats. Wien, Walter Krieg Verlag, 1945—. Irreg.

Book Collector. London, Shenval Press, 1952—. Quarterly.

Bulletin du Bibliophile et du Bibliothécaire. Paris, 1834—. Quarterly.

Clique. The Antiquarian Bookseller's Medium. London, Clique Ltd., 1890—. Weekly.

The Library Bookseller. (TAAB Weekly) Fairless Hill, Pa., Albert Salfer, Editor, 1945—. Weekly.

Nordisk Tidskrift för Boch-och Biblioteksväsen. Uppsala, Almqvist und Wiksell, 1914—. Quarterly.

Philobiblon. Für Buch und Graphik Samler. Hamburg, Ed. Ernst Hanswell, 1957—. Quarterly.

University Bookman. New York, Ed. Russel Kirk, 1960—. Quarterly.

b. Reprints

Placing Orders

Altman, F. "The Antiquarian Reprint Dealer Looks at Acqusitions," Library Resources and Technical Services, 11:207-210, Spring, 1967.

Belzer, S. A. "Remarks on Reprinting," Reprint Expediting Service Bulletin, 9:1-41, Spring, 1964.

Fessler, Aaron, L. "Bring Them Back Alive," A. L. A. Bulletin, 50:559-561, October, 1956.

The operations of the Reprint Expediting Service explained.

__________. "Reprinted Reference Books," Library Journal, 83:691-694, March 1, 1958.

Kruse, P. "Piracy and the Britannica: Unauthorized Reprintings of the Ninth Edition," Library Quarterly, 33:313-328, October, 1963.

McClelland, J. G. "Publisher's View of Reprinting," Library Journal, 86:183-185, January 15, 1961.

Melcher, D. "New Techniques Permit the Reprinting of Books in Editions of 1 to 100 Copies," In: American Library and Book Trade Annual, 1960. New York, Bowker, 1959. Pp. 101-102.

Palmer, P. R. "Reserve Book Library and the Out-of-Print Book," ALA Reprint Expediting Service Bulletin, 2:2-9, January, 1957.

Reichmann, F. "Biographical Control of Reprints," Library Resources and Technical Services, 11:415-435, Fall, 1967.

A comprehensive treatment of the subject, international in coverage.

Rosenthal, B. M. "The Antiquarian Reprint Trade," The Antiquarian Bookman, 35:1667-1670, April 19, 1965.

Silverthorn, M. E. "Canadian Library Association, Committee on Out-of-Print Canadian Books," Reprint Expediting Service Bulletin, 8:2-4, Fall, 1963.

Whitten, J. N., and A. L. Fessler. "Hard-Cover Reprint Publishing," Library Trends, 7:82-92, July, 1958.

Gives background of the reprint business and discusses current practices.

Williams, S. P. "Interview with Sol Lewis of Argosy---Antiquarian Ltd., Discussing Some Facts and Fallacies about Reprinting with Emphasis on the Americana Field," Reprint Expediting Service Bulletin, 9:1-4, Summer, 1964.

__________. "A Short History of the Reprint Expediting Service," Library Resources and Technical Services, 10:228-232, Spring, 1966.

__________. "What is a Reprint?" Reprint Expediting Service Bulletin, 7:2, Spring, 1962.

A Selected List of Reference Aids

Books, Periodicals and Reference Works in Reprint Editions. New York, AMS Press, 1967.

The general 1967-68 catalog of one of the major reprint publishers.

Bibliographia Anastatica, Edited by P. Schippers, A. M. Hakket, B. R. Güner, Amsterdam, 1964—.

A list of monographs and serials including titles scheduled for reprinting. Includes some 200 publishers.

Catalog of Reprints in Series. 20th ed. Robert M. Orton, ed. New York, Scarecrow, 1965. 982 p.

Lists reprints of English language books and English translations available in series. Many European reprint publishers are not included and this guide is limited primarily to American publishers.

Guide to Reprints. Washington, Micro-Card Editions, 1967—. Annual.

A cumulative list to books, periodicals and other materials available in hard bound reprint from publishers in the U. S. Includes some 70 publishers. Paperbacks are omitted as a rule.

Johnson Reprints. 1967 Catalogue. Periodicals and Reference Works. New York, Johnson Reprint Corp., 1967. 72 p.

An example of a catalog prepared by one of the major reprint publishers. Covers science, medicine, law, humanities, and economics. Catalogs on other areas are also available. It should be noted, as it is true of most other catalogs, that some publications listed in this catalog are scheduled for reprint and are not available immediately.

Kawe-Katalog. Berlin, Krüger, 1959.

Includes reprints from West and East Germany.

Kraus Reprints. 3d General Katalog, 1966-67. New York, Kraus Reprint Corp., 1967. 302 p.

An example of a catalog prepared by one of the major reprint publishers. Includes periodicals, reference works and monographs. In addition, there are several supplements and specialized catalogs pertaining to different disciplines or areas.

Leipziger Bücher Katalog, 1965/66. Leipzig, Deutcher Buch Export und Import, 1966. Suppls.

Includes reprints from East Germany.

Literatur Katalog, 1966/67. Stuttgart, Köhler and Volckmar, 1967. 2482 p. — Register. 696 p.

Library ed. of the Barsortiments-Katalog, listing the holdings of one of the largest German jobbers.

Reprints. An Alphabetical List of Publications in Various Languages. General Catalogue, 1967-68. New York, Burt Franklin, 1967.

Another example of a catalog of a major reprint publisher.

The Reprint Bulletin, v. 1—. Dobbs Ferry, N. Y., Oceana Publications, 1965—. Bi-monthly.

Formerly published under the title Reprint Expediting Service Bulletin. Includes bibliography of reprints, articles and news on reprinting and librarians' lists of o. p. titles. Limited primarily to American publishers.

Reprint Information. Hauszeitschrift aus Antiquariats Dr. Martin Sändig. Wiesbaden, 1966—.

Two series: A. Geisteswissenschaften
B. Naturwissenschaften.

Covers materials in humanities, social sciences and biological sciences, international in scope, but by no means complete.

Reprint News, No. 1—. 1960—. East Ardsley, Wakefield, Yorkshire, Micro Methods and S. R. Publishers, 1960—.

Formerly published as Micro News this periodical is limited to description of the company's own publication program and the techniques and equipment used. It is a typical example of a house organ in this field.

Reprintothek. Riedensburg, Verlag der Reprintothek, 1966—.

A listing on cards of reprints of books and periodicals

with addresses of publishers. Includes titles in preparation and already out-of-print. The second edition (1967) includes 4, 500 reference cards and there will be 12 monthly supplements.

Reprints in Print. Dobbs Ferry, N. Y. Oceana Publications, 1968-?

Oceana Publications, Inc. has announced a new guide to be published in 1968, where for the first time all reprints of o. p. serials and monographic serials in print and available will be listed in one place. This guide will be published bi-annually and the Reprint Bulletin will serve as supplement.

c. Microfilms and Xerographic Prints

Placing Orders

American Library Association. Committee of the Resources and Technical Services Division. Microfilm Norms: Recommended Standards for Libraries. Chicago, American Library Association, 1966.

"Australian Newspapers on Microfilm, 1962," Australian Library Journal, 12:137-140, September, 1963.

Lists newspapers, dates on film, body responsible for filming or holding negative, remarks, also lists future microfilming plans.

Barcus, T. R. "Microreproduction of Federal Publications," Library Journal, 77:39-41, January 1, 1952.

Berry, Paul L. "United States and Canadian Government Documents on Microforms," Library Resources and Technical Services, 5:60-67, Winter, 1961.

Born, L. K. "The Literature of Microreproduction, 1950-55," American Documentation, 7:167-187, July, 1956.

Daly, Lowrie J. "Some Examples of Theological Materials Available on Microfilm," Library Trends, 9:246-252, October, 1960.

Diaz, A. "Microreproduction Information Sources," Library Resources and Technical Services, 11:211-214, Spring, 1967.

Eaton, Andrew J. "Toward a Statewide Newspaper Microfilming Program," College and Research Libraries, 14: 26-34, January, 1953.

Describes the Louisiana plan to preserve on microfilm all Louisiana newspapers that exist in and out of the state. Lists some of newspapers, describes procedures, costs, availability of film to users.

Fussler, Herman H. "A New Pattern for Library Cooperation," Library Journal, 81:126-133, January 15, 1956.

Describes a plan for cooperative microfilming of about 100 foreign newspaper titles. A committee formed by the ARL to provide for cooperative access to current foreign newspapers.

__________. "Photographic Reproduction of Research Materials," Library Trends, 2:532-544, April, 1954.

Discusses photostats, microfilming. University of Chicago is publishing in microfilm a series of manuscripts, studies of Middle American linguistics and cultural anthropology.

"A Great Step Forward--O. P. Books Newly Available," Library Journal, 83:1164-1165, April 15, 1958.

Discusses economics of combination of microfilm and xerography by University Microfilms, Inc.

"Half a Century of French Language Newspapers Now on Microfilm," Canadian Librarian, 21:141-148, November, 1964.

Hawken, William R. Copying Methods Manual. Chicago,

American Library Association, 1966. (LTP Publication No. 11). 375 p.

Discussion of the characteristics of research materials and the processes available for making copies of them.

__________. "Developments in Xerography: Copyflo, Electrostatic Prints and O-P Books," College and Research Libraries, 20:111-117, March, 1959.

__________. Enlarged Prints from Library Microforms. Chicago, American Library Association, 1963. 131 p.

A study of reader-printer machines of potential use in libraries.

__________. Photocopying from Bound Volumes; A Study of Machines, Methods and Materials. Chicago, American Library Association, Library Technology Project, 1962. Supplements. 208 p.

A guide to basic copying methods, evaluating advantages and disadvantages of each.

Heinz, G. "Case Study in Microfilming Documents: The NSDAP Hauptarchiv," College and Research Libraries, 26:467-476, November, 1965.

Describes 1959 Hoover Institute microfilming of 160 shelf feet of captured documents of German National Socialist Party. Gives organization and historical development of archive and its value to scholarship.

Henry, Edward A. "Books on Film: Their Use and Care," Library Journal, 57:215-217, 1932.

Describes what is available on microfilm from Library of Congress and France, predicts wide use of microfilm in research libraries.

__________. "Films Versus Books," Library Journal, 58:237-240, 1933.

Most larger libraries in Europe are rich in rare

books and manuscripts. Lists major U.S. Libraries that had no film reproductions of books or manuscripts. Lists microphotography projects in process, mentions it is cheaper than photostat.

Jolley, Leonard. "The Use of Microfilm for Completing Sets," *Journal of Documentation*, 4:41-43, June, 1948.

McReynolds, H. *Microforms of United States Government Publications*. Urbana: University of Illinois. Graduate School of Library Science, December, 1963. (Occasional Papers No. 69).

Microfilms of Latin American Documents," *UNESCO Bulletin for Libraries*, 14:88, March, 1960.

"Notre Dame Microfilms Vatican Papers Dealing with Catholic Church in U.S.," *Library Journal*, 87:2110, June 1, 1962.

Power, Eugene. "O-P Books; A Library Breakthrough," *American Documentation*, 9:273-276, October, 1958.

This article gives a brief history of microfilming as a means of reproducing the printed word. It, also, presents a detailed explanation of the Xerox process used at University Microfilms, Inc., Ann Arbor, Michigan.

Price, M.O. "Photocopying by Libraries and Copyright: A Precis," *Library Trends*, 8:432-447, January, 1960.

Riggs, J.A. "State of Microtext Publications," *Library Trends*, 8:372-379, January, 1960.

Shepard, Stanley A. "Libraries in Microform," *Bookmark (Idaho)*, 17:87-89, December, 1964.

Describes Early American Imprints 1639-1800, English Books 1641-1700, U.S. Serial Set, The Plains and the Rockies.

Simonton, Wesley. "Bibliographical Control of Microforms," Library Resources and Technical Services, 6:29-40, Winter, 1962.

Sullivan, R. C. "Library Microfilm Rate Indexes," Library Resources and Technical Services, 11:115-119, Winter, 1967.

Tate, Vernon D. "Microreproductions and the Acquisitions Programs," Library Trends, 3:432-447, April, 1955.

Indicates the usefulness of microfilm in limited areas only---not for advanced bibliographic work. A logical acquisitions program must be formulated for the proper items. Bibliography. Has table of typical library uses of microtechniques.

Thompson, L. S. "The Microfacsimile in American Research Libraries," Libri, 8:209-222, 1958.

__________. "Microforms as Library Resources," Library Trends, 8:359-371, January, 1960.

Varmer, B. Photoduplication of Copyrighted Material by Libraries. Washington, Copyright Office, 1959. (General Revision of the Copyright Law: Study No. 19).

A Selected List of Reference Aids

American Studies Association. Committee on Microfilm Bibliography. Bibliography of American Culture, 1493-1875. Ann Arbor, Mich., University Microfilms, 1957.

Includes 5000 items filmed by University Microfilms in the American Culture Series and 1500 titles not schedules for filming as they have been reprinted after 1900.

Ballou, H. W., ed. Guide to Microproduction Equipment. 3d ed. Annapolis, Md., National Microfilm Association, 1965.

Canadian Library Association. Microfilm Committee. Canadian Newspapers on Microfilm. Ottawa, 1959—. Loose-leaf.

Diaz, A. J., ed. "Microcards," 1944-1958. A Selected Bibliography," Microcard Foundation, Microcard Bulletin, 19:7-19, 1959.

Dissertation Abstracts, v. 1—. 1938—. Ann Arbor, Mich., University Microfilms, 1938—.

> Published under the title Microfilm Abstracts 1938-1951, title changed in 1952 in view of enlarged scope. Currently this service abstracts doctoral dissertations of most major universities in the U. S. and beginning with July 1966 is issued in two sections: A-Humanities and Social Sciences and B-Sciences and Engineering. Dissertations are available on microfilm or in xerographic prints.

Duopage Out-of-Print Books. Cleveland, Bell and Howell Co., Micro Photo Div., 1965-66. Suppls.

> Publisher's catalog listing titles available either as Duopage reproductions or on microfilm.

Guide to Microforms in Print. Washington, Microcard Editions, 1961—. Annual.

> A cumulative listing of books and serials available on microfilm and other microforms. 1967 ed. lists material from 50 U. S. publishers. Theses and dissertations are not included.

Maison des Sciences de l'Homme, Paris. Service Bibliothèque-Documentation. Périodiques et Publications en Série Concernant les Sciences Sociales et Humaines. Liste de Reproductions Disponibles dans le Commerce. Paris, Maison des Sciences de l'Homme, 1966. 2 v.

> A list of an extensive collection of periodicals and serials in the social sciences and humanities. Supplements planned.

Microcard, Microfiche Catalog, No. 1—. July 1959—. Washington, Microcard Editions, 1959—. Annual.

Lists microcards, microfilms and microfiche available or published by Microcard Editions. Other publishers issuing material on microcard and microfiche are also included.

Micro Library. Tumba, Sweden. International Documentation Center, 1958-59. 2 v.

A short-lived attempt to list all books, periodicals and manuscripts available on microforms, serving as a clearing house of all the materials listed. This list was published every two months.

Newspapers on Microfilm. 10th ed. Cleveland, Bell and Howell Co., 1967.

The latest edition includes listings of nearly 1000 newspapers now being filmed by the company's Micro Photo Division. It also includes over 4000 newspaper backfiles stored in microfilm archives and available for reproduction.

Poole, M. E. Index to Readex Microprint Edition of Joint Publications Research Service Reports. New York, Readex Microprint Corp., 1964.

Readex Microprint Corporation. Readex Microprint Publications, 1965-66, New York, 1965. 144 p.

Publisher's catalog.

Subject Guide to Microforms in Print. Washington, Microcard Editions, 1962—. Annual.

A subject index to Guide to Microforms in Print.

Tilton, E. M. A Union List of Publications in Opaque Microforms. 2d ed. New York, Scarecrow Press, 1964. 744 p.

Contains 7600 entries available from 26 American and European publishers, with an index. Not a union list (no library locations are provided) but rather an alphabetical listing.

U. S. Library of Congress. National Register of Microfilm Masters, Sept. 1965—. Washington, Govt. Print. Off., 1965—.

Includes foreign and domestic books, serials, newspapers and foreign dissertations for which master negatives exist and identifies those which are designated as master preservation negatives.

U. S. Library of Congress. Newspapers on Microfilm. Washington, Govt. Print. Off., 1st ed. 1948—.

The 5th ed. (1963) includes some 16, 000 domestic and foreign newspapers. Locations are provided for both negative and positive copies.

University Microfilms. Microfilm Catalog. Ann Arbor, Mich., 1965.

A guide to periodicals, books and newspapers available from U. M. Includes description of special projects, e. g. STC and Wing series.

University Microfilms. Modern Periodicals on Microfilm. Ann Arbor, Mich., 1965.

Publisher's list of periodicals available. Separate catalogs are published for Chinese and Russian titles.

University Microfilms. O. P. June 1965 Cumulation. Ann Arbor, Mich., 1965. Supplements.

A guide to books microfilmed by U. M. and available from the company. Also in Xerox prints. Note that some foreign books listed in the catalog may be still available from original publishers. Separate catalogs by subject are also issued, e. g. History and Political Sciences, Fine Arts and Architecture, Russian language books, etc. Semi-annual supplements.

Verry, H. R. Microcopying Methods. London: Focal Press, 1964. 175 p.

Practical aspects of microrecording.

d. Foreign Purchases

Placing Orders

"Acquisition of Latin American Library Materials," Library Journal, 85:2747-2749, August, 1960.

5th Seminar, 1960, New York: Report.

Archer, B. J. "Acquiring Soviet Literature," Special Libraries, 53:199-200, April, 1962.

"Are Some Imports Priced Too High? Can Publication Be More Prompt?" Publishers' Weekly, 161:681, 683, February 2, 1952.

Benson, N. L. "Latin American Books and Periodicals," Library Trends, 15:589-598, January, 1967.

Beyerly, E. "Acquisition Methods and Sources of Soviet Medical Publications," Medical Library Association Bulletin, 47:124-131, April, 1959.

Blaustein, A. P. "Panel on Foreign Law: Selection of Foreign Materials, Periodicals," Law Library Journal, 55:350-364, November, 1962.

Brunswick, S. R. "Acquisition of Hebrew and Yiddish Books," Library Resources and Technical Services, 9:377-379, Summer, 1965.

Cave, R. "Translations and the Book Selection Problem," Library World, 62:32-35, August, 1960.

Chiu, A. K. "Problems of Acquiring Far Eastern Publications for American Libraries," Special Libraries, 48:19-25, January, 1957.

Coppola, Dominick. "Breakthrough in Latin American Acquisitions," Stechert-Hafner Book News, 17:1-2, September, 1962.

__________. "The International Bookseller Looks at Acquisitions," Library Resources and Technical Services, 11:203-206, Spring, 1967.

Daniels, M. Seminars on the Acquisition of Latin American Library Materials: A Seven Year Report, 1956-1962. Washington, Pan American Union, 1962.

Fall, J. "Problems of American Libraries in Acquiring Foreign Publications," The Library Quarterly, 24:101-113, April, 1954.

A detailed discussion of the myriad problems involved. Concludes with the suggestion that a newsletter is needed by both acquisitions librarians and by dealers, in order to keep them informed about sources, problems, prices and techniques.

"Foreign Language Books," News Notes of California Libraries, 55:363-386, Fall, 1960.

Gorokhoff, B. I. Providing U. S. Scientists with Soviet Science Information. Rev. ed. Washington, National Science Foundation, 1962.

A concise guide to the sources and availability of Soviet scientific literature.

"Importation Problems, Rules Governing Appraisal of Books for Duty," Publishers' Weekly, 178:38-44, July 18, 1960.

"Inter-American Seminar on University Libraries," UNESCO Bulletin for Libraries, 15:345-346, November, 1961.

Keller, D. B. "Acquisition of Library Materials from East Europe," Library Resources and Technical Services, 7:34-37, Winter, 1963.

Kurth, W. H. "Acquisitions from Mexico," Library Resources and Technical Services, 2:96-114, Spring, 1958.

Lucas, R., and G. Caldwell. "Joint Publications Research Service Translations," College and Research Libraries, 25:103-110, March, 1964.

McNiff, Philip J. "Acquisition of Library Materials from the Middle East," Library Resources and Technical Services, 7:22-27, Winter, 1963.

__________. "Foreign Area Studies and Their Effect on Library Development," College and Research Libraries, 24:291-296, July, 1963.

The development of area study programs since World War II has created a critical need for adequate library resources. Need for research on the selection and acquisition of the area study collection exists. Mentions reports, development, and surveys on this problem.

Martin, R. L. "Foreign Scientific Literature in Translation," American Documentation, 11:135-150, April, 1960.

Miller, R. A. Purchasing of Books and Journals in Europe. Urbana, Ill., Illinois University Library School, 1953. (Occasional Papers, No. 30).

Orne, J. "Resources of Foreign Scientific Literature: Acquisition on a National Scale," American Documentation, 14:229-233, July, 1963.

Panofsky, Hans E. "Acquisition of Library Materials from Africa," Library Resources and Technical Services, 7:38-46, Winter, 1963.

Reichmann, Felix. "Acquisition of Library Materials from Southeast Asia," Library Resources and Technical Services, 7:13-21, Winter, 1963.

Reiss, Reuben. "Problems in the Acquisition of Foreign

Scientific Publications," _Department of State Bulletin_, 22: 151-155, January, 1950.

Ruggles, M. J., and V. Mostecky. _Russian and East European Publications in the Libraries of the United States._ New York, Columbia University Press, 1960. 396p.

A survey of the existing collections of East European materials in American libraries with a description and analysis of techniques used in handling.

Schick, F. L. "Acquiring Books from Abroad," _Library Resources and Technical Services_, 3:46-50, Winter, 1959.

Seminar on the Acquisition of Latin American Library Materials. Berkeley, California, 1958. 3d ed. Final Report and Papers of the Third Seminar of the Acquisition of Latin American Library Materials, July 10-11, 1958. Berkeley, General Library, University of California, 1959.

Stevens, Robert D. "Library of Congress Public Law 480 Programs," _Library Resources and Technical Services_, 7:176-188, Spring, 1963.

Thompson, L. S. "Continental European Literature," _Library Trends_, 15:573-588, January, 1967.

Tsuneishi, Warren M. "Acquisition of Library Materials from China, Japan, and Korea," _Library Resources and Technical Services_, 7:28-33, Winter, 1963.

Vasilenko, V. I. "Distributing Centers for Libraries in the U. S. S. R.," _UNESCO Bulletin for Libraries_, 20:136-139, May, 1966.

Wallach, K. "Problems of Acquisitions and Ordering of Foreign Law," _Law Library Journal_, 55:365-77, November, 1962.

West, Stanley L. "Acquisition of Library Materials from Latin America," _Library Resources and Technical Services_, 7:7-12, Winter, 1963.

A Selected List of Directories and Guides

(Including Guides to Serials and Periodicals)

Adressbuch des Deutschsprachigen Buchhandels. Buchhandelsadressbuch für die Bundesrepublik Deutschland und West-Berlin, Österrich und die Schweiz. Frankfurt am Main, Buchhänder Vereinigung, 1966. 1091 p.

Older edition published in 1962 covering 1962-63. Covers West Germany.

Adressbuch des Volkbuchhandels der Deutschen Demokratischen Republik. Stand 30 Juni, 1965. Leipzig, Volksbuchhandel der DDR, 1965. 96 p.

Covers East Germany.

American Book Trade Directory. Lists of Publishers, Booksellers, Periodicals, Trade Organizations, Wholesalers, etc. New York, Bowker, 1915—. Biennial.

American Library Association. International Subscription Agents. Chicago, American Literary Association, 1963. 84 p.

A directory of subscription agents compiled as a result of questionnaires from ninety-four libraries.

Annuaire International de la Presse Française et Etrangere et du Monde Politique. Paris, 1878—. Title varies.

Anschriften Deutscher Buchhandlungen. Bundesgebiet einschl. West Berlin mit Neuen Postleitzahlen. 1. Jg. Marbach/Neckar, Verlag d. Schiller-Buchhandlung Banger, 1962. 241 p.

Anschriften Deutscher Verlage, Ausländische Verlage mit Deutschen Auslieferungsstellen. . . mit Neuen Postleitzahlen. 14Jg. Marbach/Neckar, Verlag der Schiller-Buchhandlung Banger, 1964. 220 p.

Anschriften Deutschsprachigen Zeitschriften Bundesgebiet,

SB2, Österrich, Schweiz. 8. Jg. Marbach/Neckar, Verlag der Schiller-Buchhandlung Banger, 1964. 392 p.

Das Buch in der Rumänischen Volksrepublik. Bukarest, Grafica, 1965.

Das Buch in Ungarn. Budapest, Kultura, 1965.

Cassell's Directory of Publishing in Great Britain, The Commonwealth, Ireland and South Africa. London, Cassell, 1962. 443 p.

Directory-type information on book publishers and services related to the publishing trade (i. e. translators, microfilm, shipping).

Clegg's International Directory of the World's Book Trade. Ser. I, 1886-1914; New Series, 1927—. London, Clarke; New York, Bowker, 1927—.

Conover-Mast Purchasing Directory. 48th ed. New York, Conover-Mast Publications, 1965.

Directory of Asian Book Trade. Bombay, Popular Prakashan, 1964. 478 p.

Directory of Bookshops in Russia. London, Flegon Press, 1965. 18 p.

A Directory of British Publishers. 2d ed. London, Booksellers Association of Great Britain, 1961. 268 p.

Gregory, W., ed. List of the Serial Publications of Foreign Governments, 1815-1931. New York, Wilson, 1932.

Guia de Editores y de Libreros de Espana. Madrid, Inst. National del Libro Espanol, 1961. 744 p.

Publishers and bookstores are separately listed.

International Library Directory; A World Directory of Libraries. 2d ed. A. P. Wales, ed. London, The A. P. Wales Organization, 1966. 1203 p.

Listing by country of libraries---including public, university, government, and special.

International Literary Market Place. European Edition, 1967-68. New York, Bowker, 1967. 161 p.

A directory of European publishers, personnel, addresses, foreign representatives, bookstores and book production statistics.

Internationales Verlagsadressbuch. 2. Auf. München-Pullach, Verlag Dokumentationen der Technik, 1965. 810 p. (Handbuch der Technischen Dokumentation und Bibliographie, Bd. 7).

A comprehensive list of some 15,000 publishers in 110 countries.

Kawe-Katalog. Berlin, Krüger, 1959.

German titles, providing author, title, and subject index.

Leipziger Bücher Katalog, 1965/66. Lepzig, Deutcher Buch-Export und Import, 1966. Suppls.

An extensive listing of books from East Germany.

Mason's Publishers; An Annotated Directory of the Publishing Trade. London, K. Mason Publications, 1965. 152 p.

Merrill, J. C. *The Foreign Press.* Baton Rouge, La., State University Press, 1964. 256 p.

Panoramic view of world's press systems described by country.

Nachdruckverzeichnis von Einzelwerken, Serien und Zeitschriften aus Allen Wissensgebieten. Wiesbaden, G. Nobis, 1965.

Neverman, F. J., comp. *International Directory of Back Issue Periodical Vendors.* Albany, N. Y., State University Bookstore, 1964. 45 p.

Orne, J. The Language of the Foreign Book Trade: Abbreviations, Terms, Phrases. 2d ed. Chicago, American Library Association, 1962.

Dictionary of foreign terms as they are used in the book trade. Each of eight languages is presented separately.

Publisher's International Yearbook: World Directory of Book Publishers. 4th ed. London, Alexander P. Walls, 1966. 597 p.

Directory of publishers and booksellers arranged geographically.

Publishers' World. New York, Bowker, 1965.

Repertoire des Éditeurs et Liste des Collections. Paris, Cercle de la Librairie, 1963. 294 p. Loose-leaf.

Stamm, Willy. Wer und Was in Presse und Werbung. Essen, Stamm Verlag, 1963. 227 p.

Sythoff's Adresboek voor de Boekhandel en Uitgeverij. Leiden, A. W. Sythoff, 1967.

Annual directory of the Dutch booksellers and publishers.

Willing's British Press Guide, 93rd ed., New York, Bowker, 1968.

Willing's European Press Guide, 1968/69. New York, Bowker, 1968.

2d rev. expanded edition. Contains 20, 000 more listings than 1st ed. 50,000 newspapers, periodicals and annuals in 11 Continental countries.

A Selected List of Verification Aids

British National and Trade Bibliographies

Last Week:

British Books, Incorporating the Publishers' Circular and Booksellers' Record. London, Publishers' Circular, 1959—.

The Bookseller; The Organ of the Book Trade. London, J. Whitaker, 1858—.

British National Bibliography. London: Council of the British National Bibliography, 1950—.

Last Half-Year:

Whitaker's Cumulative Book List; A Classified List of Publications. London, J. Whitaker, 1924—.

Books in Print:

Reference Catalogue of Current Literature. London: J. Whitaker, 1874—. Since 1966 published under the title British Books in Print.

German National and Trade Bibliographies

Last Week:

Deutsche Bibliographie; Wöchentliches Verzeichnis, bearb. von der Deutschen Bibliothek. Frankfurt/am Main, Buchhändler-Vereinigung, 1953—.

Last Half-Year:

Deutsche Bibliographie, Halbjahresverzeichnis. Frankfurt/am Main, Buchhändler-Vereinigung, 1951—.

Last Year:

Deutsche Nationalbibliographie; Gesamtverzeichnis des im Deutschland Erschienenen Schrifttums und der Deutschsprachigen Schriften des Auslands. Leipzig, Deutsche Bücherei, 1931—.

Jahresverzeichnis des Deutschen Schrifttums. Bearb. und hrsg. von der Deutschen Bücherei und dem Börsenverein der Deutschen Buchhändler zu Leipzig, Bd. 1—. 1945/46—. Leipzig, Verlag des Börsenvereins des Deutschen Buchhändler, 1948—.

Deutsches Bücherverzeichnis . . . bearb. von der Deutschen Bücherei, 1911—. Leipzig, Börsenverein der Deutschen Buchhändler, VEB Verlag für Buch und Bibliothekswesen, 1916—.

French National and Trade Bibliographies

Last Week:

Bibliographie de la France. Paris, Cercle de la Librairie, 1811—.

Last Month:

Biblio: Catalogue des Ouvrages Parus en Langue Française dans le Monde Entier, Octobre 1933—. Paris Hachette, 1933—.

Last Year:

La Librairie Française; les Livres de l'Annee, 1930—. Paris, Au Cercle de la Librairie, 1931—.

Soviet National Bibliographies

Books in Print:

Knizhnaia Letopis; Organ Gosudarstvennoi Bibliografii SSSR. Moskva, Vsesoiuznaia Knishnaia Palata, 1907—.

Ezhegodnik Knigi SSSR; Sistematicheskii Ukazatel. Moskva, Vsesoiuznaia Knizhnaia Palata, 1927—.

Spanish National and Trade Bibliographies

Bibliografia Hispanica. Madrid, Instituto Nacional de Libro Espanol, 1942-1957.

El Libro Espanol; Revista Mensual. Madrid, Instituto National del Libro Espanol, 1958—.

Bibliografia Espanola. Madrid, Ministerio de Educacion Nacional, 1959—.

Books in Print:

Libros en Venta en Hispanoamerica y Espana. New York, Bowker, 1964.

Fichero Bibliographico Hispanoamericano. New York, Bowker, 1964—.

Italian National and Trade Bibliographies

Florence. Biblioteca Nazionale Centrale. Bolletino delle Publicazioni Italiane Ricevute per Diretto di Stampa. Firence, Biblioteca, 1886-1957.

Centro Nazionale per il Catalogo Unico delle Biblioteche Italiane e per le Informazioni Bibliografiche. Bibliografia Nazionale Italiana. Nuova Serie del Bolletino delle Publicazioni Italiani Recevuti per diritto di Stampa. Firence, Biblioteca Nazionale Centrale, 1958—.

Books in Print:

Associazione Italiana Editori: Catalogo Collectivo della Libreria Italiana. Milano, Soc. Anonima per Publicazioni Bibliografico-Editoriali, 1948—.

Library Catalogs

(Note: In addition to the Library of Congress, the following British and French National library catalogs are frequently consulted to verify foreign out-of-print and in-print materials.)

British Museum. Department of Printed Books. Catalogue of Printed Books. London, W. Clowes, 1881-1900. 95 v.

__________. Supplement. London, W. Clowes, 1900-1905. 13 v.

British Museum. General Catalogue of Printed Books. London, W. Clowes, 1931-1955. 51 v. (A-DEZ)

__________. General Catalogue of Printed Books. Photo-lithographic edition to 1955. London, Printed by the Trustees of the British Museum, 1959-1966. Vol. 52-263. (DF-Z).

British Museum. Department of Printed Books. General Catalogue of Printed Books: Additions, 1963—. London, Trustees of the British Museum, 1964—.

Paris Bibliotheque Nationale. Catalogue General des Livres Imprimes: Auteurs. Paris, Imprimerie Nationale, 1900—.

e. Government Publications

Placing Orders

Andriot, J. L. "Documents Expediting Project," Library Journal, 77:693-695, April 15, 1952.

Andriot, J. L. Guide to U.S. Government Statistics. 3d ed. Arlington, Va.: Documents Index, 1961.

Archer, J. H. "Acquisition of Canadian Provincial Government Documents," Library Resources and Technical Services, 5:52-59, Winter, 1961.

Aufdenkamp, J. A. "Aids in Ordering Government Documents," Special Libraries Association. Business and Financial Division. Bulletin, 3:9-17, April, 1961.

Berry, P. L. "United States and Canadian Government Documents on Microforms," Library Resources and Technical Services. 5:60-67, Winter, 1961.

Bertalan, F. J. "Selection and Reference Use in the Special Library," Library Trends, 15:143-156, July, 1966.

Boyd, Anne M. United States Government Publications. 3d ed. Rev. by Elizabeth Rips. New York, Wilson, 1949. 627 p.

> Primarily a textbook for library school students. Discusses each government department and its publications.

Brimmer, B., et al. Guide to the Use of United Nations Documents. New York, Oceana, 1962. 272 p.

> Includes methods and problems of research as well as available tools and guides for using the U. N. publications.

Brown, E. S. Manual of Government Publications, United States and Foreign. New York, Appleton-Century-Crofts, 1950. 121 p.

> Emphasis is on American and British government publications and international affairs.

Buckley, C. W. "Implementation of the Federal Depository Library Act of 1962," Library Trends, 10:27-36, January 1962.

Buckley, C. W. "The New Depository Program and College Libraries," _College and Research Libraries,_ 26:18+, January, 1965.

Caldwell, G. "University Libraries and Government Publications; A Survey," _College and Research Libraries,_ 22:30-34, January, 1961.

California. State Library. _California State Publications;_ Manual for Acquisition, Processing, Use. 2d ed. Sacramento, Dept. of Finance, Organization and Cost Control Division, 1961.

Carrol, M. J. "League of Nations Documents and Publications Comparable with or Continued in United Nations Publications," _College and Research Libraries,_ 13:44-52, January, 1952.

Childs, J. B. "Bibliographic Control of Federal, State, and Local Documents," _Library Trends,_ 15:6-26, July, 1966.

Provides numerous bibliographic references. Of special interest is information on bibliographic control of state publications.

__________. "Current Bibliographical Control of International Intergovernmental Documents," _Library Resources and Technical Services,_ 10:319-331, Summer, 1966.

__________. "Government Publications," _Library Trends,_ 15:378-97, January, 1967.

__________. "United States of America Official Publications," _Annals of Library Science,_ 9:84-91, June, 1962.

Connor, John M. "The Need for Documentation to Government Specifications," _Special Libraries,_ 47:152-155, April, 1956.

A discussion of the irregularities in size, printing, paper, binding, dating, bibliographic control, and number systems found in technical reports. This paper also contains suggested standards for the physical format and bibliographical control.

Curran, N. E. "Yours for the Ordering," Wilson Library Bulletin, 37:342-344, December, 1962.

Darling, R. L. "Selection and Reference Use in the School Library," Library Trends, 15:87-92, July, 1966.

Delhi Library Association. "Seminar on Acquisition of Documents and Other Reading Materials," Library Herald, 5:174-184, October, 1962 - January, 1963.

Downs, R. B. "Government Publications in American Libraries," Library Trends, 15:178-194, July, 1966.

Fukuda, N. "Japanese Government Publications." Library Resources and Technical Services, 9:249-250, Spring, 1965.

Groesbeck, J. "United Nations Documents and Their Accessibility," Library Resources and Technical Services, 10:313-318, Summer, 1966.

Holbrock, F. K. "Checklist of Current State, Federal and Canadian Publications, Revised to June 1, 1965," Law Library Journal, 58:326-340, August, 1965.

Jackson, Ellen P. A Manual for the Administration of the Federal Documents Collection in Libraries. Chicago, American Library Association, 1955. 108 p.

Discusses sources, acquisitions, classification, and bibliographies relating to government documents.

Jacobsen, Edna L. "State and Local Government Archives," Library Trends, 5:397-405, January, 1957.

Kirkpatrick, L. H. "Public Document Charges," Library Journal, 79:733-735, April 15, 1954.

Klahre, E. S. "Ordering Government Publications," Special Library Association Business and Financial Division Bulletin, 18:14-18, October, 1955.

Kuhlman, A. F. "The Need for a Comprehensive Check-List Bibliography of American State Publications," Library Quarterly, 5:31-58, January, 1935.

Kumar, S. "Sources for the Selection of British Government Publications," Annals of Library Science, 9:115-118, September, 1962.

Lane, M. T. "List of Current State Documents Checklists," Library Resources and Technical Services, 10:504-506, Fall, 1966.

Lane, M. T. "State Documents Checklists," Library Trends, 15:117-134, July, 1966.

Leavitt, E. P. "Government Publications in the University Library," Library Journal, 86:1741-1743, May 1, 1961.

Lee, C. E. "Selected Bibliography of Acquisition Tools for Government Publications," News Notes of California Libraries, 51:501-507, October, 1956.

Lloyd, Gwendolin. "The Status of State Document Bibliography," Library Quarterly, 18:192-199, July, 1948.

McCamy, J. L. Government Publications for the Citizen. New York, Columbia University Press, 1955.

Examines present machinery for publication and distribution of government documents. Includes recommendations for a new system in which the public library would be involved.

McDonald, M. J. "Ordering UN, OEEC, and Foreign Documents," Special Library Association Business and Financial Division Bulletin, 18:18-20, October, 1955.

McReynolds, H. Microforms of United States Government Publications. Urbana, University of Illinois Graduate School of Library Science, 1963. (Occasional Papers, No. 69.)

Mahler, J. H. "Selection and Reference Use in the Public Library," Library Trends, 15:93-106, July, 1966.

Maybury, C. "Dealers and Documents," Library Resources and Technical Services, 6:184-186, Spring, 1962.

Merritt, L. C. The United States Government as Publisher. Chicago, University of Chicago Press, 1943. 179p.

General picture of the material to be found in U. S. public documents including an analysis of past and present trends.

Murra, K. O. International Scientific Organizations; A Guide to Their Library, Documentation and Information Services. Washington, Superintendant of Documents, 1962. 794p.

Olle, J. G. An Introduction to British Government Publications. London, Association of Assistant Librarians, 1965.

Powell, Benjamin E. The Books of a New Nation; U. S. Government Publications, 1774-1814. Philadelphia, University of Pennsylvania Press, 1957. 170p.

Three bibliographic essays of the early years of U. S. Government publications.

Powell, Benjamin E. "New Depository Library Legislation," ALA Bulletin, 57:36-39, January, 1963.

Schell, M. "Acquisition, Handling and Servicing in State Libraries," Library Trends, 15:135-142, July, 1966.

Schmeckebier, Laurence F., and Roy B. Eastin. Government Publications and Their Use. Rev. ed. Washington, Brookings Institution, 1961. 476p.

Describes the basic guides to government publications.

Scott, P. "The Present and Future of Government Documents in Microfilm," Library Trends, 15:72-86, July, 1966.

Shaw, T. S. "Distribution and Acquisition," Library Trends, 10:37-49, January, 1962.

Shore, P.D. "Evaluation of U.S. Document Bibliography," Library Resources and Technical Services, 4:34-43, Winter, 1960.

Sims, E.M. "Selection and Reference Use in the College and University Library," Library Trends, 15:107-116, July, 1966.

Temple, Phillips L. Federal Services to Libraries. Chicago, American Library Association, 1954. 227 p.

An attempt to analyze and describe programs and policies of the federal government in its relations with libraries.

Thibault, Charles D. "Survey of Specialized Acquisitions Procedures in a Technical Documents Center; A Survey Conducted at the Engineering Research and Development Laboratories. Fort Belvoir, Virginia." Unpublished Master's thesis, Catholic University of America, Washington, 1956.

U.S. Congress. House Committee on House Administration. Sale and Distribution of Government Publications by the Superintendent of Documents. Washington, Govt. Print. Off., 1956.

U.S. Congress. Joint Committee on Printing. Government Printing and Binding Regulations. Washington, Govt. Print. Off., 1965.

U.S. Government Printing Office. 100 GPO Years: 1861-1961. Washington, Govt. Print. Off., 1961. 164 p.

A history of United States public printing.

Wilcox, J.K. "The Acquisition of Government Publications," Library Trends, 3:403-413, April, 1955.

__________., ed. Manual on the Use of State Publications. Chicago, American Library Association, 1940. 342 p.

Wynar, B. S. Introduction to Bibliography and Reference Work, 4th ed. Rochester, N. Y., Libraries Unlimited, 1967. Pp. 267-304.

A Selected List to Guides, Bibliographies and Purchasing Aids

(U. S. Government Publications)

Ames, John G. Comprehensive Index to the Publications of the United States Government, 1881-1893. Washington, Govt. Print. Off., 1905.

Andriot, John L. Guide to Popular U. S. Government Publications. Washington, Documents Index, 1960. 125 p.

> Selective listing of approximately 2, 000 government publications compiled with medium and small-sized library in mind.

Andriot, J. L. Guide to U. S. Government Serials and Periodicals. 1964 ed. McLean, Va., Documents Index, 1964-65. 3 v.

> v. 1. Current Serials and Periodicals of Washington Agencies, 1964.
>
> v. 2. Releases and Other Ephemeral Material, 1964.
>
> v. 3. Field Agency Publications, 1965.

Bowker, R. R. comp. State Publications; A Provisional List of the Official Publications of the Several States of the United States from their Organization. New York, The Publishers' Weekly, 1908 4 v.

"Current Checklists of State Publications as of May 1962, " Library Resources and Technical Services, 6:357-359, Fall, 1962.

Hirshberg, Herbert S. Subject Guide to U. S. Government Publications. Chicago, American Library Association, 1947. 228 p.

Selective list of those books and pamphlets published 1927-1947 of most value to libraries.

Jenkins, W. S. Collected Public Documents of the States. A Check-List. Boston, National Association of State Libraries, 1947.

Leidy, W. Philip. A Popular Guide to Government Publications. New York, Columbia University Press, 1968. 367 p.

A subject listing of 3000 titles of popular government publications; 1000 titles retained from 1963 edition.

MacDonald, G. E. Check-List of Legislative Journals of States of the United States of America. Compiled for the Public Document Clearing House Committee of the National Association of State Libraries. Providence, The Oxford Press, 1938.

— Suppl. comp. by E. H. Pollack. Boston, National Association of State Libraries, 1941.

— Suppl. Comp. by W. S. Jenkins. Boston, National Association of State Libraries, 1943.

Poore, B. P. Descriptive Catalogue of the Government Publications of the United States, September 5, 1774-March 4, 1881. Washington, Govt. Print. Off., 1885.

United States Government Organization Manual, 1935—. Washington, Govt. Print. Off., 1935—.

U. S. Superintendent of Documents. Catalog of Public Documents of Congress and of All Departments of the United States for the Period March 4, 1893-December 31, 1940. Washington, Govt. Print. Off., 1896-1945. 25 v.

United States Superintendent of Documents. Checklist of United States Public Documents, 1789-1909. 3d ed., rev. and enl. Washington, Govt. Print. Off., 1911.

U. S. Superintendent of Documents. Price Lists. Washington, Govt. Print. Off., Nos. 1-85.

U. S. Superintendent of Documents. Selected United States Government Publications. Washington, Govt. Print. Off., 1928—.

U. S. Superintendent of Documents. United States Government Publications: Monthly Catalog, 1895—. Washington, Govt. Print. Off., 1895—.

Wilcox, J. K. Bibliography of New Guides and Aides to Public Documents Use, 1953-1956. New York. Special Library Association, 1957 (SLA Bibliography, No. 2).

Continues the series published in Special Libraries, e.g. 40:371-77, Nov. 1949; 40:406-412, Dec. 1949; 45:29-36, Jan. 1954.

Wood, Jennings. United States Government Publications: A Partial List of Non-G. P. O. Imprints. Prepared under the Direction of the Interdivisional Committee on Public Documents of the American Library Association. Chicago, American Library Association, 1964.

f. Rare Books, Incunabula, Manuscripts and Other Related Material

Placing Orders

Baughman, R. "The Selection and Acquisition of Rare Books and Related Materials at Columbia University," Library Resources and Technical Services, 2:271-278, Fall, 1958.

Brewer, F. J. "Friends of the Library and Other Benefactors and Donors," Library Trends, 9:453-465, April, 1961.

Burke, F. G. "Manuscripts and Archives," Library Trends, 15:430-445, January, 1967.

Byrd, C. K. "Collecting Collections," Library Trends, 9:434-436, April, 1961.

__________. "Rare Books in University Libraries," Library Trends, 5:441-450, April, 1957.

Cahoon, H. "Literary Manuscripts and Autographs," Library Trends, 9:430-433, April, 1961.

Carter, J. "Book Auctions," Library Trends, 9:471-482, April, 1961.

__________. "Reflections on Rarity," New Colophon, 1:134-150, April, 1948.

Cochran, Thomas C., et al. "Report of Ad Hoc Committee on Manuscripts Set Up by the American Historical Association in December 1948," American Archivist, 14:229-240, July, 1951.

Gingerich, M. "Effective Acquisition Program for the Religious Archives," American Archivist. 29:515-18, October, 1966.

Goff, F. R. "Incunabula and Sixteenth Century Imprints," Library Trends, 15:446-458, January, 1967.

Howell, W. R. "California and Western Americana," Library Trends, 9:423-429, April, 1961.

Howes, Wright. "A Rare Book: Its Essential Qualifications," Library Trends, 5:489-494, April, 1957.

Jackson, W. A. "Universities and Rare Books," Courier of the Syracuse University Library Associates, 2:1-12, October, 1962.

Kane, L. "Manuscript Collecting," In: W. B. Hesseltine and D. R. McNeils, eds. In Support of Clio: Essays in Memory of Herbert A. Kellar. Madison, State Historical Society of Wisconsin, 1958.

Kerabian, J. S. "Book Appraisals," Library Trends, 9: 466-470, April, 1961.

King, Jack. "Collecting Business Records," American Archivist, 27:387-390, July, 1964.

Lehmann-Haupt, H., ed. "Current Trends in Antiquarian Books," Library Trends, 9:387-492, April, 1961.

The whole issue covers certain aspects of antiquarian and rare book market.

Lovett, Robert L. "Care and Handling of Non-Governmental Archives," Library Trends, 5:380-387, January, 1957.

Marston, T. "Incunabula and Postincunabula," Library Trends, 9:406-416, April, 1961.

Munby, A. N. L. "Acquisition of Manuscripts by Institutional Libraries," Bibliographical Society of America Papers, 54:1-15, 1960.

Nye, W. J. "Trends in Rare Book Library Facilities," College and Research Libraries, 24:377-82, September, 1963.

The findings of a questionnaire sent to 70 public, special and academic libraries in U. S.

Pargellis, S. "Book Supply and the Book Market," Library Quarterly, 23:199-204, July, 1953.

Peckham, H. H. "Acquisition of Rare Materials," In: Archer, H. R., ed. Rare Book Collections, Chicago, American Library Association, 1965. Pp. 35-50.

__________. "Policies Regarding the Use of Manuscripts," Library Trends, 5:361-368, January, 1957.

Powell, William S. "Local Material for Reference---Their Acquisition and Administration," The Southeastern Librarian, 11:293-296, Winter, 1961.

Shafer, E. "Books with a Past and Present and a Future Are Rare Books," Wilson Library Bulletin, 34:138-144, October, 1959.

Silver, R. G. "The Training of Rare Book Librarians," Library Trends, 9:446-452, April, 1961.

Weighs the various aspects of training rare book librarians. Implications: scholarship, librarianship, social grace, and business sense are required.

Thompson, L. S. "Facsimiles and the Antiquarian Trade," Library Trends, 9:437-445, April, 1961.

Walsh, M. J. "Basic Americana," Library Trends, 9:417-422, April, 1961.

Wing, D. G., and R. Vosper. "The Antiquarian Bookmarket and the Acquisition of Rare Books," Library Trends, 3:385-392, April, 1955.

Discusses the problems associated with the acquisition of rare books, primarily from abroad.

Witten, L. "Collecting Medieval and Renaissance Manuscripts Today," Library Trends, 9:398-405, April, 1961.

Book Collecting and Collectors

Antiquarian Booksellers Association of America. Books and Values. New York, The Association, 1953. (Publication No. 4).

Ashton, John. Chap-books of the Eighteenth Century. Notes and Introduction by John Ashton. New York, Blom, 1966. [1882].

Archer, R. Rare Book Collections. Chicago, American Library Association, 1965. (ACRL Monograph No. 27). 128 p.

Ten essays of theoretical and practical suggestions for working with rare book collections.

Augerville, Richard. Philobiblon; a Treatise on the Love of Books, by Richard de Bury [pseud.] The English Translation thereof made by John Bellingham Inglis with Introduction by Charles Orr. New York, Meyer, 1899.

Bennett, James O'Donnell. Much Loved Books; Best Sellers of the Ages. New York, Liveright, 1927.

Bennett, P. A., ed. Books and Printing. A Treasury for Typophiles. Cleveland, World, 1951.

Bennett, W. Practical Guide to Book Collection, 1663-1940. New York, Bennett Book Studies, 1941.

Berry, W. T., and H. E. Poole. Annals of Printing. A Chronological Encyclopedia from the Earliest Times to 1950. London, Blandford Press, 1966. 315 p.

Bordin, R. B., and R. M Warner. The Modern Manuscript Library. Metuchen, N. J., Scarecrow Press, 1966. 152 p.

Boutell, H. S. First Editions of Today and How to Tell Them; American, British and Irish. 4th ed. rev and enl. Berkeley, University of California Press, 1965. 227 p.

Listing of publishers in U. S. and England with information on how their first impressions may be identified.

Bowers, F. Principles of Bibliographical Description. New York, Russel and Russel, 1962.

Bradley, Van Allen. Gold in Your Attic. New York, Fleet, 1958, 277 p.

An informal handbook for book collectors including a brief glossary of terms and a price index and guide to forty-two valuable U. S. books.

__________. More Gold in Your Attic. New York, Fleet, 1961. 415 p.

Guide to over 2500 rare and valuable American books.

Brewer, Reginald. The Delightful Diversion; The Whys and Wherefores of Book Collecting. New York, Macmillan, 1935.

Briggs, M.H. Buying and Selling Rare Books. New York, Bowker, 1927.

Carlson, Pearl Gertrude. Choice of Editions. Chicago, American Library Association, 1942. 69p.

Cannon, Carl L. American Book Collectors and Collecting From Colonial Times to the Present. New York, Wilson, 1941.

Carter, J. ABC for Book-Collectors. 2d rev. ed. New York, Knopf, 1953. 196p.

A dictionary of terms commonly used in book-collecting.

__________. Books and Book-Collectors. New York, World Publishing, 1957. 196p.

A collection of reprints of previously published essays on book collecting.

__________. Taste and Technique in Book Collecting; A Study of Recent Developments in Great Britain and the United States. Cambridge, Eng., Cambridge University Press, 1949. 201p.

Evaluation of present state of book collecting and examination of current methods and techniques.

Carter, John and Pollard, Graham. An Enquiry into the Nature of Certain Nineteenth Century Pamphlets. London, Constable; New York, Scribner, 1934.

Currie, Barton. Fishers of Books. Boston, Little Brown, 1931.

De Ricci, Seymour. English Collectors of Books and Manuscripts (1530-1930) and Their Marks of Ownership. Cambridge: University Press, 1930. (Sandars Lectures, 1929-1930).

Dibdin, Thomas Frognall. *A Bibliographical, Antiquarian, and Picturesque Tour in France and Germany*. 2d ed. London, Robert Jennings and John Major, 1829. 3 v.

__________. *Bibliomania; or, Book-Madness.* A Bibliographical Romance. New and improved ed., to which are added preliminary observations and a supplement including a key to the assumed characters in the drama. London, Chatto and Windus, 1876.

Dore, John Read. *Old Bibles: An Account of the Early Versions of the English Bible*. 2d ed., with the Preface to the Version of 1611 added at the request of the . . . [London] Eyre and Spottiswoods, 1888.

Downs, Robert B. *Famous Books, Ancient and Medieval.* New York, Barnes and Noble, 1964.

__________. *Famous Books Since 1492*. New York, Barnes and Noble, 1961. [former title was: Molders of the Modern Mind.]

Emmison, F. G. *Archives and Local History*. London, Methuen, New York, Barnes and Noble, 1966. 112 p.

> Although intended primarily for British students as a guide to the location and use of their local archives, it will also interest American students and librarians containing helpful hints on arrangement and acquisitions of archival material.

Esdaile, A. *A Student's Manual of Bibliography*. Rev. by Ray Stokes. New York, Barnes and Noble, 1954.

Ettinghausen, Maurice L. *Rare Books and Royal Collectors; Memoirs of an Antiquarian Bookseller*. New York, Simon and Schuster, 1966.

Gillett, Charles Ripley. *Burned Books; Neglected Chapters in British History and Literature*. Port Washington, N. Y., Kennikat Press, 1964. [c 1932]. 2 v.

Glaister, G. A. Glossary of the Book. London, Allen and Unwin, 1960. 484 p.

> Definitions of terms used in papermaking, printing, bookbinding and publishing, with notes on illuminated manuscripts, bibliophiles, private presses and printing societies.

Haight, Anne Lyon. Banned Books. Informal notes on some books banned for various reasons at various times in various places. 2d ed., rev. and enl. New York, Bowker, 1955.

Hamilton, Charles. Collecting Autographs and Manuscripts. Norman, Okla., University of Oklahoma Press, 1961. 269 p.

> Practical guide to the recognizing and collecting of autographs and manuscripts.

Hazlitt, W. Carew. The Book-Collector; General survey of the pursuit and of those who have engaged in it at home and abroad from the earliest period to the present time. An account of public and private libraries, anecdotes of their founders or owners and remarks on bookbinding and on several copies of books. London, Grant, 1904.

Hoebler, K. Handbuch der Inkunabelkunde, Leipzig, Hiersemann, 1925. 187 p.

> A standard handbook on the literature, history and printing of incunabula.

Hobbs, John L. Local History and the Library. London, Andre Deutsch, 1962. 338 p.

> Includes chapters on the collection, its care, problem of organization, cataloging, staffing, etc.

Jackson, Holbrook. The Anatomy of Bibliomania. London, Soncino Press, 1930-31. 2 v.

Jenkinson, Hilary. A Manual of Archive Administration. 2d rev. ed. London, P. Lund, Humphries, 1965.

Johnson, M. de V. American First Editions. 4th ed. New York, Bowker, 1942.

Jordan-Smith, Paul. For the Love of Books: The Adventure of an Impecunious Collector. New York, Oxford University Press, 1934.

Kirchner, J., ed. Lexikon des Buchwesens. Stuttgart, Hiersemann Verlag, 1952-1956. 4 v.

McKerrow, R. An Introduction to Bibliography for Literary Students. Oxford, Clarendon Press, 1927. 358 p.

Muir, Percival H. Book-Collecting as a Hobby, in a Series of Letters to Everyman. New York, Knopf, 1947.

__________. Book-Collecting: More Letters to Everyman. Chester Springs, Pa., Dufour Editions, 1950.

__________. Points, Second Series, 1866-1934. London, Constable; New York, Bowker, 1934.

__________. Talks on Book Collecting.... Chester Springs, Pa., Dufour Editions, 1952.

Newton, Alfred Edward. The Amenities of Book-Collecting and Kindred Affections. Boston, Atlantic Monthly Press, 1918.

__________. End Papers; Literary Recreations. Boston, Little Brown, 1933.

__________. A Magnificent Farce and Other Diversions of a Book-Collector. Boston, Atlantic Monthly Press, 1921.

__________. Rare Books, Original Drawings, Autograph Letters and Manuscripts, Collected by the Late A. Edward Newton . . . For public sale by order of the executors under the will . . . at the Parke-Bernet galleries. New York, Printed by Maynard Printing Corp., 1941. 3 v.

Newton, Alfred Edward. _This Book-Collecting Game_. Boston, Little Brown, 1928.

Nineteenth-Century English Books; Some Problems in Bibliography. Gordon N. Ray, Carl J. Weber, John Carter. Urbana, University of Illinois Press, 1952. (3d annual Windsor lectures in librarianship).

Partington, Wilfred G. _Forging Ahead; The True Story of the Upward Progress of Thomas James Wise, Prince of Book Collectors, Bibliographer, Extraordinary and Otherwise_. New York, Putman, 1939.

Pearson, Edmund L. _Books in Black or Red_. New York, Macmillan, 1923.

Philadelphia. Free Library. Rare Book Dept. _Four Talks for Bibliophiles_, by George Allen, Catherine Drinker Bowen, Merle M. Odgers, Michael J. Walsh. With an introduction by C. Barton Brewster. Philadelphia, Free Library of Philadelphia, 1958.

Powell, Lawrence C. _Books in My Baggage; Adventures in Reading and Collecting_. Cleveland, World, 1960.

__________. _A Passion for Books_. Cleveland, World, 1958.

Rosenback, Abraham S.W. _A Book Hunter's Holiday; Adventures with Books and Manuscripts_. Boston, Houghton Mifflin, 1936.

__________. _Books and Bidders: The Adventures of a Bibliophile_. Boston, Little Brown, 1927.

Rumball-Petre, E. _Rare Books: An Introduction for Collectors and a Descriptive Check-List_. New York, Philip C. Duschnes, 1938.

Sawyer, Charles J. and F.J. Harvey Darton. _English Books, 1475-1900; A Signpost for Collectors_. Westminster, Charles J. Sawyer, 1927. 2 v.

Sayers, W. C. Berwick. Library Local Collections. London, G. Allen and Unwin, 1939. 128 p.

Covers various aspects of local history collecting.

Schneider, G. Theory and History of Bibliography, tr. by R. R. Shaw. New York, Columbia University Press, 1934.

Slater, J. Herbert. How to Collect Books. London, George Bell, 1905. 205 p.

Handbook for beginners in book collecting.

Storm, C., and H. Peckham. Invitation to Book Collecting; Its Pleasures and Practices. New York, Bowker, 1947. 281 p.

A book aimed at the beginner with several chapters on techniques of acquisition and evaluation.

Targ, W. American Books and Their Prices: A Handbook for Collectors, Booksellers, and Librarians. Chicago, Black Archer Press, 1941.

__________. Modern First Editions and Their Prices. Chicago, Black Archer Press, 1932. 108 p.

Selective list of 2,000 English first editions published between 1860 and 1931.

__________, and H. F. Marks. Ten Thousand Rare Books and Their Prices. New York, H. F. Marks, 1936.

Taylor, H. Book Catalogues: Their Varieties and Uses. Chicago, Newberry Library, 1957. 284 p.

Essay discusses bibliographic value of catalogues of printed books. Primary emphasis is prior to 1800.

Thompson, Lawrence S. Notes on Bibliokleptomania. New York, New York Public Library, 1944. (Also contained in the September 1944 issue of the Bulletin of the New York Public Library and in Marshall, John D., comp. Books Libraries and Librarians. Hamden, Conn., Shoe String Press, 1955.)

Tredwell, Daniel M. *A Monograph on Privately Illustrated Books, A Plea for Bibliomania.* Flatbush, Long Island, Privately Printed, 1892.

U. S. Library of Congress. Manuscript Division. *Handbook of Manuscripts in the Library of Congress.* Washington, Govt. Print. Off., 1918.

West, Herbert F. *Modern Book Collecting for the Impecunious Amateur.* Boston, Little Brown, 1936.

Winterich, John T. *The Fales Collection; A Record of Growth.* New York, New York University Libraries, 1963.

__________, and Randall, D. A. *A Primer of Book Collecting.* 3d rev. ed. New York, Crown, 1966.

Wolf, Edwin. *Rosenbach.* Cleveland, World, 1960.

Guides and Verification Aids

See also O. P. Books, pp. 167-169.

Bibliographical Society of America. *Census of Fifteenth Century Books owned in America.* New York, New York Public Library, 1919.

Burger, K. *Supplement zu Hain und Panzer*, Beiträge zur Inkunabelbibliographie . . . Leipzig, Hierseman, 1904. 440 p.

Brunet, Jacque Charles. *Manuel du Libraire et de l'Amateur de Livres.* 5th ed. Paris, Firmin Didot Freres, 1860-80, 9 v.

> This is a universal bibliography of rare, important or noteworthy books. It is strongest in French and Latin titles and for publications before the nineteenth century.

Butler, Pierce, comp. *A Check List of Fifteenth Century*

Books in the Newberry Library and in other Libraries of Chicago. Chicago, The Newberry Library, 1933.

Carnegie Institution, Washington. Guides to Manuscript Materials for the History of the United States. Washington, 1906-42. 23 v.

Copinger, W. A. Supplement to Hain's Repertorium Bibliographicum... London, Sotheran, 1895-1902. 2 v. in 3.

Lists corrections and additions to Hain's Repertorium.

Grässe, J. G. T. Tresor de Livres Rares et Precieux. Dresden, R. R. Kuntze, 1859-69. 7 v.

Hain, L. I. T. Repertorium Bibliographicum, in quo Libri Omnes ab Arte Typographica Inventa usgue ad Annum M. D.. Stuttgart, Cotta, 1826-38. 2 v. in 4.

A basic list arranged alphabetically with items numbered. These "Hain numbers" are frequently referred to in many later bibliographies of incunabula.

Hamm, R. A., ed. J. Norman Heard: Bookman's Guide to Americana. 4th ed. New York, Scarecrow Press, 1967. 494 p.

"The present volume contains 6,702 priced entries, condenced from the 1964-65 catalogs of an unnamed number of unnamed out-of-print dealers in U. S. and Canada." (Library Journal).

Harvard University. The Houghton Library, 1942-1967; a Selection of Books and Manuscripts in Harvard Collections. Cambridge, The Harvard College Library, 1967.

Lowndes, William Thomas. Bibliographer's Manual of English Literature. New edition revised, corrected and enlarged by H. G. Bohn. London, G. Bell, 1883. 6 v. in 11.

McKay, G. L., ed. American Book Auction Catalogues, 1713-1914. New York, New York Public Library, 1937.

Suppl. 1946 and 1948.

A union list of some 10,000 American auction catalogs.

National Union Catalog of Manuscript Collections 1959/61-1962. Hamden, Conn., Shoe String Press, 1962-64, 3 v.

Panzer, G. W. F. Annales Typographici ab Artis Inventae Origine ad Annum 1500. Norimbergae, Zeh, 1793-97. 5 v.

__________. . Ab Anno 1501-ad Anum 1586. Norimbergae, 1798-1803. 6 v.

Proctor, R. Index to the Early Printed Books in the British Museum; with notes of those in the Bodleian Library. London, K. Paul, 1898-1938. 6 v.

__________. Supplements 1898-1902. London, 1900-1903. 5 parts.

Ransom, W. Private Presses and Their Books. New York, Bowker, 1929. 493 p.

A history of private presses and an attempt at a comprehensive listing of their books.

__________. Selective Check Lists of Press Books. New York, Philip C. Duschnes, 1963. 420 p.

A selective listing of private presses and their books.

Stillwell, M. B. Incunabula and Americana 1450-1800. 2d ed. New York, Cooper Square Publishers, 1961. 483 p.

A bibliographical study for the beginner covering printing of the 15th century, Americana from 1492-1800, and a reference section which includes a list of over 1200 titles of bibliographic importance.

Trade Prices Current of American First Editions, 1937-1941. New York, Bowker, 1941.

Reichling, D. Appendices ad Hainii-Copingeri Repertivm Bibliographicvm; Additones et Emendationes. Monachii, Rosenthal, 1905-11. 7 v. Supplement, 1914.

Sonnenschein, W. S. The Best Books, A Reader's Guide. New York, Putnam, 1910-1935. 6 v.

U. S. National Archives. Guide to Records in the National Archives. Washington, Govt. Print. Off., 1948. 684 p.

__________. National Archives Accessions, 1947—. Wash ington, 1947—. Quarterly.

U. S. National Historical Publications Commission. A Guid to Archives and Manuscripts in the United States. Ed. P. M Hamer. New Haven, Yale University Press, 1961.

Watt, Robert. Bibliotheca Britannica; or, A General Index to British and Foreign Literature. Edinburg, Printed for N. Constable, 1824. 4 v.

Wemyss, S. General Guide to Rare Americana. Philadelphia, S. Wemyss, 1950. 323 p.

> Selected list of rare and notable books relating to America published from 1493 to 1943. Includes information about auction records where available.

Serials and Periodicals

See also Serials and Periodicals, p. 171.

American Book Collector. Chicago, W. B. Thorsen, Editor and Publisher, 1950—. Monthly.

Archives and Manuscripts. Brisbane, Archives Section, Library Association of Australia, 1955—. Semi-Annual.

Archives et Bibliothiques de Belqique. Brussels, Association des Archivistes et Bibliothécaires de Belqique, 1923— Semi-Annual.

<u>Beiträge zur Inkunabelkunde</u>. Dritte Folge, Heft 1—. Berlin, Akademie Verlag, 1965—.

The third series, first issued in 1907, contains articles based on original research on incunabula.

Bibliographical Society of America. <u>Papers</u>. New York, 1904—. Quarterly.

Official organ of the Bibliographical Society of America. American counterpart of <u>Transactions</u> published by Bibliographical Society in England. The most important American publication in the area of descriptive and analytical bibliography. Contains material on history of printing and related subjects.

<u>Book Collector</u>. London, Shenval Press, 1952—. Quarterly.

Cambridge Bibliographical Society. <u>Transactions</u>. New York, Cambridge University Press, 1949—. Irregular.

One of the scholarly publications in the area of descriptive bibliography. Contains material on history of libraries and printing esp. connected with Cambridge and Cambridge libraries.

<u>The Colophon</u>. A Book Collector's Quarterly. New York, The Colophon, Ltd., Feb. 1930 - March 1935, v. 1-5. <u>New Series</u>. New York, Pynson Printers, Summer 1935-Autumn 1938, v. 1-3; <u>New Graphic Series</u>, 1939-40, v. 1, nos. 1-4; For description see <u>The New Colophon</u>.

<u>The Dolphin</u>. A Journal of the Making of Books. New York, The Limited Editions Club, 1933-1940, Nos. 1-4. (No. 4 in four parts.)

One of the most important serials in the area of history of printing, collecting, booktrade and related subjects.

<u>Gutenberg Jahrbuch</u>. Mainz, Gutenberg Geselschaft, 1926—. Annual.

One of the most important serials in the area of the

history of printing and libraries, book design, history of the book trade and related subjects. Articles in several languages. Gutenberg Gesellschaft also publishes "Veröffentlichungen" und "Kleine Drucke."

Het Boek. Hague, Martinus Nÿhoff, 1912—. Irregular.

"Devoted to the study of books, old and new, typography."

Huntington Library Quarterly. A Journal for the History and Interpretation of English and American Civilization. San Marino, Calif. Huntington Library and Art Gallery, 1937—. Quarterly.

Journal of the Printing Historical Society. London, St. Bride Institute, 1964—. Annual.

History of printing and related subjects.

La Bibliofilia. Rivista di Storia del Libro e di Bibliografia Florence, Leo S. Olschki, Publisher, 1899—. Three time a year.

Leading Italian journal in history of printing and book trade. Contains material on historical and descriptive bibliography.

Librarium. Zeitschrift der Schweizerischen Bibliophilen-Gesellschaft. Zurich, 1958—. Three times a year.

Contains information on history of book trade, printir and libraries.

The Library. (Transactions of the Bibliographical Society) London, Oxford University Press, 1888—. Series I, v.1-1 Series II, v.1-10; Series III, v.1-10. Fourth Series, v.1-26 1920-1946. Fifth Series, v.1—. 1947—.

Published by the Bibliographical Society in England. One of the most important publications in the area of historical, analytical and descriptive bibliography; contains materials on history of printing, history of the book and book trade, and history of libraries and book collections.

Manuscripts. Carbonadle, Ill., Manuscript Society, Morris Library, Southern Illinois University, 1948—. Quarterly.

The New Colophon. A Book Collector's Quarterly. New York, Duschnes Crawford, Jan. 1948—Feb. 1950. v. 1-2. Pts. 1-8. A Book-Collectors' Miscellany, 1950. 1 v.

> Continues The Colophon. One of the most important serials in the area of graphic arts, fine printing, book collecting and related subjects.

Nordisk Tidskriftför Bok-och Biblioteksväsen. Uppsala, Almqvist and Wiksell, 1914—. Quarterly.

> A leading journal on book collecting with materials in Danish, English, German, Norwegian and Swedish.

Princeton University Library Chronicle. Princeton, N. J., Princeton University Library, 1939—. Three times a year.

Scriptorium. Brussels, Bibliotheque Royale de Belgique, 1946/47—. Twice a year.

> International review of manuscript studies.

Yale University Library Gazette. New Haven, Conn., Donald C. Gallup, Editor, 1926—. Quarterly.

g. Paperbound Books

Placing Orders

Bob, M. L. "Paperback Utopia," Library Journal, 88: 1941-1942, May 15, 1963.

Buckstaff, J. B. "World of the Paperback," Library Journal, 87:165-168, January 15, 1962.

Cohen, Arthur A. "Paperbacks in the College," College and Research Libraries, 24:109-112, March, 1963.

De Young, C. D. "Operation Paperback: A Second Look," Library Journal, 85:3023-3026, September 15, 1960.

Enoch, K. "The Paperbound Book - Twentieth Century Publishing Phenomenon," Library Quarterly, 24:211-25, 1954.

Flower, D. "The Paper-Back: Its Past, Present and Future," Library Association Record, 62:175-184, June, 1960.

Forman, S. "A Look at the Future: Hardbound Myth and Paperback Reality," In: V. Anderson, ed. Paperbacks in Education. New York, Teachers College, University of Columbia, 1966. Pp. 175-180.

__________, and R. L. Collins. "The Paperback Book," Library Trends, 15:347-349, January, 1967.

Holtman, E. A. "Paperbacks and the Academic Library," Ohio Library Association Bulletin, 33:23-24, October, 1963

Klingmeyer, F. M. "Paperbacks and Hardbacks," Clearing House, 34:415-416, March, 1960.

Laskey, H. H. "Continuing Paperback Revolution," Mountain Plains Library Quarterly, 4:3-5, Winter, 1960.

Melcher, D. "Paperbounds: The Revolution in Book Distribution Patterns," Library Journal, 85:179-182, January 15 1960.

Sadler, G. E. "Technology in Paperbacks: ICA Develops Little Libraries of Technical Literature," Library Journal, 85:3027-3028, September 15, 1960.

Schick, F. L. "Library's Use of Paperbacks: Are They Measuring Up?" Pennsylvania Library Association Bulletin 17:195-196, Summer, 1961.

__________. "Paperbacks---A Primary Reprint Service," Reprint Expediting Service Bulletin, 6:2-3, Winter, 1961.

Schick, F. L. The Paperbound Book in America: The History of Paperbacks and Their European Background. New York, Bowker, 1958. 262 p.

Covers the history of paperbacks in Europe and the United States, the current publishing scene, and specific paperback publishers.

Stone, E. O., and M. B. Melvin. "Paperbounds Go to College," Library Journal, 80:1644-1649, August, 1955.

Reviews three years of paperback service at Southern Illinois University Library.

Thompson, L. S. "European Paperbacks," Books Abroad, 36:147-149, Spring, 1962.

Guides and Directories

Andrews, D. H. and T. J. Hillman, comp. Latin America. A Bibliography of Paperback Books. Washington, Library of Congress, 1964. (Hispanic Foundation Bibliographic Series, No. 9).

Morehouse, C. T., comp. Paperbound Books on Asia. New York, Foreign Materials Center, University of the State of New York, 1963.

Paperback Goes to School. New York, Bureau of Independent Publishers and Distributors, 1964.

A selective list of paperbacks for junior and senior high schools. Compiled by NEA and AASL committee. Free.

Paperbacks in Print. 11th ed. London, Whitaker, 1967.

The English counterpart to Bowker's publication, listing some 20,000 titles in print.

Paperbound Book Guide for Colleges. New York, Bowker, 1967. 260 p. Annual.

Lists 15,400 paperbacks.

Paperbound Book Guide for Elementary Schools. New York, Bowker, 1967. 64 p. Annual.

List 800 paperbacks for pre-school through 6th grade. Arranged by subject and grade level.

Paperbound Book Guide for High Schools. New York, Bowker, 1967. 136 p. Annual.

Lists about 6500 paperbacks under 45 subject headings Includes an introduction on locating suppliers and information on discounts.

Paperbound Books in Print. A Guide to Available Paperbacks Indexed by Author, Title, and Subject. New York, Bowker, 1955—. Monthly.

Lists 44,000 paperbacks arranged by author with cumulative author, title and subject indexes. Annotated previews of the month ahead in paperbacks, with complete order information.

Rosenblum, P., comp. Checklist of Paperbound Books on Africa. Albany, Office of the Foreign Area Studies, State University of New York, 1964.

Spector, S. D., comp. Checklist of Paperbound Books on Russia. Albany, Office of the Foreign Area Studies, State University of New York, 1964.

h. Audio-Visual Materials

Placing Orders

Alvarez, E. R. S. "Working Bibliography of Commercially Available Audio-visual Materials To Be Used in Conjunction with the Teaching of Library Science," In: National Conference on the Implications of the New Media for the Teaching of Library Science. Proceedings of the Conference Held at the Sheraton-Chicago Hotel, Chicago, Ill., May 27-29, 1963. Urbana, University of Illinois, 1963. Pp. 121-163.

"Audio Services and Facilities, A Panel Discussion," In: Library Equipment Institute, 1964. St. Louis. Library Environment: Aspects of Interior Planning. Chicago, American Library Association, 1965. Pp. 41-50.

"Audiovisual Selection Aids," Wisconsin Library Bulletin, 62:180-181, May, 1966.

Bradley, C.J. Manual of Music Librarianship. Ann Arbor, Mich., Music Library Association, School of Music, University of Michigan, 1966. 140 p.

Includes chapter on acquisitions.

Brown, James W., et al. A-V Instruction: Materials and Methods, 2d ed. New York, McGraw-Hill, 1964.

__________, and Thornton, J.W. New Media in Higher Education. Washington, Association for Higher Education and the Division of Audiovisual Instructional Service of the National Education Association, 1963.

Bryant, E.T. Collecting Gramophone Records. New York, Focal Press, 1962.

Clarke, Virginia. Non-Book Library Materials. Denton, Texas, North Texas State College Print Shop, 1953.

Coover, J. "Reference Bibliography in the Music Library," Library Trends, 8:519-528, April, 1960.

Curral, F.J., ed. Phonograph Record Libraries: Their Organization and Practice. Hamden, Conn., Archon Books, 1963. 182 p.

A volume of essays on record collections written primarily by British music librarians.

Dana, John Cotton. The Picture Collection. New York, Wilson, 1943.

deKieffer, Robert, and Lee W. Cochran. Manual of Audio-Visual Techniques. 2d ed. Englewood Cliffs, N.J., Prentice-Hall, 1961.

Duckles, V. "Music Literature, Music and Sound Recordings," Library Trends, 15:494-521, January, 1967.

Edinger, L. "Technology in Education," Wilson Library Bulletin, 41:72-75, September, 1966.

Erickson, Carlton W. H. Administering Audio-Visual Services. New York, Macmillan, 1959.

__________. Fundamentals of Teaching with Audiovisual Technology. New York, Macmillan, 1965.

Goldstein, H. "A/V: Has It Any Future in Libraries?" Wilson Library Bulletin, 36:670-673, April, 1962.

__________, ed. "Audiovisual Issue," Illinois Libraries, 48:69-136, February, 1966.

Hagist, B. "Resistance and Reluctance in Record Selection Library Journal, 93:518-520, February 1, 1968.

A survey of public libraries policies.

Harrison, K. C. "Gramophone Record Library," UNESCO Bulletin for Libraries, 14:197-201, September, 1960.

Howell, W. "Let's Keep in Step," Illinois Libraries, 44: 154-155, February, 1962.

Hulfish, J. W. "Audio-Visual Media for Librarians," Illinois Libraries, 47:99-103, February, 1965.

Ireland, Norma Olin. The Picture File. Boston, Faxon, 1952.

Kinder, James S. Audio-Visual Materials and Techniques. 2d ed. New York, American Book Company, 1959.

Krummel, D. W. "Observations on Library Acquisitions of Music," Notes, 23:5-16, September, 1966.

Lieberman, I. "Reference Service and Audiovisual Materials: Recommended Books, Pamphlets and Periodicals for a Library and Audiovisual Materials Information Collection As Well As Tools for Selection of Materials," In: National Conference on the Implications of the New Media for the Teaching of Library Science. Proceedings of the Conference Held at the Sheraton-Chicago Hotel, Chicago, Ill., May 27-29, 1963. Urbana, University of Illinois, 1963. Pp. 164-178.

Limbacher, James, ed. Using Films: A Handbook for Program Planners. New York, Educational Film Library Association, 1967.

Mason, D. Primer of Non-Book Materials in Libraries, with an Appendix on Sound Recordings by J. C. Cowan. London, Association of Assistant Librarians, 1958.

Nolan, J. L. "Audio-Visual Materials," Library Trends, 10:261-272, October, 1961.

Oppenheim, H. L. "Audio Visual Material in the Library," Cape Librarian, 7-9, February, 1964.

Orrego-Salas, J. A. "Acquisitions of Latin American Books and Music," Music Library Association Notes, 22:1008-13, March, 1966.

Overton, C. David. The Gramophone Record Library. London, Grafton, 1951. 123 p.

Practical aspects of a record collection.

Pearson, M. D. Recordings in the Public Library. Chicago, American Library Association, 1963. 153 p.

Emphasis is on administering a collection of disc recordings in a small and medium sized public library.

Peters, W. "Audio-Visual Materials in the Public Library, Library Trends, 16:241-250, October, 1967.

Quinly, W. "The Selection, Processing and Storage of Non-Print Materials: Aids, Indexes and Guidelines," Library Trends, 16:274-282, October, 1967.

Preggi, W. C. "Local Production Center, A Time and Mone Saver," In National Conference on the Implications of the New Media for the Teaching of Library Science. Proceedin of the Conference Held at the Sheraton-Chicago Hotel, Chicago, Ill., May 27-29, 1963. Urbana, University of Illinois 1963. Pp. 49-52.

Scourzo, Herbert. Practical A-V Handbook for Teachers. West Nyack, N. Y., Parker Publishing Co., 1967.

Shepard, B. "Building a Collection to Meet the Needs of Research Scholars in Music," Library Trends, 8:539-546. April, 1960.

Shera, J. H. "Cult of the Audio-Visual," Wilson Library Bulletin, 36:251, November, 1961.

Simons, W. W. "Choosing Audio-Visual Equipment," Library Trends, 13:503-516, April, 1965.

Stevenson, G. "The Cost of Imported Scores," Library Resources and Technical Services, 6:320-331, Fall, 1962.

Stone, C. W. "Development of Professional Tools for the Materials Center," In: Mahar, M. H., ed. School Library as a Materials Center. Washington, U. S. Education Office 1963. Pp. 7-11.

__________. "Listening Facilities in the Library," In: Library Equipment Institute, 1964. St. Louis. Library Environment: Aspects of Interior Planning. Chicago, American Library Association, 1965. Pp. 34-40.

Thomas, R. M., and S. G. Swartout. Integrated Teaching

Materials: How to Choose and Create Them. Rev. and enl. ed. New York, McKay, 1963. 559 p.

Intended primarily for the elementary and secondary school teacher.

Thompson, M. D. "Growing Pains for Audio-Visual Co-ordinators," Illinois Libraries, 42:236-237, April, 1960.

VanderMeer, A. W. "Fear of the Newer Media," ALA Bulletin, 55:798-802, October, 1961.

Veslak, E. "Audiovisuals in a Library System," Wisconsin Library Bulletin, 62:158-159, May, 1966.

Welch, H. M. "Cost of Library Materials," Library Trends, 11:384-394, April, 1963.

Wittich, W. A., and C. F. Sculler. Audiovisual Materials: Their Nature and Use, 4th ed. New York, Harper, 1967.

Zigrosser, C., and C. M. Gaehde. Guide to the Collecting and Care of Original Prints. New York, Crown, 1965. 120 p.

Guides and Directories

American Library Association. Audio Visual Committee. Films for Libraries. Chicago, ALA, 1962. 81 p.

Intended as a guide to the best films available for library collections. Graded, annotated list of 400 16mm films.

Audio Visual Instruction. Washington, National Education Association, 1956—. Monthly.

Includes reviews of current material.

Bartran, M. Guide to Color Reproductions. New York, Scarecrow Press, 1966. 382 p.

Blue Book of Audio-Visual Materials. Chicago, Educational Screen, 1922—.

This annual has appeared under this title since 1954. It lists films, filmstrips, recordings, slides and can be kept up to date by reference to Educational Screen and Audio-Visual Guide, issued monthly.

The British Catalogue of Music. London, Council of the British National Bibliography, 1957—. Annual.

Listings are based upon the works received at the Copyright Office.

Brooke, Milton, and Henry J. Dubester. Guide to Color Prints. Washington, Scarecrow Press, 1953.

Dimmitt, R. D. A Title Guide to the Talkies. New York, Scarecrow Press, 1965. 2 v.

Gives titles to about 16,000 feature-length films released between 1927 and 1963. Supplements.

Educational Film Guide. New York, Wilson, 1936-1962.

The last cumulation was for 1954-1958 with annual supplements through 1962. These cover 13,416 16mm educational films. The 11th edition, 1953, covers 11,000 16mm films.

Educational Media Index. New York, McGraw-Hill, 1964. 14 v. No supplements issued to date.

The first attempt to provide a multi-media index to films, filmstrips, videotapes, models, programed learning materials, phonodiscs, cross-media sets, etc. Entries are organized by subject and educational level and include source, content and price. A new edition is in progress.

Educational Screen and Audiovisual Guide Magazine. Chicago, Ed. D. A. Wenger, 1922—. Monthly.

Listings of audio-visual materials released. Important source for school materials.

Educators Guide to Free Films. Randolph, Wisc., Educators Progress Service, 1941—.

An annual listing of sponsored films of educational value. Subject arrangement.

Educators Guide to Free Slide Films. Randolph, Wisc., Educators Progress Service, 1949—.

An annual listing of slide films, sound films, and some slides.

Educators Guide to Free Tapes, Scripts, and Transcriptions. Randolph, Wisc., Educators Progress Service, 1955—. Annual.

Fawcett, M. An Index to Films in Review, 1960-64. New York, National Board of Review of Modern Pictures, 1966. 196p.

Film Evaluation Guide, 1946-1964. New York, Educational Film Library Association, 1965. 528p.

Comprehensive listing of motion picture film and filmstrips. 4500 films evaluated by EFLA; includes all essential information for purchase; gives recommendations. An annotated list of 205 16mm films is also available: Films for Children, The Association, 1961, 56p. Can be kept current by listings in Film Review Digest, issued bimonthly since 1953.

Film Strip Guide. New York, Wilson, 1948-1962.

This guide listed 35mm filmstrips released between 1948 and 1962.

Finn, J.D. Audiovisual Equipment Manual. New York, Dryden Press, 1957.

Contains 1400 illustrations, giving comprehensive and detailed information.

Instructional Television Materials. New York, National Instructional Television Library, 1962—.

Lists programs for elementary grades, secondary schools, colleges, and for adults and teachers.

Landers, Bertha, ed. *Foreign Language Audiovisual Guide.* Landers Associates, 1961.

McKune, L. E., comp. *National Compendium of Televised Education.* East Lansing, Mich., Michigan State University, 1953—. Annual.

Lists tape recordings by subject and title.

Music Trade Directory and Guide, 2d ed. London, Tofts and Woolf, 1966.

National Audio-Visual Association. *The Audio-Visual Equipment Directory.* Fairfax, Va., The Association, 1967.

This comprehensive directory of dealers and manufacturers of a-v equipment is published annually. Includes illustrations, descriptions and prices of equipment.

National Council of Teachers of English. *An Annotated List of Recordings In the Language Arts.* Champaign, Ill., National Council of Teachers of English, 1964. 83 p.

Covers literature, composition, linguistics, speech and associated areas for elementary, secondary and college levels.

National Tape Recording Catalog, 1962-63. 3d ed. Washington, Department of Audio-visual Instruction, National Education Association, 1963. 138 p.

__________. *Supplement I.* 1965. 38 p.

Lists 5000 tapes available from the National Tape Repository. Includes description, subject classification, grade level. Is the basic source for tape recorded educational radio programs produced by United States school systems. Covers all major curriculum areas on elementary and secondary levels.

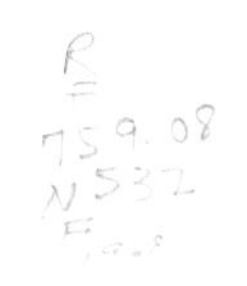

New York Graphic Society. Fine Art Reproductions of Old and Modern Masters. Greenwich, Conn., 1961.

New York Library Association. Films for Children; A Selected List. New York, New York Public Library, 1966. 30 p.

Annotated list; special attention to relating film and specific book titles.

__________. Films For Young Adults; A Selected List. New York, New York Public Library, 1966.

__________. Recordings For Children; A Selected List. 2d ed. New York, New York Library Association, 1964. 64 p.

Selected and annotated list of best recordings of music and literature.

Osborn, M. B., and B. Miller. Sources of Free Pictures, rev. ed. Riverside, Calif., Bruce Miller Publications, 1963. 31 p.

Rufsvold, M. I., and C. Guss. Guides to Newer Educational Media. 2d ed. Chicago, American Library Association, 1967.

Annotated guide to the catalogs, lists, professional organizations, and specialized periodicals which systematically provide information on films, filmstrips, kinescopes, phonodiscs, slides, transparancies and videotapes. This is a revision of the 1961 edition and covers guides through April 1, 1967.

Schwann Long Playing Record Catalog. Monthly Guide to Mono and Stereo Records. Boston, W. Schwann, 1949—. Monthly.

Special Libraries Association. Picture Division. Picture Sources; edited by Celestine G. Frankenberg, 2d ed. New York: The Association, 1964. 216 p. (Earlier edition, 1959.)

A bibliography listing 700 sources; classified arrangement. Information for each source includes: name; address; description of picture collection, size, subjects; regulations; charges.

U. S. Copyright Office. Motion Pictures. 1912-1939; 1940-1949; 1950-1959. Washington, Library of Congress, 1951-1960.

Catalog of copyright entries.

U. S. Library of Congress. Library of Congress Catalog-Motion Pictures and Filmstrips, 1953-1957, 1958-1962. Ann Arbor, Mich., Edwards, 1958-63. 2 v.

A cumulative list of works represented by Library of Congress printed cards.

U. S. Library of Congress. Library of Congress Catalog-Music and Phonorecords. Washington, 1953—. Semi-annua

U. S. Office of Education. United States Government Films for Public Education Use. Washington, Govt. Print. Off., 1940—.

Issued irregularly as a circular of the Office of Education.

UNESCO. Catalog of Colour Reproductions of Paintings. Paris, UNESCO, 1963. 2 v.

__________. Mass Communication Techniques Division. World Film Directory: Agencies Concerned with Educationa Scientific, and Cultural Films. Paris, 1962.

A directory of sources.

University of Southern California. National Information Center for Educational Media. Index to 16mm Educational Films. New York, McGraw-Hill, 1967. 955 p.

Library Film Quarterly, V. 1 —. Greenwich, Conn., Film Library Information Council, 1967/68—.

Broad coverage of public library a/v services; includes film and book reviews.

i. Maps

Placing Orders

Bahn, Catherine E. "Map Libraries---Space and Equipment," Special Libraries Association Geography and Map Division Bulletin, 46:3-17, December, 1961.

Bartlett, Dorothy W. "New Government Maps for Everyone: A Select List," Special Libraries, 54:24-28, January, 1963.

"Bibliographies on Maps and Map Making," Special Libraries Association Geography and Map Division Bulletin, 51:19-21, March, 1963.

Bowman, Nellie M. "Publications, Maps, and Charts Sold by U. S. Government Agencies Other Than the Superintendent of Documents," Special Libraries, 44:53-65, February, 1953.

Bryan, Mary M. "Harvard College Library Map Collection," Special Libraries Association Geography and Map Division Bulletin, 36:4-10, April, 1959.

DeWald, Ernest. "Map Procurement in Government Agencies," Special Libraries, 44:175-178, May-June, 1953.

Dowd, Sheila T. "Map Collection of the University of California at Berkeley," Special Libraries Association Geography and Map Division Bulletin, 43:13-14, February, 1961.

Drazniowsky, R. "Bibliographies as Tools for Map Acquisition and Map Compilation," The Cartographer, 3:138-144, December, 1966.

__________. "Cartography," Library Trends, 15:710-717, April, 1967.

Espenshade, Edward. "Maps for the College Library," College and Research Libraries, 8:132-137, April, 1947.

__________. "No One Source for Acquiring Maps," Library Journal, 75:431-436, March 15, 1950.

Recommends training in geography for map librarians. Discusses three kinds of issuing agencies, 1) government or official, 2) commercial or private, and 3) institutions and organizations.

Felland, N. "Geography," Library Trends, 15:704-709, January, 1967.

__________. "Periodical Aids to Map Acquisition," Library Journal, 75:438, March 15, 1950.

Ferrar, A. M. "Management of Map Collections and Libraries in University Geography Departments," Library Association Record, 64:161-165, May, 1962.

Gluck, Harold. "Maps Practically for the Asking," Journal of Geography, 39:39-36, January, 1940.

Goodman, Marie C. "Map Producers," Special Libraries Association Geography and Map Division Bulletin, 27:4-11, February, 1957.

Hagen, C. B. "The UCLA Map Library," Special Libraries Association Geography and Map Division Bulletin, 51:18, March, 1963.

Hammond, Caleb D. "Maps on Parade," Library Journal, 83:1475-1480, May 15, 1958.

Harrison, Richard Edes. "Evaluation of Modern Maps," Special Libraries, 44:45-47, February, 1953.

Detailed discussion of three points about maps, 1) source material, 2) design, and 3) execution.

Irish, Kathleen. "What About Gazeteers?" Library Journal, 75:447-449, March, 1950.

"List of Articles on Maps and Their Use In Geographic Education," Journal of Geography, 49:188-300, October, 1950.

Masten, Floyd E. "The Army Map Service Library," Special Libraries, 35:83-88, March, 1944.

Mueller, Anne. "Map Collection of the Los Angeles Public Library," Special Libraries Association Geography and Map Division Bulletin, 43:17-19, February, 1961.

Porter, R. E. "How to Select an Atlas," Library Journal, 86:3747-3750, November 1, 1961.

Riesner, Marianna. "Acquisition of Map Materials for a College Library." Unpublished Master's thesis, University of Michigan, Ann Arbor, 1948.

Ristow, Walter W. "Maps in Libraries, a Bibliographical Summary," Library Journal, 71:1101-1107, September 1, 1946.

Rogers, Joseph W. "Copyright Catalog is Useful Tool," Library Journal, 75:444-446, March 15, 1950.

Wolter, J. A. "The Current Bibliography of Cartography, an Annotated Selection of Serials," SLA Geography and Division Bulletin, 58:9-13, December, 1964.

Woods, Bill. "Map Information Reference Service," Special Libraries, 45:103-106, March, 1954.

__________. "Map Librarianship," Special Libraries Association Geography and Map Division Bulletin, 23:9-12, February, 1956.

__________. "Training for Map Librarianship," Special Libraries, 43:87-88, March, 1952.

Description of workshop at University of Illinois for selected students on maps and cartobibliographical aids, with suggestions for revision of the program.

Yonge, Ena L. "Map Procurement in the Special Library," Special Libraries, 44:173-174, May-June, 1953.

A Selected List of Guides and Directories

American Congress on Surveying and Mapping. Surveying and Mapping. Washington, October, 1941—.

Published monthly through May, 1942, and quarterly thereafter.

American Geographical Society. Library. Research Catalogue. Boston, Hall, 1962. 15 v. and map suppl.

Bibliographie Cartographique Internationale, 1936—. Paris, Colin, 1938—. Annual. (Irregular).

Bibliotheca Cartographica. Bibliographie des Kartographischen Schrifttums... Remagen, 1957—. Semiannual.

International in coverage.

Current Geographical Publications. Addition to the Research Catalogue of the American Geographical Society. New York, The Society, 1938—. Monthly except July and August.

Geographisches Jahrbuch. Gotha, Perthes, 1886—. Annual (Irregular)

Olson, Everett C. Foreign Maps. New York, Harper, 1944. 237 p.

Discusses methods of studying foreign language maps and includes glossaries of terms and representative maps.

Orbis Geographicus. World Directory of Geography... Wiesbaden, F. Steiner, 1960—.

Lists geographical societies, congresses, institutes, and includes a directory of geographers.

Royal Geographical Society, London. *New Geographical Literature and Maps*. London, 1951—. N. S. v.1—. Semiannual.

Special Libraries Association. Geography and Map Division. Map Resources Committee. *Map Collections in the United States and Canada*. New York, Special Libraries Association, 1954.

Thiele, Walter. *Official Map Publications*. Chicago, American Library Association, 1938. 356p.

An historical sketch and bibliographical handbook of current maps and mapping services of selected countries.

U. S. Copyright Office. *Catalog of Copyright Entries. Maps and Atlases.* Third series, part 6. Washington, Govt. Print. Off., 1948—. Semiannual.

U. S. Library of Congress. *Library of Congress Catalog. A Cumulative List of Works Represented by Library of Congress Printed Cards: Maps and Atlases.* Washington, 1953-55. 3 v.

Before 1953 and after 1955 entries are included in the *National Union Catalog*.

U. S. Library of Congress. Map Division. *A List of Geographical Atlases in the Library of Congress, with Bibliographical Notes*. Washington, Govt. Print. Off., 1909-63. v. 1-6 (In progress).

World Cartography. V. 1— 1951—. New York, United Nations, Department of Social Affairs, 1951—.

Wright, J. K., and Platt, E. T. *Aids to Geographical Research: Bibliographies, Periodicals, Atlases, Gazetteers and Other Reference Books*. 2d ed. New York, Publ. for the American Geographical Society by Columbia University Press, 1947. 331 p.

Outdated but still useful for general orientation.

j. Technical Reports and Ephemera

Placing Orders

Boylan, Nancy G. "Identifying Technical Reports Through U. S. Government Research Reports and Its Published Indexes," College and Research Libraries, 28:175-183, May, 1967.

Provides information about changes of title, publisher and numbering for government reports series and indexes.

Burkett, J., and T. S. Morgan. Special Materials in the Library. London, Library Association, 1963. 177 p.

Good chapters on technical reports and ephemera literature.

Cole, Betty Joy. "Acquisition of Technical Reports," In: Fry, B. M., and J. J. Kortendick, eds. The Production and Use of Technical Reports. Washington, The Catholic University Press, 1955.

Curran, N. E. "Yours for the Ordering," Wilson Library Bulletin, 37:342-344, December, 1962.

Fry, B. M. Library Organization and Management of Technical Reports Literature. Washington, Catholic University of America, 1953. (Catholic University of America. Studies in Library Science, No. 1.)

Gray, Dwight E. "Technical Reports I Have Known," Physics Today, 13:24-32, November, 1960.

Heald, J. H. "ASTIA and the Information Revolution," Special Libraries, 54:40-44, January, 1963.

International Federation for Documentation. "The Content, Influence and Value of Scientific Conference Papers and Proceedings," UNESCO Bulletin for Libraries, 16:113-126, May-June, 1962.

Jenkins, F. B. "The Acquisition of Scientific and Technological Material," Library Trends, 3:414-421, April, 1955.

This paper gives procedures used in acquiring all forms of scientific literature, e.g. books, journals, technical reports, patents, thesis, etc. Bibliographic tools used in locating technical reports are listed along with the dissemination methods used by government agencies.

King, I. "The Pamphlet in the University Library," Library Resources and Technical Services, 10:51-56, Winter, 1966.

Miller, Eugene E. "The Distribution-Acquisition Problem in Technical Reporting," In: Egan, Margaret E., ed. The Communication of Specialized Information. Chicago, University of Chicago, 1954. Pp. 22-33.

A discussion of the problems and techniques of distribution of technical reports with particular emphasis on the ASTIA and NACA procedures.

Miller, S. "AFL-CIO Publications: A Guide to Acquiring and Using Them," American Library Association, Library Service to Labor Newsletter, 13:1-3, Summer, 1960.

Murray, May P. "The Report and Document Library of Armour Research Foundation," Special Libraries, 49: 153-156, April, 1958.

A review of the methods in which internal and external reports are processed at the Armour Research Foundation.

Pfoutz, Daniel R. "Guide to Report Literature," Library Journal, 84:3363-3366, November, 1959.

A good review of indexes, abstracts and bibliographies listing technical reports. This paper also lists the major documentation centers and the methods by which reports may be obtained from them.

Smith, Maurice H. "Reports Acquisition as a Service Element," In: Fry, B. M., and J. J. Kortendick. The Production and Use of Technical Reports. Washington, The Catholic University of America Press, 1955. Pp. 65-74.

A review of the acquisitioning, indexing and cataloging, circulation, reference, literature searching, and distribution of acquisition lists of technical reports at the James Forrestal Research Center.

Spence, Barbara A. "The Librarian and the Procurement Problem," Sci-Tech News, 13:6-7, Fall, 1959.

The need for rapid acquisition of technical reports is stressed in this paper. Clearing houses for technical reports and methods of acquisition are also given.

Tallman, J. "History and Importance of Technical Reports," Sci-Tech News, 15:44-46, Summer, 1961; 15:164-172, Winter, 1962.

Weil, B. H., ed. The Technical Report, Its Preparation, Processing and Use in Industry and Government. New York, Reinhold, 1954.

A Selected List of Reference Aids

(Note: For a more comprehensive listing of reference aids for technical reports see: Acquisition of Special Materials ed. by I. Jackson. San Francisco, SLA, San Francisco Bay Region Chapter, 1966.)

American Society for Testing and Materials. Book of A. S. T. M. Standards, With Related Material, 1939—. Philadelphia, 1939—. Annual.

Carter, L. F., et al. National Document Handling Systems for Science and Technology, New York, Wiley, 1967.

An outgrowth of a study undertaken for Committee on Scientific and Technical Information (COSATI).

This guide describes the present system of document handling.

Clarke, E. A Guide to Technical Literature Production. A Concise Handbook of Production Methods. River Forest, Ill., TW Publishers, 1961. 182 p.

Harwell, G. C. Technical Communication. New York, Macmillan, 1960. 332 p.

Houghton, B. Technical Information Sources. A Guide to Patents, Standards and Technical Reports Literature. Hamden, Conn., Archon Books, 1967. 101 p.

Redman, H. F., and L. E. Godfrey, eds. Dictionary of Report Series Codes. New York, Special Libraries Association, 1962. 648 p.

U. S. Atomic Energy Commission. Standard Distribution Lists for Unclassified Scientific and Technical Reports. 19th ed. Oak Ridge, Tenn., February, 1963. (TID 4500)

U. S. Atomic Energy Commission. Standard Distribution Lists for Classified Scientific and Technical Reports. 40th ed. Oak Ridge, Tenn., May 15, 1965. (M. 3679)

U. S. Atomic Energy Commission. Technical Information Services of the United States Atomic Energy Commission. 4th ed. Oak Ridge, Tenn., 1962. 119 p.

U. S. Atomic Energy Commission. What's Available in the Atomic Energy Literature. Oak Ridge, Tenn., April, 1966. (TID-4550).

Describes various sources available for locating information on the subject.

U. S. Clearinghouse for Federal Scientific and Technical Information. Government-Wide Index to Federal Research and Development Reports. Springfield, Va., 1965—. Monthly.

U.S. Defence Documentation Center. Technical Abstract Bulletin. Alexandria, Va., September, 1957—. Semi-monthly.

Originally published under its former name, ASTIA.

U.S. Patent Office Official Gazette, 1872—. Washington, Govt. Print. Off., 1872—. v.1—. Weekly.

Weil, B. H. The Technical Report: Its Preparation, Processing and Use in Industry and Government. New York, Reinhold, 1954. 485 p.

k. Ordering for School Libraries

Guides and Reference Aids

The following are selective lists of important or well known book selection tools for school libraries. The "General Tools" includes selected aids useful to elementary schools, junior and senior high schools, and curriculum libraries. Separate lists are included for Elementary Schools, Junior and Senior High Schools, and Special Readers. Limitation of space prohibits inclusion of many titles; tools going beyond the limit of "school libraries" were for the most part omitted although they are useful to the school librarian. For example Books for College Libraries, prepared under the direction of M. J. Voight and J. H. Treyz, Chicago, American Library Association, 1967. 1056 p. This list of some 53,410 monographs selected for the basic undergraduate libraries of the University of California New Campuses Program is of value to many large school libraries seeking to further expand and enrich their collections for college bound students and merit scholars. Other sections of this chapter should be consulted for additional information useful to school libraries, e.g. Verification Aids, pp. 150-151, General Guides to Reference Aids, pp. 151-153, Out of Print Materials, pp. 169-170, Government Publications, pp. 202-204.

General

See also, Paperbound Books pp. 223-224, and Audio-Visual Materials pp. 229-234.

Association for Supervision and Curriculum Development. Curriculum Materials, 1966. Washington, National Education Association, 1966. 98 p.

Lists guides and programs in all curriculum areas, kindergarten through senior high school, produced in local school systems. Materials listed were exhibited at 1966 ASCD Annual Conference.

Best Books for Children, 1967. New York, Bowker, 1967. 238 p.

The 9th edition of an annual list; annotates 4000 children's books in-print for preschool through high school. Arranged within grade level by subject. Entries include: title, author, illustrator, grade level, price, annotation and code indicating recommendations from standard reviewing media and catalogs.

Children's Books for Schools and Libraries, 1966-1967. New York, Bowker, 1967. 487 p.

Published annually in fall. Author-title index to 18,000 books in publishers' reinforced editions; a selection of recommended books in trade editions are included. Entries include publisher, price, grade level, recommending source. The catalog represents titles for which LJ Book Processing Kits are available. Formerly Publishers' Library Bindings In Print.

Dobler, Lavinia G. The Dobler World Directory of Youth Periodicals. Schulte Publisher, 1966. 37 p.

Lists and annotates 400 periodicals in five groups: general, religious, school, foreign-in English, foreign-language. Includes price, grade level, publisher, circulation, purpose. Successor to Dobler International List.

Educators Guide to Free Guidance Materials. 6th ed. Randolph, Wisc., Educators Progress Service, 1967. 238 p.

One title in a series of guides to free materials and sources published annually. This guide lists 861 items from 346 sources.

Educators Guide to Free Social Studies Materials. Randolph, Wisc., Educators Progress Service, 1967.

Educators Guide to Free Science Materials. Randolph, Wisc., Educators Progress Service, 1967.

Hopkins, Shirley L. *Instructional Materials for Teaching the Use of the Library*; A Selected, Annotated Bibliography of Films, Filmstrips, Books and Pamphlets, Tests, and Other Aids. San Jose, Calif., Claremont House, 1966. 59 p.

How-To-Do-It-Books: A Selected Guide. 3d ed. rev. New York, Bowker, 1963. 265 p.

Lock, Muriel. *Reference Material for Young People.* Hamden, Conn., 1967. 189 p.

Survey of reference and non-fiction for all age groups through adolescence, including titles from U. S. and Commonwealth countries.

Michigan Association of School Librarians. *Recommended Materials for a Professional Library in the School.* Ann Arbor, Mich., The Association, 1962. 187 p.

Lists and annotates books, periodicals, films for teachers' library. Classified arrangement.

Modern Language Association of America. *MLA Selective List of Materials*; For Use By Teachers of Modern Foreign Languages in Elementary and Secondary Schools. New York, Modern Language Association of America, 1962. 162 p.

List of teaching materials; includes some trade books.

North Carolina. Department of Public Instruction. *Refer-*

ence Materials for School Libraries; Grades 1 through 12, 2d ed. North Carolina Department of Public Instruction, 1965. 166 p.

1000 books are annotated. Discusses criteria for selecting reference books and building a collection.

Perkins, Ralph. Book Selection Media; A Descriptive Guide to 175 Aids for Selecting Library Materials. Champaign, Ill., National Council of Teachers of English, 1966. 188 p.

Covers aids in children's work and young adult as well as college and adult. Tabular form; shows author index, classed indexes, table of contents.

The Teachers Library. Washington, National Education Association, 1966. 204 p.

The first edition of a selected, annotated list of materials for a professional library. Books and pamphlets are in classed arrangement. Films, filmstrips, journals are in separate lists. Prices are included. Pp. 9-11 "Selection of Materials," lists and describes some selection tools, indexes, periodicals and guides, to aid in locating current materials.

Textbooks in Print, 1967. New York, Bowker, 1967. 506 p.

An annual index to 1400 elementary, junior and senior high school textbooks and pedagogical materials. Classified by subject with author and title indexes. 207 U.S. publishers included. A separate listing for adult education and five sections on programed learning materials.

United Nations Educational, Scientific and Cultural Organization. Source Book for Geography Teaching. Paris, UNESCO, 1965. 254 p.

Contains lists of teaching materials and bibliographies.

Vertical File Index. New York, Wilson, 1935—. Monthly except August.

Annual cumulation in December lists about 4500 titles

of pamphlets, maps, posters and other inexpensive material of value to libraries; ranges from elementary to highly technical. U. S. government publications not included but lists state and local government materials and publications of foreign information services locate in the United States.

Elementary School

American Library Association. *A Basic Book Collection for Elementary Grades.* 7th ed. Chicago, American Library Association, 1960.

Annotated list of 1000 titles; now dated.

__________. *Books for Children, 1960-1965.* Chicago, American Library Association, 1965. 448p.

__________, __________, 1965-1966. Chicago, American Library Association, 1966. 128p.

__________, __________, 1966-1967. Chicago, American Library Association, 1967.

This book selection and buying guide lists books recommended and reviewed in *Booklist and Subscription Books Bulletin.* The 1966-1967 list includes 800 books for preschool through junior high school in classified subject arrangement. Entries give complete buying and cataloging information plus original *Booklist* review. Author, subject, title index.

Baker, Augusta. *Books About Negro Life for Children.* New York, New York Public Library, 1965.

Chase, Judith W. *Books to Build World Friendship*; An Annotated Bibliography of Children's Books from Preschool to 8th Grade: Europe. Dobbs Ferry, N. Y., Oceana, 1964. 76p.

296 selected titles, mostly fiction, devoted to building friendship among peoples. Criteria for selection stated in Introduction.

Child Study Association of America. The Children's Bookshelf: A Guide to Books For and About Children. New York, Bantam, 1965.

__________. Books of the Year for Children. New York, The Association, 1965.

An annual list of selected titles.

Children's Catalog, Eleventh Edition. New York, Wilson, 1967. With 4 annual suppl.

Covers 4274 books; additional 1200 titles to be added in supplements.

Deason, Hilary J., comp. The AAAS Science Book List For Children. 2d ed. Washington, American Association For the Advancement of Science, 1963. 201 p.

An authoritative guide to selected, annotated and graded (primary, intermediate, advanced) science books for children. Updated by Science Books; A Quarterly Review since 1965.

Eakin, Mary K., comp. Good Books For Children; A Selection of Outstanding Children's Books Published 1948-1961. Rev. and enl. Chicago, University of Chicago Press, 1963. 362 p.

Introduction discusses selection and evaluation of children's books. Selection of 1306 best books published 1948-1961 based on recommendations from Bulletin of Center For Children's Books. Long descriptive reviews.

Gaver, Mary V., ed. The Elementary School Library Collection Phases 1-2-3. 2d ed. Newark, N.J., Bro-Dart Foundation, 1966.

Contains 6757 selected titles; cut-off date of titles listed is December 30, 1965. The annual volume is updated by a supplement. Selection policy and classification principles and policies are discussed in introductory pages. Presents 1748 titles in Phase 1--minimum for any elementary collection; Phases 2 and

3 add 5592 titles plus a/v and professional listings. Section I contains a reproduction of annotated catalog card with full cataloging information and prices. Arrangement is classified: reference, non-fiction, fiction, easy, a/v, periodicals, professional tools. Cards are marked Phase 1, 2 or 3. Section II contains author, title, subject indexes.

__________. __________. Supplement to the Second Edition. Newark, N.J., Bro-Dart Foundation, 1966. 1293 p.

The supplement covers the gap between editions, e.g. this supplement covers January 1, 1966-November 15, 1966. Two parts: classified catalog, indexes. The supplement is intended as a "current guide to materia[ls] for grades from pre-school through sixth, listing those titles published during the year just ended." (Preface) Titles included in the supplement are re-evaluated before being included in the annual edition: some titles may be omitted in the annual edition. The 1966 supplement contains 980 titles; includes books in 18 pt type.

Guilfoile, Elizabeth. Books For Beginning Readers. Champaign, Ill., National Council of Teachers of English, 1962. 73 p.

A selective bibliography of easy to read books for primary grades with critical and descriptive commen[ts]. A supplement reprinted from Elementary English, April, 1963 is available: "One Hundred More Books for Beginning Readers," 4 p. All this material is reprinted in Adventuring With Books.

Heller, Frieda M. I Can Read It Myself! Some Books For Independent Reading in the Primary Grades. Columbus, College of Education, The Ohio State University, 1965. 46 p.

Arranged in 3 reading levels. Includes older as well as recent books.

Huus, Helen. Children's Books to Enrich the Social Studie[s] for the Elementary Grades. Rev. ed. Washington, Nation[al]

Council for the Social Studies, 1966.

An annotated bibliography.

Independent Schools Education Board. *Current Books: Junior Booklist.* Concord, N. H., The Board, 1967.

An annual graded, annotated list for leisure reading; preschool to grade 9.

Kircher, Clara J., comp. *Behavior Patterns in Children's Books: A Bibliography.* Washington, Catholic University of America Press, 1966. 132 p.

Based on earlier work, "Character Formation Through Books." Lists and describes 500 titles for preschool to grade 9 which demonstrate desirable character traits.

Metzner, Seymour. *American History in Juvenile Books; A Chronological Guide.* New York, Wilson, 1966. 329 p.

Comprehensive list of trade books to 1964/65. Chronological arrangement by period. Indicates level of difficulty.

National Art Education Association. *Bibliography of Children's Literature.* Washington, National Education Association, 1965.

National Council of Teachers of English. *Adventuring With Books: A Book List for Elementary Schools.* New York, New American Library, 1966.

A selective guide to 1250 books for children 3-14 years of age. 32 subject groups. Includes price, publisher, descriptive annotation. Intended for parents but useful for school libraries. Includes *100 Books for Beginning Readers* and supplement. The chapter "Books for Beginning Readers" lists independent reading level for each title; other entries indicate interest level. A directory of publishers is included.

Pellowski, Anne. *The World of Children's Literature.*

New York, Bowker, 1967.

A comprehensive bibliography of materials dealing with children's literature, historical backgrounds and current trends throughout the world. Arranged by country within broad geographic areas.

Junior and Senior High School

American Library Association. *African Encounter:* A Selected Bibliography of Books and Other Materials for Promoting an Understanding of Africa Among Young Adults. Chicago, American Library Association, 1963. 80 p.

Includes fiction and non-fiction for ages 13-19. Long descriptive annotations discuss content, use and reading level.

__________. *A Basic Book Collection for High Schools.* 7th ed. Chicago, American Library Association, 1963. 192 p.

A list of 1400 titles of fiction, non-fiction and periodicals.

__________. *A Basic Book Collection for Junior High Schools.* 3d ed. Chicago, American Library Association, 1960. 144 p.

1000 titles of fiction, non-fiction and periodicals.

__________. *Doors to More Mature Reading: Detailed Notes on Adult Books for Use With Young People.* Chicago, American Library Association, 1964. 192 p.

150 titles with long annotations summarizing story, suggesting uses for the book, notes on reader guidanc For more mature reader than the similar guide *Book Bait* (1957).

__________. *Paperbacks for a Home Library.* Chicago, American Library Association, 1966.

Paperbound books for young adults.

American Library Association. Richer by Asia; A Selected Bibliography of Books and Other Materials for Promoting West-East Understanding Among Young Adults. Chicago, American Library Association, 1959. 64p.

A supplement updates it to 1960, In: Top of the News, 17:47-54, December, 1960.

Deason, Hilary J., comp. The AAAS Science Book List for Young Adults. Washington, American Association for Advancement of Science, 1964. 250p.

An annotated list of 1376 science and mathematics titles for school, college and public libraries. Updated by Science Books; A Quarterly Review since 1965.

__________, and W. Blacklow. A Guide to Science Reading. 2d rev ed. New York, New American Library, 1966. 288p.

Fiction Catalog, Seventh Edition. New York, Wilson, 1960. 650p.

__________, 1961-1965. New York, Wilson, 1966. 299p. With 4 annual suppl.

The Seventh Edition lists 4097 works of fiction; the bound cumulative volume, 1961-1965, lists 1524 titles; the four annual supplements will cover about 1200 additional titles. Recommended books for young adults are marked "y".

Forrester, Gertrude. Occupational Literature: An Annotated Bibliography. 1964 ed. New York, Wilson, 1964. 674p.

Describes 58 series; main index lists 4850 references to current occupational literature classified under 500 occupational and industrial titles. Annotates 1800 publications under 18 topics. Directory of publishers. Index.

Independent Schools Education Board. Current Books: Senior Booklist. Concord, N.H., The Board, 1967.

An annual list published in March by the National

Association of Independent Schools. Also, Current Books: Junior Booklist.

Jones, Howard M., and Richard M. Ludwig. Guide to Ame ican Literature and Its Backgrounds Since 1890. 3d ed. rev and enl. Cambridge, Harvard University Press, 1964. 240

A comprehensive bibliography and guide in two parts: historical backgrounds and intellectual setting of American literature; and selected titles in American literature in 51 groups.

Junior High School Library Catalog. New York, Wilson, 1965. 768 p. With 4 suppl.

The first edition lists 3278 books; 1100 titles to be added in four annual supplements.

Logasa, Hannah, comp. Historical Fiction; A Guide for Junior and Senior High Schools, Colleges, Also for General Reader. 8th rev. and enl. ed. Philadelphia, McKinley, 196 368 p. (McKinley Bibliographies, Vol. 1).

Classified subject list; arranged chronologically. Author and title index. Brief annotations.

__________. Historical Non-Fiction; An Organized, Annotated, Supplementary Reference Book for the Use of Schools Libraries, General Reader. 8th rev. and enl. ed. Philadelphia, McKinley, 1964. 328 p. (McKinley Bibliographies Vol. 2).

__________. World Culture. Philadelphia, McKinley, 196 384 p. (McKinley Bibliographies, Vol. 3).

National Council of Teachers of English. Books for You; A Reading List for Senior High School Students. Edited by Richard S. Alm. New York, Washington Square Press, 1964. 344 p.

A reading list of 2000 books for grades 9 through 12. Brief annotations note value, recommended edition. Recommendations of classics and special listings for the mature reader.

National Council of Teachers of English. The College and Adult Reading List of Books in Literature and Fine Arts. New York, Washington Square Press, 1962. 446p.

760 titles selected and critically annotated to direct the reader to books worth reading for pleasure or knowledge, arranged alphabetically by author under 40 areas.

__________. Your Reading; A Book List for Junior High Schools. Edited by Charles B. Willard. New York, New American Library, 1966.

National Association of Independent Schools. 3000 Books for Secondary School Libraries. 2d ed. New York, Bowker, 1968.

A new revision of the 1961 edition prepared by the Library Committee of the Independent Schools Education Board. Titles arranged by subject; author-title index.

New York Public Library. Books For the Teen Age, 1967. New York, New York Public Library, 1967.

Revised annually. A list of high interest books for leisure reading. Some titles for easy reading.

New York State Education Department. Careers in Fact and Fiction. Albany, State Department of Education, 1961.

__________, New York Public Library and Lincoln Center Council on Educational Programs. An Invitation to the Performing Arts. New York, New York Public Library, 1966.

The Reader's Adviser, 11th Edition. Edited by W. E. Courtney. New York, Bowker, 1968-1969. 2 vols. (in preparation).

An announced expansion and revision of the 10th edition of Hoffman's Reader's Adviser and Bookman's Manual. Volume I Literature; Volume II Religion, Science, Philosophy, Social Sciences, History.

Schaaf, William L., comp. The High School Mathematics Library. Champaign, Ill., National Council of Teachers of Mathematics, 1963. 55p.

Senior High School Library Catalog, 9th ed. New York, Wilson, 1967. 1044p. With 5 annual supplements through 1972.

Formerly Standard Catalog For High School Librarie 4231 books entered; 15,678 analytical entries.

University Press Books for Secondary School Libraries: First Annual Bibliography, 1967. New York, American University Press Services, Inc., 1967.

Wiltz, John E. Books in American History; A Basic List for High Schools. Bloomington, Indiana University Press, 1964. 150p.

Special Readers

American Library Association. Children's Services Divisio Selected Lists of Children's Books and Recordings. Washington, Office of Economic Opportunity, 1966. 48p.

Includes lists for Head Start Programs, Spanish-speaking children, and other special needs, e.g. books for the 12-16 year olds who need special encouragement.

Dunn, Anita E., and Mabel E. Jackman. Fare for the Reluctant Reader. 3d ed. Albany, N.Y., Capitol Area School Development Association, State University of New York, 1964.

Emery, Raymond C., and Margaret B. Houshower. High Interest - Easy Reading for Junior and Senior High School Reluctant Readers. Champaign, Ill., National Council of Teachers of English, 1965.

Bibliography arranged by interest groups. Notes reading and interest levels and provides descriptive annotation. Includes lists of series and book clubs.

Horn, Thomas D., ed. Books for the Partially Sighted Child... Champaign, Ill., National Council of Teachers of English, 1965. 76p.

Lists fiction and non-fiction. Entries include trade information, grade levels, annotation and type size. Introduction discusses special aspects of selection: type size, leading, colors, etc.

Newton, Mary Griffen. Books for Deaf Children; Graded, Annotated, Bibliography. Washington, Alexander Graham Bell Association for the Deaf, 1962. 172p.

Includes discussion of techniques of selection of materials for the deaf.

Spache, George D. Good Reading for Poor Readers, Champaign, Ill., Garrard, 1964.

Discusses selection of books to help solve reading problems. Lists simplified editions, texts, workbooks, trade books, series and periodicals.

Strang, Ruth. Gateways to Readable Books; An Annotated Graded List of Books in Many Fields for Adolescents Who Find Reading Difficult. 4th ed. New York, Wilson, 1966. 245p.

1000 titles arranged by subject. Annotations are written to attract young people; reading levels indicated; most books between 5-7th grade reading difficulty.

U.S. Library of Congress. Division for the Blind. Catalog of Talking Books for Juvenile Readers. Washington, Govt. Print. Off., 1961. 118p.

CHAPTER V

COOPERATIVE ACQUISITIONS, GIFTS, AND EXCHANGES

---

1. COOPERATIVE ACQUISITIONS

a. General Problems

Allardyce, A. "Cooperation between Libraries. The British National Centre," UNESCO Bulletin for Libraries, 14:157-159, 188, July-August, 1960.

Description of a duplicate exchange plan coordinated by the British National Centre (BNBC) in which the participating libraries subscribe to book lists and periodical lists. The requests are sent to BNBC which decides which library should get the material. This plan is now also available to foreign libraries and national exchange centers.

American Library Association. Resources and Technical Services Division. Regional Processing Committee. "Guidelines for Centralized Technical Services," Library Resources and Technical Services, 10:233-240, Spring, 196

Anderson, LeMoyne W. "Feasibility Study for Establishing Cooperative Program for State Academic Libraries," Library Research in Progress, 8:5, March, 1963.

Barkman, M. W. "Sheboygan (Wis.) Centralized Book Purchasing for Neighboring Village Libraries," PLD Reporter 5:38, November, 1956.

Biller, F. E. "Centralized Purchasing of Books and Supplies in the Fort Loudon (Tenn.) Region," PLD Report, 5:35-36, November, 1956.

Brennan, E. F. "Centralized Purchasing of Supplies in the Worcester (Mass.) Area," PLD Reporter, 5:36-37, November, 1956.

Cahalan, T. H. "Regional Cooperation in the Acquisition of Foreign Dental Periodicals," Medical Library Association Bulletin, 45:30-33, January, 1957.

Carlson, W. H. "Cooperation: An Historical Review and a Forecast," College and Research Libraries, 13:5-13, January, 1952.

Clapp, V. W. "Cooperative Acquisitions," College and Research Libraries, 8:99-100, April, 1947.

Corey, Patricia B., and Violet F. Myer. Cooperative Film Services. Chicago, American Library Association, 1956.

A report of present methods of cooperative film services among libraries.

David, C. W., and R. Hirsch. "Cooperation and Planning from the Regional Viewpoint," Library Trends, 3:356-375, April, 1955.

Downs, R. B. "American Library Cooperation in Review," College and Research Libraries, 6:407-415, September, 1945.

Esterquest, R. T. "Aspects of Library Cooperation," College and Research Libraries, 19:203-208, May, 1958.

__________, ed. "Building Library Resources Through Cooperation," Library Trends, 6:257-383, January, 1958.

__________. "Cooperation and the Physical Book," College and Research Libraries, 9:115-119, April, 1950.

Frizzell, M. "Book Selection in a Cooperative Group," North Country Libraries, 6:8-10, March, 1963.

Galloway, R. D. "Cooperative Acquisitions for California's Libraries," California Librarian, 24:183-187, July, 1963.

Hoffman, H. H. "Co-operative Acquisitions in German Research Libraries, 1800-1930," Library Quarterly, 34:249-257, July, 1964.

Juchoff, R. "Cooperation on the Continent," Library Trends, 6:365-376, January, 1958.

Kaser, D. E. "Interdependence of Academic Libraries," Kentucky Library Association Bulletin, 25:3-9, April, 1961

Kingery, R. E. "Latin-American Cooperative Acquisitions Project," Stechert-Hafner Book News, 14:65-66, February 1960.

Lowell, M. A. College and University Library Consolidatio Eugene, Oregon State System of Higher Education, 1942.

McAnally, A. M. "Recent Developments in Cooperation," College and Research Libraries, 12:123-132, April, 1951.

McEldowney, W. J. "Subject Specialization in New Zealand University Libraries," New Zealand Libraries, 27:189-197 August, 1964.

Maihl, V. R. "Cooperation in Book Buying and Lending," PLD Reporter, 5:39, November, 1956.

Mercer, A. E. "Cooperative Book Buying in the Waikato," New Zealand Libraries, 24:133-135, July, 1961.

Metcalf, Keyes D. "Survey of Possible Cooperation Among the Larger Academic and Public Libraries of Maine," Library Research in Progress, 5:8, March, 1961.

Meyerhoff, Eric. "Medical Library Center of New York: An Experiment in Cooperative Acquisition and Storage of Medical Library Materials," Medical Library Association Bulletin, 51:501-506, October, 1963.

Oertel, Dieter. "Co-ordinating the Acquisitions of Researc Libraries in the Federal Republic of Germany," UNESCO Bulletin for Libraries, 17:285-289, September-October, 1963.

Describes history of the Library Committee of the Deutsch Forschungsgemeinschaft (German Research

Association). This association is the central organization for the promotion of research and coordination of acquisitions. Several large German libraries concentrate on certain fields in accordance with a joint plan.

Ramakrishna, Rao, K. "Library Co-operation in the United States," Bibliographical Indian Librarian, 17:19-26, June 26, 1962.

Sanborn, F.M. "Example of Regional Cooperation in West Angeles," California Librarian, 21:41-44 , January, 1960.

Vosper, R.G. "Cooperation a l'Echelon National Pour la Selection et l'Acquisition des Livres Courants Entrangers; Une Experience Recente des Bibliotheques de Recherche aux Etats-Unis," Bulletin des Bibliotheques de France, 7:461-474, September, 1962.

Title translated: Cooperation at the National Level for the Selection and Acquisition of Current Foreign Books; A Recent Experience in the United States Research Libraries.

b. Farmington Plan and Scandia Plan

Ash, Lee Michael. "Farmington Plan Junk," Library Journal, 85:3050, September 15, 1960.

"Association of Research Libraries Considering Farmington Planning," Library Journal, 84:810-811, March 15, 1959.

Association of Research Libraries. Farmington Plan Survey. Chicago, The Association, 1959.

Barcus, T.R., and V.W. Clapp. "Collecting in the National Interest," Library Trends, 3:337-355, April, 1955.

David, C.W., and Rudolf Hirsch. "Importations of Foreign Monographs under the Early Influence of the Farmington Plan," College and Research Libraries, 11:101-105, April, 1950.

Downs, Robert B. "Report on Farmington Plan Program," College and Research Libraries, 23:143-145, March, 1962.

"Farmington Plan Survey," Library Journal, 83:568, February 15, 1958.

"Farmington Plan to be Reviewed," Antiquarian Bookman, 21:150, January 20, 1958.

Gibb, I. P. "Foreign Book Procurement, the Decennial Farmington Plan Survey and Afterwards," Journal of Documentation, 16:1-9, March, 1960.

Kleberg, Tonnes. "Cooperation in Acquisitions," Library Journal, 88:4319-4322, November 15, 1963.

> Outlines history of Scandia Plan. Discusses its present goals and dispersion of interest in countries. The responsibility for acquiring materials for subject coverage of certain literature from foreign countries is divided among the participating libraries.

__________. "Some Notes on the Scandia Plan; Paper Read to the Section of National and University Libraries at the IFLA-Council Meeting, Edinburgh, 1961," Libri, 12:76-84, 1962.

Metcalf, K. D., and E. E. Williams. "Proposal for a Division of Responsibility among American Libraries in the Acquisition and Recording of Library Materials," College and Research Libraries, 5:105-109, March, 1944.

> Beginning of the Farmington Plan.

Nitecky, A. "Polish Books in America and the Farmington Plan," College and Research Libraries, 27:439-49, November, 1966.

Pearce, D. J. "Survey of Books in French, Published in 1952, Received by the Catholic University of America Library from the Bibliotheque Nationale under the Farmington Plan." Unpublished Master's thesis, Catholic University of America, 1955.

"Report on the Farmington Plan Program," College and Research Libraries, 23:143-145, March, 1962.

Strom, Folke. "Interlibrary Cooperation in Sweden and the Medical Part of the Scandia Plan," Medical Library Association Bulletin, 52:287-293, January, 1964.

Talmadge, Robert L. "Farmington Plan," Canadian Library Association Bulletin, 16:209-212, March, 1960.

__________. "The Farmington Plan Survey: An Interim Report," College and Research Libraries, 19:375-383, September, 1958.

Evaluates the results of the Plan in its first ten years.

Thompson, M. O. "Examination of the Farmington Plan Based on American Acquisitions of Swedish Publications in 1959." Unpublished Master's thesis, University of North Carolina, 1964.

Tveteras, H. L. "Scandia Plan; a Plan for Co-operative Acquisitions of Materials," UNESCO Bulletin for Libraries, 14:153-156, July-August, 1960.

Vosper, Robert G. Farmington Plan Survey: A Summary of the Separate Studies of 1957-1961. Urbana, University of Illinois, Graduate School of Library Science, 1965. 45p. (Occasional Paper No. 77).

__________. "International Book Procurement; or Farmington Extended," College and Research Libraries, 21:117-124, March, 1960.

Discusses the survey of the Farmington Plan conducted under the auspices of the Council on Library Resources. 1959 report recommended that Farmington Plan should become world wide. It was also suggested that it be strengthened by area subcommittees.

__________, and R. Talmadge. Report of a Survey of the First Ten Years of the Farmington Plan. Cambridge, Mass., Association of Research Libraries, 1959.

Williams, E. E. What is the Farmington Plan. Cambridge, Mass., Harvard University Printing Office, 1959.

Wisdom, D. F. Foreign Government Publications in American Research Libraries; A Survey Prepared for the Farmington Plan Committee of the Association of Research Libraries Cambridge, Mass., Association of Research Libraries, 1961.

Zimmerman, I. "Reference Problems; the Farmington Plan and Florida, 1954," Florida Libraries, 5:7-8 , September, 1954.

c. Recent Trends

Coffin, L. C. "P. L. 480 in Africa," Law Library Journal, 60:34-40, February, 1967.

Conferences Abroad on Shared Cataloging and Acquisition Programs, In: "Poland and in the U. S. S. R.," Library of Congress Information Bulletin, 25:780-82, December 22, 1966.

Cronin, J. W. "Library of Congress National Program for Acquisitions and Cataloging," Libri, 16:113-117, 1966.

__________, et al. "Centralized Cataloging at the National and International Level," Library Resources and Technical Services, 11:27-49, Winter, 1967.

Library of Congress plans for implementation of the new centralized acquisitions and cataloging program under Title II-C, Higher Education Act.

Hamer, E. E. "Conferences in Europe on Shared Cataloging and Acquisition Program," Library of Congress Information Bulletin, 25:721-22, November 17, 1966.

Holmes, R. R. "RTSD Resources Committee ACRL Joint Program: NPAC: a Progress Report on Developments under Title II-C of the Higher Education Act of 1965," Library of Congress Information Bulletin, 26:487-89, July 20, 1967.

Kaplan, L. "Public Law 480," ACLS Newsletter, 17:3:8-9, March, 1966.

Contrasts the objectives and methods of the P. L. 480 Program and the Farmington Plan.

Kaser, D. E. "Acquisition Work in the Next Twenty Years," Southeastern Librarian, 15:90-94, Summer, 1965.

"Public Law 480," Library Trends, 15:327-31, October, 1966.

Library of Congress P. L. 480 program of cooperative acquisitions.

Skipper, J. E. "Future Implications of Title II-C, Higher Education Act of 1965," Library Resources and Technical Services, 9:46-49, Winter, 1967.

Considers Title II-C, among other topics, as an extension of the Farmington Plan.

Skipper, J. E. National Planning for Resource Development," Library Trends, 15:321-34, October, 1966.

2. GIFTS AND EXCHANGES

a. Gifts

American Library Association. Association of College and Research Libraries. Rare Book Section. "Statement of Recommended Library Policy Regarding Appraisals," Antiquarian Bookman, 26:2205, December 19, 1960.

"America's Future Promotes Library Gift Book Package," Library Journal, 90:2800 , June 15, 1965.

Avicenne, P. "The Mission of the National Exchange Services," UNESCO Bulletin for Libraries, 18:253-58, November-December, 1964.

Shows how the Brussels and UNESCO conventions on the exchange of publications came into being.

Baughman, R. "Our Growing Collections," Columbia Library Columns, 9:39-45, November, 1959.

"Book Drives," ALA Bulletin, 57:191-192, February, 1963.

"Books USA," Higher Education, 19:16-17, May, 1963.

"Books USA: A Program in International Sharing," School Librarian, 14:33-36, October, 1964.

"Brazilian Books and Business Ledgers Presented to NYU and Harvard," Library Journal, 87:4162-4163, November 15, 1962.

Brewer, Frances J. "Friends of the Library and Other Benefactors and Donors," Library Trends, 9:453-465, April, 1961.

Describes activities of various "Friends" groups in the U. S.

__________. "Twenty Years of Giving, A Few of the Many Treasures Made Possible by the Friends," Among Friends, (Detroit Public Library) 28:7-13, Fall, 1962.

"Canadian Overseas Book Centre; A Progress Report," Ontario Library Review, 43:276, November, 1959.

Clark, Edward C. "Disposition of Gift Books by Libraries in Ohio." Unpublished Master's thesis, Kent State University, Kent, Ohio, 1952.

Conference on International Cultural, Educational, and Scientific Exchanges. Princeton University, Nov. 25-26, 1946. Chicago, American Library Association, 1947. 210p.

Includes chapters on cooperative acquisitions and specialization, international exchange of documents, international commercial exchanges, etc. Now of historical interest only.

"Gifts to Libraries Proposed Revision of Income Tax Regulations," ALA Washington Newsletter, 15:2-3, July 2, 1963.

Hektoen, F. H. "Kenya Project in Wisconsin," Top of the News, 20:16-17, October, 1963.

Henry, M. C. "Books for Africa, a Growing Program," Top of the News, 20:12-16, October, 1963.

LaCroix, F. S. "Gift Policy of North Carolina Public Libraries." Unpublished Master's thesis, University of North Carolina, 1963.

Lancour, H. "Exporting Gift Horses," Library Journal, 83:3194-3197, November 15, 1958.

"Librarian of Congress Asks for Tax Break for L. C.," Library Journal, 88:1636, April 15, 1963.

"Library Donors and the 1964 Tax Law," Bookmark, 23: 235-236, May, 1964.

Logan, George King. "New Orleans Public Library Reviews Its Gifts," Library Journal, 82:2093-2096, September 15, 1957.

Lowenberg, C. "Books and Library Aid to Asia," Wilson Library Bulletin, 35:452-454 , February, 1961.

Moorhead, J. "Books for the Mountain Children; Providing Libraries in the Schools of Appalachia," PTA Magazine, 59:2-3, March, 1965.

Mumford, L. Q. "Testimony of the Librarian of Congress Before the Committee on Ways and Means of the House of Representatives (March 7, 1963)," Antiquarian Bookman, 31:1183-1184, March 25, 1963.

"1,000,000 Books for the Needy," Wilson Library Bulletin, 39:608, April, 1965.

"$1 Million Gift for Exhibits to Performing Arts Library," Library Journal, 91:77, January 1, 1966.

Paddock, C. "Gifts and Exchanges," Louisiana Library Association Bulletin, 20:127-130, Summer, 1957.

Perkins, H. A. T. "Exchange and Gifts," Medical Library Association Bulletin, 50:407-417, July, 1962.

Powell, B. E. "Sources of Support for Libraries in American Universities," In: Tennessee. University. Library. Library Lectures, Numbers Ten, Eleven, and Twelve, 1958-1960. The University, 1961. Pp. 1-22.

Richards, Benjamin B. "How to Handle Gift Books and Magazines," Illinois Libraries, 39:137-139, May, 1957.

The policy of the library should prevent the acceptance of gifts which bear little or no relation to the purpose of the library.

Ruckman, Kathleen Margaret. "Gifts and Exchanges in the University of Illinois Library." Unpublished Master's thesis, University of Illinois, Urbana, 1936.

Stein, J. W. "Fate of a Private Collection," ALA Bulletin, 56:357-359, April, 1962.

"Ten Million Dollar Gift to University of Chicago for New Graduate Research Library," Library Journal, 90:5224, December 1, 1965.

Thompson, D. E. "Gifts," In: Rutgers University. Graduate School of Library Service. State of the Library Art. New Brunswick, N. J., Rutgers University Press, 1961. Vol. 1, Pt. 4. (Bibliography).

Thompson, L. S. "Of Bibliographical Mendicancy," College and Research Libraries, 14:373-378, October, 1953.

Problems in gift solicitation.

Willging, E. P. "Book Aid to Foreign Missions," Catholic Library World, 31:290-291, February, 1960.

Willging, E. P., and C. A. Field. "Of Bread Stones, and Serpents: Books for the Missions Program," Catholic Library World, 36:599-602, May, 1965.

"Yale Libraries on Gift Trail," Library Journal, 88:2477-2478, June 15, 1963.

b. Exchanges

Adoption of New Conventions on the Exchange of Publications," UNESCO Bulletin for Libraries, 13:29-35, February, 1959.

Avicenne, P. "Mission of the National Exchange Services," UNESCO Bulletin for Libraries, 18:253-258, November, 1964.

Backus, O. P. "Recent Experiences with Soviet Libraries and Archives," College and Research Libraries, 20:469-473 , November, 1959.

Bakulin, K. D. "International Book Exchanges of the Ukrainian S. S. R. Academy of Science Library," UNESCO Bulletin for Libraries, 19:169-170, May, 1965.

Banerjea, B. M. "National Exchange Services," Herald of Library Science, 2:134-141, July, 1963.

Blake, Fay M. "Expanding Exchange Services," College and Research Libraries, 24:53-56, January, 1963.

Busse, Gisele Von. "National Exchange Centre; A Practical Guide," UNESCO Bulletin for Libraries, 13:36-47, February, 1959.

"Conference on the International Exchange of Publications in Europe," UNESCO Bulletin for Libraries, 15:7-10 , January, 1961.

Cox, W. "New Exchange Conventions," UNESCO Bulletin for Libraries, 15:171-177, July, 1961.

Daniels, M. "The Contribution of the Organization of American States to the Exchange of Publications in the Americas," *The Library Quarterly*, 28:45-55, January, 1958.

__________. "International Exchange of Publications," *ALA Bulletin*, 51:124-125, February, 1957.

A summary of the 1956 Havana Conference on the international exchange of publications.

Dargent, J. L. "FIAB---Commission des Echanges de Publications depuis 1947," *Libri*, 14:81-85, no. 1, 1964.

Title translated: IFLA's Commission for Exchange of Duplications Since 1947.

__________. "Les Exchanges," In: *International Congress of Libraries and Documentation Centres*. Brussels, Conference, 1955. V. 1:118-126; Discussion: V. 2A:222-225.

Diakonova, O. A. "International Book Exchange of Soviet Libraries," *Libri*, 15:180-185, No. 2, 1965.

Draft Conventions Concerning the International Exchange of Publications. Paris, UNESCO, 1958.

"Duplicate Exchange Union of ACRL," *College and Research Libraries*, 17:511, November, 1956.

Obtaining backfiles of books, documents, etc., for cost of transportation.

"Duplicates Exchange Union," *Library Resources and Technical Services*, 8:333, Summer, 1964.

"The Exchange of Publications in Latin America," *UNESCO Bulletin for Libraries*, 10:112-113, May-June, 1956.

Describes preparatory activities for the Havana Conference by Brazil, Chile, the Dominican Republic, and Uruguay.

"Exchange of Publications: Statistics," *UNESCO Bulletin for Libraries*, 16:206-208, July, 1962.

Franklin, Robert D., and John W. Snyder. "A Cordial Exchange with Leningrad Librarians," Library Journal, 87: 720-722, February 15, 1962.

Hallett, R. "International Book Exchange and International Book Exchange Library Clubs," Library Association Record, 65:22-24, January, 1963.

"Hungarian Decree on International Exchanges," UNESCO Bulletin for Libraries, 14:227-228, September, 1960.

"International Exchange Activities, 1957-1958," UNESCO Bulletin for Libraries, 13:53-55, February-March, 1959.

Kanevskii, B. P. "International Exchange of Publications at the Lenin State Library," UNESCO Bulletin for Libraries, 13:48-52, February, 1959.

Khan, M. Siddig. "Events at Tokyo, Seminar on the International Exchange of Publications and the AFLA Conference," Libri, 8:141-153, No. 2, 1958.

Lane, A. H. "The Economics of Exchange," Serial Slants, 3:19-22, July, 1952.

A paper presented at the Acquisitions Round Table, ALA, 1952, contains a discussion of the cost of exchange procedures at Columbia University Library with an economic evaluation.

__________. "Exchange Work in College and University Libraries." Unpublished Master's thesis, Columbia University, New York, 1950.

MacIver, I. "The Exchange of Publications as a Medium for the Development of the Book Collection," The Library Quarterly, 8:491-502, October, 1938.

Discusses the above at the University of California.

Maichel, Karol. "The Russian Exchange Program at Columbia University," Library Resources and Technical Services, 2:254-258, Fall, 1958.

Martinez, J. M. "Present Status of Exchanges in Argentina, In: Acquisition of Latin American Materials. Seminar, 3d, 1958, Berkeley, Final Report and Papers. Berkeley, University of California Library, 1959. Pp. 206-217.

Mora, J. A. "Free Cultural Exchange," Library Journal, 84:3531-3533, November 15, 1959.

Discusses problems encountered by Latin American Libraries in building up collections.

Newell, A. "British-American Exchange; Books for Better Understanding," Times (London) Educational Supplement, 2488:143, January 25, 1963.

Novak, V. "Let's Exchange Profitably," Library Resources and Technical Services, 9:345-351, Summer, 1965.

Paddock, C. "Gifts and Exchanges," Louisiana Library Association Bulletin, 20:127-130, Summer, 1957.

The practice of the exchange of publications between libraries.

Perkins, H. A. T. "Exchange and Gift," Medical Library Association Bulletin, 50:407-417, July, 1962.

Peterson, E. N, "Steps Toward the Adoption of New Conventions for the Exchange of Official and Non-Official Publications," Libri, 7:296-308, No. 4, 1958.

Poynter, F. N. L. "Organization of the International Exchange of Medical and Scientific Periodicals," In: International Congress of Libraries and Documentation Centres. Brussels, Conference, 1955. v. 2A:317-321.

"Regional Seminar on Bibliography, Documentation and Exchange of Publications in Latin America," UNESCO Bulletin for Libraries, 15:139-143, May, 1961.

Rozsa, G. "International Exchange of Publications with Afro-Asian Countries," UNESCO Bulletin for Libraries, 16:141-143, May, 1962.

Ruckman, Kathleen Margaret. "Gifts and Exchanges in the University of Illinois Library." Unpublished Master's thesis, University of Illinois, Urbana, 1936.

Ruff, B., and H. A. Izant. "International Scheme for Duplicate Medical Literature," Medical Library Association Bulletin, 52:283-286, January, 1964.

Sabzwari, I. H. "National Exchange Centre," Pakistan Library Review, 3:44-47, March, 1961.

Sheel, P. "Exchange of Publications in South and South East Asia," Annals of Library Science, 5:52-54, June, 1958.

Terry, Juanita. "Exchanges as a Source of Acquisition with Special Emphasis on College and University Collection." Unpublished Master's thesis, Columbia University, New York, 1939.

Thom, Ian W. "Duplicates Exchange: A Cost Analysis," Library Resources and Technical Services, 1:81-84, Spring, 1957.

Results of a survey at Northwestern University Library of participation in the Duplicates Exchange Union.

Thompson, D. E. "Exchanges," In: Rutgers University Graduate School of Library Service. State of the Library Art. New Brunswick, N. J., Rutgers University Press, 1961. V. 1, Pt. 5.

"Two UNESCO Exchange Conventions Ratified by U. S. S. R.," Library Journal, 87:4506-4507, December 15, 1962.

United Nations Educational, Scientific and Cultural Organization. Conference on the international exchange of publications. (4th Regional Conference, 1960, Budapest).

United Nations Educational, Scientific and Cultural Organization. "Exchange of Publications: Statistics for the Year 1960," UNESCO Bulletin for Libraries, 16:206-208, July, 1962.

UNESCO, "Report of the Intergovernmental Committee on Exchange of Publications," Canadian Library Association Feliciter, 4:7-11, October, 1958.

Von Busse, Gisela. "Access to Books," UNESCO Bulletin for Libraries, 10:271-278, November-December, 1956.

Emphasizes UNESCO's role in aiding war-devastated countries to continue exchange programs and build up damaged collections after the war. Outlines important conventions on the international exchange of publications.

Waersegger, Charles de. "Multilateral Conventions Concerning the International Exchange of Publications," UNESCO Bulletin for Libraries, 17:53-62, March, 1963.

Welch, Helen M. "Publications Exchange," Library Trends, 3:423-431, April, 1955.

Discusses recent developments in the field of exchanges on both the national and international levels with due credit to UNESCO. Includes bibliography.

White, H. L. "Australian Experience in International Exchange of Publications," Australian Library Journal, 7: 9-12, April, 1958.

Williams, Edwin E. "Exchange between Exchanges," Library Journal, 86:186-189, January 15, 1961.

__________. "Exchanges: National and International," Library Trends, 2:562-572, April, 1954.

Describes briefly a number of current exchange programs. Includes bibliography.

__________. A Serviceable Reservoir; Report of a Survey of the United States Book Exchange. Washington, The United States Book Exchange, 1959.

Williams, Edwin E. "USBE---What's in a Name?" Canadian Libraries, 16:206-209, March, 1960.

U. S. Book Exchange.

Zwartz, E. "International Book Exchange: British National Book Centre," New Zealand Librarian, 25:131-134, June, 1962.

3. A SELECTED LIST OF REFERENCE AIDS

Farmington Plan Newsletter. Washington, Association of Research Libraries, No. 1—. March, 1949—.

Published irregularly (No. 25, May, 1967). Contains articles on activities, current notices on the Farmington Plan, Farmington Plan bibliography and statistics. Of special interest are bibliographic listings of foreign reference tools, usually in regional arrangement.

United Nations Educational, Scientific and Cultural Organization. Handbook on the International Exchange of Publications. 3d ed., edited and rev. by Gisela von Busse. Paris, UNESCO, 1964. 767 p.

Discusses types of exchanges and the organization of exchange services. Contains a directory of publications.

__________. Handbook of International Exchange. Paris, UNESCO, 1967. 1102 p.

Includes chapters on international organizations and their activities,(295) national organizations, (4, 750) and on agreements concerning international relations and exchanges. The first edition of the Handbook was published in 1965. The new edition is more complete and covers 131 countries.

Williams, E. E. Farmington Plan Handbook. Rev. to 1961 and abridged. Ithaca, N. Y., Association of Research Libraries, 1961. 141 p.

Brings the history and bibliographies of the 1953 edition up-to-date. Includes tables of the countries and subjects for which the individual libraries are responsible.